The Complete Idiot's Reference

Great Goals Generate Great Results

➤ **Get ready to set goals.** You need data, very good data, to set great goals. Col... from past performance. Clearly state your needs and make sure everyone agrees these really are needs.

➤ **Get specific.** So many goals fail to inspire and guide action because of vagueness. Have the courage to ask for exactly what you want—define it so well that everyone knows where the start and finish lines are located.

➤ **Bring your measuring tape.** The specifics need to be measurable. If not, you will not know where you are or whether you have finished.

➤ **Is it doable?** No one likes to go on a career suicide mission. Goals can be a stretch but people need to know the reasons a goal is achievable. The building blocks to goal setting need to be logical and understandable.

➤ **Does it fit?** One last question before you launch: "Is this goal compatible with other current or envisioned goals?" If the answer is not an easy "Yes," retool before you launch.

➤ **Slave or Master?** Make goals your servants by embracing problems as learning opportunities that lead to more, not less, success.

Tips on How to Be a Super Successful Sales Person

➤ **Have passion for the product AND people.** Love your product and your customers. Passion is persuasive.

➤ **What does the customer really need?** It is not always what they say they need. Be a detective by asking great questions.

➤ **Talk their language.** "When in Rome . . ." You know the saying but use this classic advice to learn the special language a customer uses.

➤ **Will the real buyer please stand up?** This can be where you earn your detective's badge. It is not always obvious, so never assume you know. Confirm, and then confirm again, who the decision-maker is, or you will waste enormous amounts of time.

➤ **Slow down, don't need it.** It is OK if a customer really does not need your product now. Do not be angry or upset, but plant the seeds for future sales. In sales, patience is a tough-earned virtue.

➤ **Obstacles are your best friends.** Obstacles only mean you do not know everything you need to know. Expect obstacles, expect to learn from them, and you can expect success.

➤ **Add value.** Under-promise and over-deliver is a great way to make the current sale turn into one hundred future sales.

➤ **Be you.** Do not be an actor, which is another profession entirely. Be yourself and you will do your best. It is that easy.

Six Conditions for the Five-Minute Manager to Flourish

➤ **Vision and Mission.** They define an inspiring end point that focuses everyone's efforts.

➤ **Shared Values.** They are the culture and what everyone is held accountable for.

➤ **Trust.** It is the glue that holds a company together.

➤ **Listening.** When a company listens well, it hears almost twice as much as others do.

➤ **Cooperation.** When people cooperate, not compete, they produce their best results.

alpha
books

tear here

Seven Ways to Discover the Hidden Leverage Your Company Has

- ➤ **Customers are your best friends (no offense, Fido).** This oft forgotten asset is your number one asset. They will be the first to try your new products, and they can tell you how to make your current products even better.

- ➤ **Cash.** What if you were to focus all available cash on your number one opportunity? If you did it perfectly, you might be much better off than spreading the cash to several projects.

- ➤ **Market share.** If you are number one, two, or three in a category, you can leverage this with potential customers. Customers are curious about why so many people buy from the leaders—they must know something.

- ➤ **Reputation.** Conduct research, and if customers rank you number one in service or quality, you have a great message for potential consumers. Many of them will want to try your products.

- ➤ **Momentum.** If you are the fastest growing business, tell potential customers. They will want to learn for themselves why so many people are switching to your business.

- ➤ **Key staff with hidden skills.** You will be amazed at the hidden talents your employees have acquired from previous jobs and hobbies. Your challenge will be how to use them—a nice challenge to have.

- ➤ **Unique systems.** You have developed unique processes, equipment, and even software adaptations. It is guaranteed that they exist in your business. Can they become a product of their own?

Eight Ways to Have Your Best Year Ever

- ➤ **Do what you really, really want to do.** When you do what you really want to do, you do your best work and have fun doing it.

- ➤ **Power personal days.** Do those special fun projects that are just for you.

- ➤ **Set a vacation record.** Take two weeks at a time and buy additional vacation time if you need to. It is a great investment in you.

- ➤ **Commit to the dream.** You have always wanted to do _____. As the ads say, just do it!

- ➤ **Expand your vision.** Buy four provocative books. Expand your horizons by learning something important you did not know before. Now use it to have your best year ever.

- ➤ **Build your reserves.** Nothing helps make happiness a constant companion like enough financial and personal energy reserve.

- ➤ **Renew, rebuild friends and family.** They were rich once and they can be again. Be amazed when you rekindle those fun relationships.

- ➤ **Be kind.** Being kind to others is the surest way to have others be kind to you. The act of being kind to others is soothing and exhilarating at the same time.

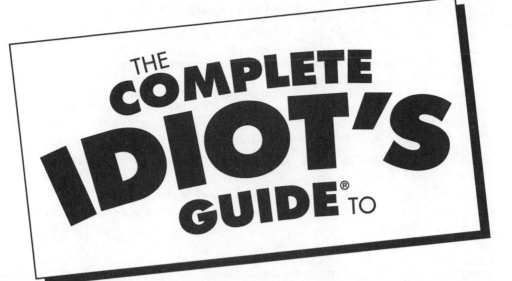

THE
COMPLETE IDIOT'S GUIDE® TO

Five-Minute Managing

by Richard Haasnoot

alpha books

Macmillan USA, Inc.
201 West 103rd Street
Indianapolis, IN 46290

A Pearson Education Company

Alpha Development Team

Publisher
Marie Butler-Knight

Editorial Director
Gary M. Krebs

Associate Managing Editor
Cari Shaw Fischer

Acquisitions Editors
Randy Ladenheim-Gil
Amy Gordon

Development Editors
Phil Kitchel
Amy Zavatto

Assistant Editor
Georgette Blau

Production Team

Development Editor
Al McDermid

Production Editor
Michael Thomas

Copy Editor
Melody Layne

Cover Designer
Mike Freeland

Photo Editor
Richard H. Fox

Illustrator
Brian Mac Moyer

Book Designers
Scott Cook and Amy Adams of DesignLab

Indexer
Lisa Lawrence

Layout/Proofreading
Angela Calvert
Diana Moore

Contents at a Glance

Part 1: The Five-Minute Foundation   **1**

1 Unveiling of the Five-Minute Manager   3
Introducing the Five-Minute Manager

2 The Guiding Lights: Vision and Mission   11
The power of everyone headed in the same direction

3 Shared Values   21
Agreeing on what is mutually important

4 Trust: Without It You Are a Five-Hour Manager   31
Trust is the glue that holds a company together

5 Just Listen   41
Effective listening makes Five-Minute Managing possible

6 Cooperate, Don't Compete   49
Cooperation is much more effective than competition

Part 2: Five-Minute Goals   **57**

7 Key Data First, and Maybe Only   59
Collecting data and understanding benchmarks

8 Whatever You Do, Be Sure You Have the Right Strategy   71
Building a strong strategy

9 Goal of a Goal   81
Building blocks of great goals

10 Score with Your Goals   93
Setting great goals and moving into action

Part 3: Feedback   **101**

11 The Answers to "When?" and "Where?" Are Easy   103
Knowing when and where to praise people

12 Positive Feedback: Having Fun Doing It   111
Delivering praise to the right people in the right way

13 The When and Where of Criticism   121
Being timely and respecting others

14 The Who and How of Criticism for the Five-Minute Manager   129
Discretion and clear intent make it constructive

Part 4: The Five-Minute Team   **137**

15 Why Is This Collection of People in This Room?   139
Developing a team mission and defining roles

16 The Team Stages for Success   147
Knowing the stages helps address the predictable challenges of each one

Part 5: The Five-Minute Small Business Manager   **155**

17 Rev Up That Sales Engine   157
Selling the super successful way

18 Low-Cost, Highly Successful Sales: You Can Have Both!   167
The keys to professional sales and low-budget, yet powerful, marketing

19 Powerful Ideas to Develop Your Business   177
Unleash your creativity and solve the most perplexing problems

20 The Power of Working Together   187
Networking and partnerships are the power boosters many businesses need

21 Supercharge Your Business   199
Make yourself attractive and then let others see the new, improved you.

22 Leap Forward   211
Use hidden leverage to leap forward to your best year ever

23 The Effective Home Business   225
How your home business can become the powerhouse you want it to be

24 Avoid Potholes and Mistakes   241
Proven methods of preventing and handling disasters

25 Why Be Number Two When You Can Be Number One?   251
What made you Number Two may not be what you need to be Number One

26 Profitable Success for the Five-Minute Manager   263
Plan for immediate and long-term profitability

Part 6: The Five-Minute Life   **283**

27 The Five-Minute Parent, Friend, and Helper   285
Making Five-Minute managing techniques work with friends and family

28 Getting Personal   295
    A personal plan for enduring happiness

Appendices

    A Finding a Life or Business Coach   309
    B Suggested Reading   311
       Index   315

Contents

Part 1: Get the Foundation Right   **1**

1 Unveiling of the Five-Minute Manager   **3**

Standing on the Foundation 4
A Bird's Eye View of Five-Minute Managers 5
Five-Minute Speakers Value Each Word—All 750 of Them 5
Five-Minute Managers' Verbal Signposts 6
The Power of First Words 7
Five-Minute Printed Words 8
Five-Minute Managers Are Not Human Stopwatches 9

2 The Guiding Lights: Vision and Mission   **11**

The Best and Brightest 11
Just What Is a Vision and Mission Statement, Anyway? 12
The Magic Is in the Creation 12
A Mission and Vision Statement Sampler 14
   Ingram Micro 14
   University of North Carolina at Wilmington, Cameron
     School of Business 14
    The Burlington Northern and Santa Fe Railway 15
Creating a Personal Vision Statement 16
   The Online Mission 19
Vision and Mission Alignment 19

3 Shared Values   **21**

All Our Values 21
Examine Your Roots 25
   Eight Steps to Identifying Organizational Values 26
Everyday Values Brought to Life 27
The Personal Way 28
   Ryan's Evolution 29

4 Trust: Without It You Are a Five-Hour Manager   **31**

Trust—It Is Like Glue 31
Trust Recipe Ingredient Number One: Integrity 32
   Start Now to Repair Your Integrity 33
Trust Recipe Ingredient Number Two: Competency 33
Building Trust Five Minutes at a Time 34
   Step 1: Turn Goofs into Proof You Are Trustworthy 34
   Callie's Story 34
   Step 2: I Am Good and You Should Know It 35
   Step 3: Multidirectional Trust 36
An Oft Forgotten Dimension of Trust 38

5 Just Listen   **41**

Gosh! We're Not Good Listeners 41

How Difficult Can It Be? 42

Listening Made Easy 43

Create an Open Space in Which to Listen *43*

With No Expectations, Expect Success *43*

Listening to Learn 44

Validate and Mirror *45*

6 Cooperate, Don't Compete   **49**

Cooperation Is a Necessity... 49

The Science Against Competition 50

Some Myths About Competition.. 51

Competition Is Part of Human Nature *51*

Competition Is Fun! *52*

Competition Creates Greater Innovation *53*

Cooperation and the Five-Minute Manager 53

Making Cooperation Stronger at My Company.............................. 54

Share and Learn *54*

Win-Win *55*

Part 2: Five-Minute Goals   **57**

7 Key Data First, and Maybe Only   **59**

Get the Shovels Out 61

Customer Data—Usually There Is More Than Enough Data *61*

I Have the Data. Now What Do I Do? *62*

Let the Consumer's Voice Be Heard *64*

Other Consumer Voices *67*

The Internet—A Gold Mine for Many *67*

Search Engines *69*

**8 Whatever You Do, Be Sure You Have the
   Right Strategy**   **71**

What Makes Us So Good? 72

What Are Your Competitors Good at and Likely to Do? 74

Crawl in Bed with the Consumer 76

Crawling in Bed with the Consumer—a True Story *76*

Pull It Together 78

9 Goal of a Goal   **81**

The Five-Minute Manager's Data Summary 82

From Findings and Needs to More Help 83

You Better Be Specific 84
   The What Needs to Be Crystal Clear *84*
   Where Is the Start and Finish Line? *85*
   How Are You Going to Do That? *85*
   Who Is Really Going to Do What? *85*
Bring Your Measuring Tape 86
Can We Do This? 86
Does This Goal Match My Other Goals? 87
Goals—Masters or Servants 88
   Goals as Master *88*
   The Stress-Free Way—Goals as Servants *89*

10 Score with Your Goals   **93**

Starting Line Preparation 93
   Are You Sure People Agree? *94*
Rally Around 95
Act! 96
Learn and Then Learn Some More 96
Persist 97
Celebrate! 98

Part 3: Feedback   **101**

11 The Answers to "When?" and "Where?" Are Easy   **103**

Alert—It Is Coming 103
As Soon as You See or Hear It 105
   Customer Service Examples *106*
   Sales Representative Example *106*
Celebrate the Celebrations 107
The Public Wanderer 107
"Where?" Where It Is Right 108
Doing It in Public 109

12 Positive Feedback: Having Fun Doing It   **111**

How Most of Us Give One-Dimensional Praise.................... 111
   The Politician *112*
   The Whisperer *112*
   The Rare Find *113*
   The Exclaimer *113*
   The Writer *113*
   The Body *114*
   Is There an Ideal Style? *114*
Praise Those Benefits... 116

Who Should We Praise? 116
   Broaden Your Vision *117*
   Praise Your Boss *118*
   Praise: It Is Right Anywhere *118*

13 The When and Where of Criticism   121

When It Happens 121
   Make the Connection *121*
   The Trail Is Fresh *122*
   Put It Behind Everyone and Move On *122*
   Make Sure You Have the Facts Right *122*
   Bill's Experience *122*
   Lessons Learned *124*
In Private or in Public? Yes 124
   Private Works *125*
Out in the Open for Everyone 125
   Patricia's Experience *126*
   Group Criticism *127*

**14 The Who and How of Criticism for the
      Five-Minute Manager   129**

A Smaller Circle 130
   Criticizing the Boss *130*
   Cross-Functional Criticism *132*
Seven Considerations for Criticism 132
Warning! 133
It's in the Mix 133
   Performance Reviews *135*

Part 4: The Five-Minute Team   137

15 Why Is This Collection of People in This Room?   139

The Person Who Started All This 139
The Team Has a Mission 141
Role Players 142
The Five-Minute Agenda 143
   A Homework Assignment *144*
   Five Minutes Means Five Minutes *144*
Meeting Summaries—Write Them in Five Minutes 145
The Round Table 145

16 The Team Stages for Success   147

Getting the Engine Started 147
   The Right Response to the Why Me? Type *149*
   Making a Believer of Mr. I-Don't-Believe-in-This *150*
   Dealing with the "What's My Role?" Type *150*

This Is Not What I Expected 151
Building Momentum 152
Crossing the Finish Line 153

Part 5: The Five-Minute Small Business Manager   155

17 Rev Up That Sales Engine   157

Sales Myths 157
   Myth #1: You Can Be Sold Something You Don't Want 158
   Myth #2: Success Means Gimmicks 159
   Myth #3: Gotta Be Aggressive 160
   Myth #4: Born, Not Made 161
   Myth #5: Forget Ethics 162
Add Extra Value for Super Sales 162
   Let New Customers Try Before They Buy 162
   Follow Up After the Sale—Are They Happy? 163
   Communicate Regularly—Try a Newsletter 164
   How Web Sites Deliver Extra Value 164
   Celebrate Success with Your Customers 165
   Ask Your Customers What They Need 165

18 Low-Cost, Highly Successful Sales: You Can Have Both!   167

Be a Super Successful Sales Person 167
   Passion for the Product AND People 168
   What Does the Customer Really Need? 168
   Speak Their Language 169
   Will the Real Buyer Please Stand? 169
   Obstacles Are Your Best Friends 170
   Be You 171
Small Budget Marketing 171
   Past Customers—"Hello Again!" 171
   Business Cards and Public Materials—Don't Skimp 172
   Announce Everything 173
   Seminars and Workshops 173
   Alliances 174
   The World Wide Web 175

19 Powerful Ideas to Develop Your Business   177

You Are Creative—Discover Just How Creative 177
   See Yourself as Creative 178
   Create an Idea-Friendly Environment 178
   Schedule Regular Brainstorming Time 179
   Adapt and Build on Already Good Ideas 179
   Ban Negatives 180

Visual Stimulation and Mixed Brains 180
Curiosity Does Not Kill Humans 181
Open Door, Open Mind 181
Sharpen Your Problem-Solving Skills 182
The Right Attitude 182
Redefining 183
Have a System 183
Don't Let Experience Trap You 184
Tune Into Your Intuition 185
Going Beyond Just a Solution 185
Agreement 186

20 The Power of Working Together   187

Building a Referral Network 187
Be Visible 188
Join the Right Groups 188
Don't Be a Spotlight Hog 189
Be Prepared 189
Slow Down, Don't Panic or Rush 190
Building a Solid Partnership 190
Team Building—Shared Values and Mission 191
Equal, Associate, or Managing 191
Clearly Understand How Money Works 192
Talk, Don't Assume 193
Role Players 193
Survival and Success Tips for All Businesses 194
Technology 194
Have Financial Plans and Forecasts 195
Mentor and Advisory Board 196
Are You Doing What You Love? 197
Don't Gloat 197

21 Supercharge Your Business   199

Become More Attractive 199
Let Your Customers See You 200
Speak Out 201
Be a Special Volunteer 202
Product or Service Evaluation 203
Business Recharge Kit 204
Personal Values Inventory 205
360 Degree Review 205
The Really Big Picture 206
Backup Plans—A Through D 207
Objectivity Versus Interpretation 208

22 Leap Forward   211

Discover Your Company's Hidden Leverage 211
Customers Are Your Best Friends (No Offense, Fido)....................*211*
Cash Is a Pretty Good Friend, Too *212*
Market Share *212*
Reputation *213*
Momentum *214*
Staff Members with Hidden Skills *214*
Unique Systems *215*
Leap Forward in About a Week 216
Ask for What You Really Need, Not What You
  Think Is Possible *216*
Get Answers Today, Not Tomorrow *216*
Reduce Appointment Time by 50 Percent *217*
Over Respond *217*
Eliminate Toleration *218*
Truth Telling *219*
Stronger Systems *219*
How to Have Your Best Year Ever 219
Do What You Really, Really Want to Do.....................................*220*
Personal Power Days *220*
Set a Vacation Record *221*
Commit to the Dream *221*
Expand Your Vision—Buy Four Provocative Books *222*
Build Your Reserves *222*
Renew, Rebuild Friends and Family *223*
Be Kind *224*

23 The Effective Home Business   225

Working Effectively at Home 225
Deadlines as Friends *225*
Buddy or Coach *226*
Routine or No Routine *227*
Train Your Family *227*
The Perfect Home Office *228*
Great First Impressions That Turn People "On" 229
Neatness Counts *229*
It's in the Eyes *230*
Shake Like You Mean It..*230*
SMILE! *230*
Listen 75 Percent, Talk 25 Percent...*231*
Relax and Live Your Truth *231*
Bragging and Name-Dropping Not Allowed................................*231*
The Power of the Compliment *232*

Become a Confident Public Speaker and Deliver a
Great Presentation 232
Prepare Early 232
Jot and Jog 233
The Outline 233
Add a Dose of Humor 233
Practice; Then Let It Flow 234
Your Audience Wants You to Succeed 234
Physiology—Breathing and Eye Contact..........................235
Audience Participation 235
Stop on Time 236
Make the Telephone a Powerful Asset 236
Have a Purpose 236
Know Your Audience 237
First Words 237
Judge Your Tone and Theirs 237
Assertive, Not Aggressive 238
Of Course, Listen 238

24 Avoid Potholes and Mistakes   241

You Can Prevent Business Disasters 241
Who Is on Your Disaster Team?.......................................241
Vital Records 242
Assets—More Than Insurance 243
Natural and Self-Inflicted Disasters 243
Spotting Accounting Fraud 244
Never Takes a Vacation? 244
Blames Others 245
Volunteers to Handle Important Details 245
Picks Up the Mail 245
Makes Bookkeeping Complex 245
Feels They Are Owed Something 246
Recognizing Bad Thinking When You Hear It 247
Question, Question, Question 247
Just the Facts and All the Facts.......................................247
What's That Source? 248
Seek Other Perspectives 248
Verify 249

**25 Why Be Number Two When You Can Be
Number One?   251**

Mistakes That Make Companies Number Two When
They Can Be Number One...251
Thinking Chaos Is Creative 252
Relying on Gut Instincts 253

Keeping All Eyes on the Competition..*253*
Completing Something Is More Important Than How It Is Done ..*254*
A Quick Payoff Is Better Than Making an Investment *255*
New Business Opportunity Is More Important Than
   Current Customers..*256*
Common Troublesome Qualities of an Entrepreneur *257*
The Circle Runner *257*
Details—Not for Me *258*
Good Starter, Poor Finisher *258*
Failure After Failure *259*
Super Optimists...*259*
Living on the Edge..*259*
Weak Team Members *260*
The Family Suffers *260*

26 Profitable Success for the Five-Minute Manager   **263**

A Practical, Powerful Business Plan *263*
Dream—Now Make It Bigger *264*
Top 100 Obstacles *264*
Top 1,000 Solutions *265*
Advice by the Ton—Test Its Quality *266*
The Path of Least Resistance *267*
Act and Reassess *268*
So You Want to Be Profitable? *269*
REAL Customer Benefits *269*
Value, Value, Value..*271*
Service Superstar *272*
Location—Make It Easy *273*
Innovator..*274*
Reliable *276*
The Long-Term Success Guide *276*
Life Is a Journey *276*
Learn, Learn, Learn..*277*
Strong Reserves *277*
Pick Battles; Don't Burn Bridges *278*
Stretch Your Risk Muscles *278*
How's Your Balance? *279*
Success Resources You Need But Don't Have Today *279*
A Personal Coach *279*
The Latest and Best Success Books *280*
Personal Journal *281*
Power Door *281*

Part 6: The Five-Minute Life — **283**

27 The Five-Minute Parent, Friend, and Helper — **285**

The Five-Minute Parent 285
   Goals and Boundaries 286
   Look for Opportunities to Praise 288
   Negative Feedback Delivered Right 288
Social Situations—Five Minutes at a Time 289
   Is There a Purpose? Fun Is a Good One! 289
   Positive Power 290
   Clear, Unmistakable Boundaries 291
The Five-Minute Manager Helps the Community 291
   Crystal Clear Objectives 291
   Where Positive Power Really Works 292
   How You Can Help 292

28 Getting Personal — **295**

How to Become Invulnerable 295
   Be Centered 296
   In the Moment 296
   Openness 297
   Passion 297
   A Higher Power 298
Let a Personal Journal Help You 298
   Clearer Goals 299
   Life Simplification 299
   A Quieter Life 300
   Power 300
Getting Unstuck 301
   Sunshine 301
   Call a Friend 301
   Rest 302
   Music 302
   Change the Subject 303
   Do a Good Deed 303
Add a Strong Dose of "Delight" to Your Life 304
   Optimism Power 304
   100 Smiles per Day 304
   A Delightful Group 305
   A Delightful Place 305
   Clean Sweep Your Life 306
Living "Don't Worry, Be Happy" 306
   A News Fast 306
   Random Acts of Kindness 307

Appendices

A Finding a Life or Business Coach   **309**

B Suggested Reading   **311**

Index   **315**

Foreword

Five-minute managing sounds crazy but works beautifully. In one concise package, Richard Haasnoot takes us through every facet of successful management, from performance reviews, to new product development, to mentoring, to team building. He can do this because his emphasis is on quality and not quantity, on outcome and not input. *The Five-Minute Manager* cuts through the inertia, sclerosis, and pure sloth that incapacitates otherwise talented and motivated people, and helps them to exploit their abilities and competencies.

The reader might well ask, "Why does it take a whole book and several hours of time commitment to learn how to do things in five minutes?" The answer is simple: The great song delivery, football maneuver, architectural design, or speech might have taken only a few minutes, but the learning, preparation, and synthesis that created it took a lifetime of hard work. Haasnoot has done most of the hard work, and reduced a lifetime of management knowledge and application into basic and easy-to-master skills.

My favorite aspect is the structure that is provided for language and communication, whether on the job or in our personal lives. The mere act of being able to "signal" our current position and needs eliminates the misconceptions and misinterpretations that undercut communications at all levels. A simple concept, perhaps, and one readily agreed upon, but rarely applied with conviction and impact. Haasnoot enables us to do so with clear techniques before we even move on to the next page.

In fact, it seems as if every five minutes or so we've mastered a new skill that calls for us to put the book down and begin reaping the benefits. This might interfere with your reading regimen, but this is no ordinary read. This is a set of skills which, like a cafeteria, enables you to choose whatever is most appealing at the moment. Unlike a cafeteria, though, they don't take the trays away—all of the techniques remain herein for whenever they're needed.

Five-minute managers are conscious and respectful of the time of others, as well as their own time, and that is the major appeal of this book. It presents a variety of approaches to help others, to value their positions, and to help them motivate themselves to be more productive. It isn't a self-help book so much as a mutual-help book. I was surprised and gratified by the author's consistent embrace of colleagues, subordinates, customers, family, and acquaintances.

This is a work of great fun, of win/win solutions, of praise for good work, and of personal growth. The impact of all those five-minute applications is a lifetime of limitless possibilities.

Alan Weiss, Ph.D.

Alan Weiss, Ph.D. is the author of 12 books, including Million Dollar Consulting *and* The Unofficial Guide to Power Management. *He is a star of the lecture circuit, delivering more than 50 keynote speeches a year at major events. He appears regularly on radio and television to discuss productivity, performance, and behavior.*

Introduction

There is a life megatrend towards simplification. People recognize that life does not have to be complicated and heavy in material goods for them to experience happiness.

Managing everyday life and business does not have to be complicated. Some teachers and writers want you to believe that business is a complicated science, but managing a business is not complicated. The Five-Minute Manager knows that there are a few things you need to do well and that most of them can be done in five minutes or less.

The things you need to do well make common sense—you already know how to do them to some degree. For example, you have a process for setting goals, recharging yourself, and selling your products. These and other processes are at least somewhat successful for you. In this book, you will learn how to take essential skills you already use and make them better. The guidance is simple, straightforward, and low-cost. More important, it works.

In **Part 1, "The Five-Minute Foundation,"** you learn about the conditions that enable the Five-Minute Manager approach to work best. For example, many organizations have low trust; what takes five minutes in a high trust organization may take fifty minutes in an organization with a low level of trust (even that may not be enough). When there is a vision, mission, shared values, great listening, cooperation, and trust, the Five-Minute Manager flourishes.

Every company sets goals and a few actually achieve them or think that they do. In **Part 2, "Five-Minute Goals,"** you learn about the essential elements of a great goal. If any one of these elements is missing, the goal has the potential to be more of a negative than a positive for the organization. Even when you set a great goal, you need to make sure the goal is your servant and not your master.

One of the most crucial aspects of interpersonal relationships is the feedback we give each other. As crucial and as common as feedback is, it can also be tricky if you don't know some key elements. In **Part 3, "Feedback,"** you learn how to deliver truly helpful positive and negative feedback. You also learn how important frequent positive feedback is for an organization.

In business, teams represent a special and unique challenge for many managers. Teams usually are cross-functional, which means that the normal management relationships do not exist. In **Part 4, "The Five-Minute Team,"** you learn how to get a team off to a fast start and how to help a team at each critical stage.

Part 5, "The Five-Minute Small Business Manager," focuses on some of the challenges that small businesses face. If you are in a larger company, however, you probably experience the same challenges, only bigger in scale and complexity. Ideas are the lifeblood of any business, and there are proven methods for regularly turning on the flow of great ideas. When you have that great idea developed, you then need to sell it. I'll outline how to rev up your sales engine for both quick and long-term sales.

The skills that work for Five-Minute Managers in business also work in the other roles of their lives. **Part 6, "The Five-Minute Life,"** outlines how to use those skills in your family, community, and social roles. The suggestions are simple, yet powerful—like putting a turbobooster on your whole life.

How to Make This Book Work for You

As you read this book, some ideas will resonate stronger than others. Pursue and connect with those ideas that appeal most to you. In these ideas lie possibilities to make you a better manager in business and life.

When an idea appeals to you, personalize it. Contemplate how that idea will work in your life. The specific ideas that make you smile are particularly potent. Write them down and creatively develop them until you capture an idea with enough inspiration to move you forward.

Create the intent to manifest the idea that captured your imagination and inspired you. Now act on the first step that comes to mind. Do that today. Then continue to act each day guided by the inspiration and the gifts you encounter. Remember, apparent detours and falls have in them wonderful lessons. Use them to get you to where you want to be faster and easier.

As stated earlier, there is nothing complicated about the suggestions in this book. If an idea feels complicated, come back to it another day or move on to another one. Let the simplicity of the ideas in this book reveal their full power to you. Have fun with them. Fun is a tremendous power booster. Most of all, tread lightly, knowing that there are ideas in this book that will enable you to have your best year ever.

Extras

Spread throughout the book is a series of extras that build on the main material in the chapter. Pause, reflect, and have fun with them.

Consider This

These additional points of information may be relevant to your situation. Think about how they can help.

Speed Bump

These are cautions you'll want to consider. Many of them, as the name implies, are suggestions to slow down and consider some points before you take action.

Sage Advice

These are quotes from the famous and not so famous. Most of the time they build on and support points made in the text. Occasionally, they present another point of view.

Personal Coaching

These are specific, thought-provoking action suggestions you can take right now.

Special Thanks

This book has been fun to write and I hope it is fun for you to read. My family has helped to create the conditions that made this fun. Special thanks to my wife Patricia, daughters Holland and Tricia, and Sam the family Golden Retriever and Labrador mix.

Special thanks also to Coach University and their wonderful class leaders. They have opened my eyes to new ways of looking at life. Personal coaching is all about you. That spirit guided this book every day.

Trademarks

All terms mentioned in this book that are known to be or are suspected of being trademarks or service marks have been appropriately capitalized. Alpha Books and Macmillan USA cannot attest to the accuracy of this information. Use of a term in this book should not be regarded as affecting the validity of any trademark or service mark.

Part 1
The Five–Minute Foundation

Five-Minute Managers work best in businesses with strong foundations.

A business needs a clear vision of where it wants to go and what its mission is. When this exists, people share a common purpose. Sharing common values is another bond that pulls people together. An environment of trust is the glue that holds a business together. When these foundation elements are combined with a group of good listeners who value cooperation, you have the fundamental conditions necessary for Five-Minute Managers to achieve world class success.

Five-Minute Managers are certainly efficient as the name suggests, but they are much more than human stop watches. They value words and communication. They also value the simple, yet powerful steps managers can take to generate long term business success.

In this part of the book, you learn the conditions necessary to make the Five-Minute Manager system work in your business.

Chapter 1

Unveiling of the Five-Minute Manager

In This Chapter

➤ Learn what makes Five-Minute Managers so powerful

➤ Understand the power of five minutes or 750 words

➤ Start using the signposts used by some of America's most successful companies

➤ Understand how Five-Minute Managers care about people

Five-Minute Managers get more done, faster, and with less effort.

They are exceptionally efficient and dynamic. They know that less is more. They know that time is one of their most valuable assets. As managers, they could expand their communications to fill the available time, but instead they compact their words into about five minutes, because they know that this is enough time to say most things worth saying.

The Five-Minute Manager knows how to optimize the time spent by focusing on the separate parts of a project, while keeping the big picture in mind. The discipline and skills required to be a Five-Minute Manager are constantly honed razor sharp.

The rewards of Five-Minute Managing go far beyond business success; they contribute to life success as well. In life, Five-Minute Managers require less effort to succeed. In both business and life, there is more time (that most valuable of assets!) to focus on important but not urgent priorities—the second quadrant activities upon which Stephen Covey, author of the mega-bestseller *The 7 Habits of Highly Effective People,*

Personal Coaching

There have never been bigger bookstores than those found online, such as Amazon.com. Virtually every book in print is available. With a great search engine, you have no excuses. Find a book that sharpens and stretches your skills.

urges people to focus. These activities, which will be explained in subsequent chapters and are important but not urgent, often have life-long impact. Time is one of the great rewards of the Five-Minute Managing approach.

Some may view the Five-Minute Manager's approach as the ultimate time-management system, but that is sub-optimizing the idea. The Five-Minute Manager's approach is not just a matter of finding ways to do some things in less time. As you will see in the section of this book on providing positive feedback, in some areas it actually involves spending more time than most managers currently spend. In most areas, however, a Five-Minute Manager spends less time than other managers do, and they accomplish more in that time.

Five-Minute Management is about doing right things right. The single most important aspect of this is people. Everything the Five-Minute Manager does is geared toward being of the greatest assistance to others. The Five-Minute Manager does this through

➤ Short, direct, fact loaded communication.

➤ Structured and expected ways of communicating and acting.

➤ Superior listening skills and openness to new ideas.

These are powerful benefits for any person in any organization, not just managers. The Five-Minute Manager principles apply to managing others or yourself in a business or organization of any size, even a one-person home business.

Standing on the Foundation

Five-Minute Managers operate best when the foundation elements discussed in the next five chapters are healthy and growing.

Five-Minute Managers start with people aligned around a vision and mission. They share and recognize common values. If the Five-Minute Manager is in an organization that is not aligned around a vision and mission, then their task becomes very challenging. It is not unlike the challenge many managers face—an organization going in several directions at the same time, often conflicting directions. That is why the Five-Minute Manager makes it a very high priority to get their organization aligned around a vision and mission.

With these in place, everyone speaks the same language. This makes it possible to communicate key points in five minutes or less. In the Five-Minute Manager approach there is little time for repeated defining and explaining.

Consider This

Are you a manager? You might say "No," but actually you are. You manage your life—from getting up in the morning to shopping for your needs to deciding how much time to allocate to the various roles in your life.

Five-Minute Managers trust and are trustworthy. This makes a huge difference in the effectiveness of their communication. While Five-Minute Managers are talking, listeners are not wondering what their managers' alternative agendas are.

A company of great listeners enable Five-Minute Managing to work. Five-Minute Managers go to great lengths to speak in a user-friendly mode. This makes for easy listening if you are an effective, proactive listener. When a great listener communicates with a highly efficient, structured speaker, magic happens.

With all the other foundation elements in place, Five-Minute Managers love a spirit of cooperation and recognize it is a two-way street. Five-Minute Managers seek win-win solutions. When this spirit is alive and flourishing, work is fun—and there is plenty of success to go around.

A Bird's-Eye View of Five-Minute Managers

Five-Minute Managers approach any task with the objective of completing key elements of that task in about five minutes. It can take three or seven minutes, but the goal is to accomplish a lot in a short period of time.

Five-Minute Managers speak for short periods and listen for longer periods. If you listen closely or read what they have written, you see quickly that they are very organized. They focus on what is really important. Your first impression is that they are very efficient, because their communication is clear, concise, and candid. As you step back to see their results, you start to see that they are also highly effective. They are effective because they only focus on what is essential. They are not out to impress people with everything they know.

Five-Minute Speakers Value Each Word—All 750 of Them

In no place are the benefits of the Five-Minute Manager approach greater than in communication with others. We can comfortably talk at a rate of about 150 words per minute; in five minutes that adds up to 750 words. When you have read that many words in this chapter there will be a notice. That is a lot of words.

5

Consider This

You're right if you think people in television commercials talk faster than we normally do. It is not unusual for a 30–second commercial to have 90 words, which are 180 words per minute. That is 20 percent faster than the comfortable rate for most people.

These 750 words are more than enough to achieve most communication objectives, and the five minutes it takes to deliver this many words equals many people's optimal high-quality attention span. Once people understand that your five-minute communication conveys all the information they need, they pay even closer attention to what you have to say.

Five-Minute Managers recognize that they do not need to communicate everything they know on a topic. Five-Minute Managers' objective is not to impress people. Rather, they want listeners to hear the key points clearly, not to lose the key points in a jumble of less important words.

(By the way, if you are wondering how many words you can say in five minutes, at this point in the chapter you have read the number of words most people can easily say in about five minutes.)

Five–Minute Managers' Verbal Signposts

By preplanning what they want to say—often in five minutes or less of planning—Five-Minute Managers present their points in a logical, easy flowing manner. Key words signal important points.

➤ "I am proposing … " provides a quick introduction to an idea. Details come in a later section of this book.

➤ "As background … " signals that you are sharing a recap of previous key points or known important facts.

➤ "My detailed recommendation is … " makes it very clear that this is what you think should be done.

➤ "My reasons are … " starts your reasons for your recommendation. Often, numbering our reasons helps a listener, especially if we preface it with something like "I have three reasons for wanting to do this."

➤ "The next steps are … " indicates you are moving to the suggested actions necessary to gain agreement to the recommendation. The path may not be direct.

You may need to gain the agreement of others before presenting your recommendation to the final decision-maker. There may also need to be some additional fact-finding.

These cues are powerful communication aids when they become a part of the business' language. The key words become signposts that everyone understands. For example, when you say, "My reasons are … " it tells your listener that you are finished talking about the recommendation and are now going to share your reasons for wanting to do it. These tools not only provide structure, but also flow.

Personal Coaching

Try adopting a structured language at home that signals where you are and what you want. It gets everyone on the same page. Imagine how easy decisions at home would be if your child made a request by getting to the point and then backing it up with facts.

The Power of First Words

For Five-Minute Managers, the first sentence is the most important. It signals what they want the listener to do. Some examples are

➤ "I am sharing with you … " tells the listener that information is about to be shared and that a decision is not necessary now. Another version of this is "I am updating you … "

➤ "I am seeking your opinion on … " lets listeners know that their input is expected. They will evaluate what you say and formulate a reply. While a reply is being mentally processed, the listeners' involvement is a little less than when they are asked to concur with a recommendation.

➤ "I need your help … " prepares listeners to understand a request carefully. They think about how it fits with other things they have to do and formulate a reply. When they hear these opening words, they know their attention should be greater than when someone signals the purpose of the discussion is to share information.

➤ "I am seeking your agreement … " usually generates the greatest attention from listeners. The signal is that at the end of the communication they should not only share their thoughts, but they should also come to a bottom line conclusion—do they support the recommendation or not.

Sage Advice

I recommend to you to take care of the minutes, for hours will take care of themselves.
—Lord Chesterfield, English Statesman (1694–1773)

Five-Minute Printed Words

Five-Minute Managers also know the power of the printed word. The principles are the same and just as powerful.

Companies often adopt a common structure for all major forms of written communication. This is especially effective in larger companies. It helps managers in one part of the world pick up a memo from another part and quickly assimilate its contents. The structure and flow of the written communication is the same across all divisions. In addition, there are common understandings about what kinds of information will be conveyed in written communication. The information includes the key types of data that are critical for a manager to come to a conclusion.

Consider This

When you see the writing of top managers in companies that value good writing, you find they say a lot with few words. Short sentences and simple words can be exceptionally powerful.

For example, one large United States–based company uses the following requirements and sections for any memo recommending action:

➤ **Introduction:** Every memo starts "This recommends … " and proceeds to present briefly the specific recommended action. It might read, "This recommends the expansion of the test market of the improved cleaning (brand) CK formula." The reader knows now that a test market was probably successful enough to be expanded nationally. Further, they know it is a new formula of the product.

➤ **Background:** This provides the history relevant for the reader to make a decision. Continuing with our example, it might state the start date and location of the test markets, test variations, if appropriate, and a summary of any previous developments reported to management.

➤ **Recommendation:** Whereas the first paragraph includes only a brief statement, this section provides more detail. It can include expansion costs, payout and profit implications for the current and future fiscal years, timing, and key elements, such as which advertising campaign to employ.

➤ **Basis for the Recommendation:** This section usually provides up to three reasons for why the writer is making the recommendation. In our example, two reasons might be that the test market was successful and that the new formula provides a strategic and competitive advantage for the brand. Regarding the test market results, there would usually be a chart showing pre- and post-shipment and market share trends and a financial perspective.

➤ **Next Steps:** This brief section outlines the key immediate actions that will be taken with agreement to the recommendation.

In this same company, there are strict limitations on the length of various types of written communication. In many cases, the requirement is a one-page memo, which can be read easily in five minutes.

Speed Bump

Writing memos in a large company can take a long time. In some companies, it is not unheard of to rewrite a memo more than 100 times.

Five-Minute Managers Are Not Human Stopwatches

So much emphasis has been put on time that it is easy to think the Five-Minute Manager approach is all about efficiency. Nothing could be further from the truth.

Five-Minute Managers are concise out of respect for others. They know that their co-workers' time is valuable. More than that, however, Five-Minute Managers know that conciseness and clarity make it easier for listeners or readers to comprehend.

The concept of the Five-Minute Manager approach has several critical underlying attitudes that guide all actions and thinking. Five-Minute Managers want

➤ People to succeed.

➤ Win-win solutions.

➤ Work to be fun with a purpose.

➤ Personal growth to be a thrill.

➤ To praise people for good work.

➤ To provide the right management style for each person and project.

Personal Coaching

Take the list of what Five-Minute Managers want and adapt it to your personal life. Try adapting the list as a joint project with your spouse. Talk it over and try it. Seeking only win-win solutions at home is the key to more joy.

When you make a mistake, do not hide and feel ashamed. If there were a support group for people who have made mistakes in their life, everyone on the planet would be a member. "Admit and Grow" is not a bad life slogan.

As you will see in later chapters, Five-Minute Managers think about how to help people. When there is a plan, Five-Minute Managers execute it in a manner that is most helpful to others.

Five-Minute Managers do not have a need to hear themselves talk or impress people with written communication filled with everything they know about a subject. They resist the urge to expand to fill empty space. Rather, they know people are busy and have somewhat fixed levels of attention and comprehension. To optimize their chances for success, Five-Minute Managers quickly get to the point. Their usual function is that of coach or facilitator. They respect the desires of others to make a difference.

The Least You Need to Know

➤ Five-Minute Managers get more done faster, and with less effort.

➤ Five-Minute Managers know you accomplish more with fewer words and a focus on only the most important points.

➤ Preplanning is the key to increased efficiency and effectiveness.

➤ Verbal and written signposts give critical signals to listeners or readers.

➤ Five-Minute Managers are much more than human stopwatches. They care deeply about those with whom they work.

Chapter 2

The Guiding Lights: Vision and Mission

> **In This Chapter**
>
> ➤ Discover how a vision and mission statement represents the very best about you or your organization
>
> ➤ Guidelines to create powerful statements
>
> ➤ Multiple options for creating your own statement
>
> ➤ Understanding the vision and mission power that come from alignment

When organizations or individuals have a vision and mission, they have a compass. The compass lets them know where they are and what direction to go in when faced with several options.

For Five-Minute Managers, a vision and mission create a common bond and language. Alignment around a vision and mission means people share common objectives and understandings about why the objectives are important and how they will be achieved. These are critical to Five-Minute Managing because they create an environment in which cooperation and creativity can flourish.

The Best and Brightest

Creating a vision statement may be the only time a company sets out to identify what is best about itself, and how it wants to do its best to reach for an inspiring goal. If it is the only time, then developing a vision for the company becomes one of the most important events in the life of that company. Even entrepreneurs, who feel they hold the unarticulated vision in themselves, will be pleasantly surprised when they complete a conscious visioning process.

Just What Is a Vision and Mission Statement, Anyway?

A vision and mission statement represents the very best of what an organization or individual wants to be. The destination can be reaching new heights of profitability or other operational targets. Often the destination is stated in customer terms, knowing that when a superb customer target is reached, exceptional profitability will follow.

Whereas there is some inconsistency in usage of these terms, a vision is generally a lofty, inspiring statement of the ultimate destination. Typically, a company states only one vision for all its functions and divisions. There are situations, however, in which operating divisions adopt their own vision that is nonetheless consistent with the broader company-wide vision.

Speed Bump

Do not view the visioning process as something to check off your project list. Be prepared to treat this as one of the most important undertakings your business has ever tackled.

A mission statement usually has more immediacy when it exists with a vision statement. It often captures important intermediate goals, maybe five years out. A mission statement also tends to be easier to measure (100 percent customer satisfaction or 20 percent annual profit growth, for example) and more "nuts-and-bolts" (addresses key success factors, like productivity or a specific quality measure).

The language of a mission statement is often inspiring because it captures in a few words what everyone recognizes is critical to success. The language is also clear and concise while carefully avoiding words or abbreviations peculiar to only a part of an organization.

There are situations in which there is only one statement or another. When there is only a mission statement, it usually serves both purposes.

Once you begin to grasp these rules, recognize that there are no rules. Organizations tend to create statements that inspire them and reflect the culture of the company. Since there is great diversity in organizational cultures, vision and mission statements tend to reflect this diversity. There are almost as many approaches as there are statements—do what works for you.

The Magic Is in the Creation

Whereas there are no fixed rules, the following are some general process steps that help create a powerful statement:

➤ Identify the very best destination. Do not settle for the second best option.

➤ Know the unique combination of skills the organization possesses that enables it to aspire to the very best.

➤ Capture the highest principles that will guide your actions. Trust of and caring for each other is high when an organization aspires to its highest principles. The combination of principles that an organization embraces is usually unique and reflective of the culture. When realized, there will be a very high quality of life. For example, when trust is high, fun is often prevalent. People feel freer to take risks and be themselves.

➤ Determine if there is a broader community or world perspective that adds power. For example, the division of a bank might have as part of its mission taking the lead in revitalizing a rundown area of town with part of the mission addressing the need for low cost housing.

As an organization crafts its statements, it should consider the following factors:

➤ Crafting organizational statements requires broad involvement. People in all functions and various levels who know the organization well are usually the best designers.

➤ Select people who care. They can love the current organization or be a loud voice for change. In either case, they care and that is what is important.

➤ Top leaders should announce their strong support for the process and goal. If they do not support creating a vision, asking busy people to leave urgent operations will be a waste of time.

➤ Do something unusual. Go off-site to the most inspiring place the group knows.

➤ Time is flexible. Some organizations spend a day or several consecutive days crafting their statements. Others meet once a week for a month or two. Generally speaking, there needs to be ample time to consider multiple options and test them to determine if they represent the best and brightest.

Personal Coaching

For a small business, the personal vision of the owner often drives the business vision. To clarify the vision, a small business owner can go on a vision quest. There are many formal and informal programs and books that can assist with this process.

Speed Bump

Small business owners should objectively inventory all the skills of every person in the business. Be sure to include the skills people acquired before joining the business. There are sure to be some hidden gems.

➤ Select a good writer to reflect the group's thinking. The statements need to be inspiring, simple, clear, and memorable. Shorter tends to be better because it aids memory. But if it is too short, inspiration may be a casualty.

When the group and the senior management agree to a statement, sharing it in an inspiring presentation can benefit the entire organization. If the statement does not touch the heart and capture the imagination, more work may be necessary.

Some organizations have created a song to express their statements. When done well, it is memorable and fun. Do not forget that fun is an important of inspiration. If a song is not right for your organization, find other ways to make the announcement of your statements unusually positive.

A Mission and Vision Statement Sampler

Ingram Micro

Ingram Micro is the largest United States distributor. Its focus is on technology products. For example, it is Microsoft's biggest customer. It is also a leading assembler of computers for companies like Compaq and HP. Since becoming a public company under Jerre Stead's leadership, Ingram Micro has been one of the fastest growing distributors in the world.

Sage Advice

Where there is no vision, the people perish.
—Hebrew Bible, Proverbs 29:18 (quoted by President Kennedy on the eve of his assassination in Dallas)

Vision: We will always exceed expectations … with every partner, every day.

Mission: To maximize shareowner value by being the best distributor of technology for the world.

Comments: This statement is memorable. It emphasizes high standards, and the mission statement is bottom-line and has a financial orientation.

University of North Carolina at Wilmington, Cameron School of Business

Vision: The Cameron School of Business will be nationally recognized for our responsiveness to the needs of our students and the business community and service to the region.

Mission: The Cameron School of Business prepares students to become business leaders in a changing world and enhances learning and service to the community through the growth of intellectual capital.

Comments: The vision statement focuses on a broader view, whereas students are the focus in the mission statement.

The Burlington Northern and Santa Fe Railway

Vision: Our vision is to realize the tremendous potential of The Burlington Northern and Santa Fe Railway by providing transportation services that consistently meet our customers' expectations. We will know we have succeeded when

➤ Our customers find it easy to do business with us, receive 100 percent on time, damage-free service, accurate and timely information regarding their shipment, and the best value for their transportation dollar.

➤ Our employees work in a safe environment free of accidents and injuries, are focused on continuous improvement, share the opportunity for personal and professional growth that is available to all members of our diverse work force, and take pride in their association with BNSF.

➤ Our owners earn financial returns that exceed other railroads and the general market as a result of BNSF's superior revenue growth, an operating ratio in the low 70s, and a return on invested capital which is greater than our cost of capital.

➤ The communities we serve benefit from our sensitivity to their interests and to the environment in general, our adherence to the highest legal and ethical standards, and the participation of our company and our employees in community activities.

Comments: This uses a good approach to defining what the world will look like when the company achieves its vision. This is an all-purpose mission and vision statement.

Speed Bump

You want a vision to be highly memorable. If it is 25 words or less, most people can easily recall it. Too many words and it gets lost, filed away, never to be used.

Sage Advice

Viktor Frankl said we don't invent our mission, we detect it. It is within us waiting to be realized.
—Stephen Covey, *First Things First*

Consider This

When developing a vision, look for opportunities to define world class standards for your business. Meeting expectations may not be good enough for a dynamic, changing business.

Creating a Personal Vision Statement

Taking the time to create a personal vision statement is one of the best investments you can make. You discover what you really love doing and what your unique talents enable you to do better than anyone else. When you have your vision, you are ready to follow what Robert Fritz termed "the path of least resistance," in his book with the same name.

Personal Coaching

Take the family to their most loved vacation site to create your family vision. Spend the morning developing the vision and the afternoon frolicking.

Speed Bump

Recall the three times you had the most fun in each of the roles you play. Be detailed in your memory—capture emotions, thoughts, and the physical aspects. Take your time and enjoy the process.

Creating a personal vision statement can also be great preparation for developing a business mission or vision statement. You learn a critical threshold in statement development—when is it inspiring.

The following outlines a step-by-step process to discover and craft your personal vision statement. When you embark on this process with strong intent and passion, you will create your life compass—a valuable tool for your life journey.

Personal Vision Journey

For each of the following steps, invest quality time—remain quiet, calm, and center yourself in your heart, not your gut or head. DO NOT JUDGE ANYTHING THAT COMES TO YOU. Each step usually takes 30 to 60 minutes. Take no more than one step per day. This is not a race. The process benefits from the reflective time spent.

Step #1: Assess the Current Reality. As you move along the path of life, determine what in your current reality you want to make sure you keep. Typically, it is the moments of joy—time in nature, special activities, and close friends, for example. For each role you play in life, capture what is really special. Your roles may include spouse/companion, parent, son/daughter, friend, business associate, and community participant/leader.

Role:_____

Joys:_____

Role:_____

Joys:_____

Role:_____

Joys:_____

Role:_____

Joys:_____

Role:_____

Joys:_____

Step #2: Younger Years Joy. Go back to your earliest memory. If it is at about age three or four, use that as your starting point. To enrich your memory, reflect on the context of your life at the time. What town or city did you live in? What was your house like? Who were your friends, and what were your parents and other relatives doing? From your starting point, start grouping years into three year periods, ages 3 to 6, 7 to 9, 10 to 12, etc., for example. You can stop grouping the periods at about age 20, or stop whenever it feels right. For each period, identify your moments of greatest joy. What did you want to do when you grew up? Have fun with this process; do not judge anything.

Personal Coaching

As you work through Step 2, ask your parents for help. Ask them what moments they recall as your most fun. You will connect with some memories that that are not your own.

Ages:_____

Joys:_____

Ages:_____

Joys:_____

Ages:_____

Joys:_____

Ages:_____

Joys:_____

Ages:_____

Joys:_____

Step #3: Seventy-Fifth Birthday Celebration. Imagine it's your 75 birthday and you have invited all the important people from all the parts of your life—family, work, spiritual, and community, for example. Each person honors you for your accomplishments by giving a brief speech before the group. In this exercise, you write their speeches. In 25 to 50 words, write what you would love them to say about who you are and what you have achieved. Dare to write the best you could possibly aspire to. Do not hold back and, again, do not judge yourself. Use the following space to make notes for the eight to twelve people who will speak. Write each person's speech out on a separate piece of paper.

Person:_____

Speech:_____

Person:_____

Speech:_____

Person:_____

Speech:_____

Person:_____

Speech:_____

Person:_____

Speech:_____

Person:_____

Speech:_____

Person:_____

Speech:_____

Step #4: Creating a Vision. Now is the time to pull all your good work together. Take a few days between the last step and this step to reflect on the work you have done. Then ask yourself a question like this, "What can I do that utilizes my unique gifts and talents and, in doing so, allows me to experience what gives me great joy." Craft a question that feels right to you. Let your heart tell you when you have the right question. Ask the question and then listen for the answers that come immediately and over the next few days. Capture the answers as they come and DO NOT JUDGE THEM. When you feel you have gathered most of the elements of your vision, take some quality time to create your personal vision. If you are strong visually, collect pictures and create a collage that represents your vision. Annotate words in appropriate places. If you are a better writer, let the words flow. Have fun and do not edit right now. When you feel you have a good rough draft, look for opportunities to improve the language by making power words more inspiring and joyful. A thesaurus is a good friend at this stage. Keep working at it until your heart tells you that you have what you have been seeking. Revisit as needed, because this is a dynamic statement. CONGRATULATIONS!

The Online Mission

You can create a personal mission statement on the Internet. Stephen Covey, author of *The 7 Habits of Highly Effective People*, offers a step-by-step process at his Web site. Simply log on to www.franklincovey.com/customer/missionform.html and follow the steps.

Vision and Mission Alignment

When you create a personal vision or mission statement, your work is usually done. When creating these statements in an organization, more work is required.

Considerable effort goes into creating the right vision and mission statement. When it is completed, you really have only begun. The purpose is not to have a statement on a piece of paper, but to use the vision and mission statements as guides for the entire organization.

Sage Advice

Over and over again I have seen people, when reunited with their power to create, aspire to what is highest in humanity: freedom, justice, peace, love, purpose, truth. No one tells them these are the values to which they should aspire. These values emanate from what they truly care about.
—Robert Fritz, *The Path of Least Resistance*

Personal Coaching

Whereas a small business' vision may strongly reflect the owner's personal vision, it should not be a private document. Sharing it with everyone in the company helps employees understand there is a higher purpose than just accomplishing today's to-do list. An inspiring vision and mission can single-handedly elevate morale.

The power comes from everyone understanding and subscribing to the vision and mission. These statements become a part of the fabric of the organization. The culture revolves around them. All actions reflect their subtle guidance.

When they reach this point, the job of Five-Minute Managers is much easier. Instead of everyone using a different compass, everyone in an organization knows his or her own true north. There is great power in this alignment. It is worth every effort to cultivate and nurture the vibrancy of the vision and mission so that they continue to flourish and inspire.

The Least You Need to Know

➤ Typically, an individual or organization's vision and mission statement reflects lofty qualities and goals that inspire an organization that aligns with them.

➤ There are useful guidelines for developing your statements, but they are only guides, not fixed rules.

➤ Two practical, useful processes in this chapter can stimulate and shape the creation of a personal vision statement. The Covey online approach and a more personalized step-by-step journey produce a personally inspiring statement.

➤ Organizational alignment unleashes the power of your vision and mission statements.

Chapter 3

Shared Values

In This Chapter

➤ Identify your most important personal values

➤ Learn how large organizations identify their values

➤ Discover how a new company leader changed his company

➤ See how personal values changed a person's life

A good analogy for the relationship between a vision and values is that values are the foundation upon which the vision is built.

The unique combination of values that each person and organization possesses forms the distinctive appearance of each. The vision holds all this together. Without a vision, either carefully defined or assumed by default, the person or organization cannot be very strong.

All Our Values

As with most elements of our foundation, it helps if we define what we mean by values. In this case, a checklist of values shows the wide range of attributes that the word "values" represents. Use this checklist to determine what your values are. Whereas this list includes mostly personal values, a similar process with a modified list of values is helpful when identifying organizational values. Assign a "1" to designate those that are "exceptionally important" and a "2" for those that are "important to somewhat important."

Values can change over time; those values that were somewhat important may become exceptionally important in the future. The change could occur even as you are going through the list. Also, assigning "2"s will not only help you to see all of your values, it will also help you to be clear about your number "1"s. In this exercise, you will not need to deal with those values you consider vaguely important or unimportant.

Speed Bump

Pause as you work on your values list. Reflect on those things that give you the most joy. When you smile, you know you have connected with something that is valuable to you.

Within each category below (for example, ADVENTURE, BEAUTY, etc.) you will find a list of values. Use each item in the list to complete and answer the following question:

"Do I value _____?"

If your answer is "yes," you then need to decide if this value is exceptionally important (1) or only important to somewhat important (2). If your answer is "no," simply move on to the next value.

You can also put it in the form of a statement, like:

"I love _____."

ADVENTURE

____ Risk-taking	____ The Unknown	____ Thrill Seeking
____ Danger	____ The Endeavor	____ The Quest
____ Experimenting with Something New	____ The Venture	____ The Rush
____ Exhilaration		

BEAUTY

____ Grace	____ Refinement	____ Elegance
____ Attractiveness	____ Loveliness	____ Radiance
____ Magnificence	____ Taste	____ Style

INTEGRITY

____ Honesty	____ Truth-telling	____ Seeking the truth
____ Doing what's right	____ Candor	

TO HAVE AN IMPACT

____ Moving forward	____ Coaching	____ Spark
____ Encouraging others	____ Influencing others	____ Stimulating others
____ To Excite	____ Energizing others	____ Altering
____ Hard work		

HELPING

____ Serving ____ Improving ____ Augmenting ____ Assisting

____ Endowing ____ Strengthening ____ Facilitating ____ Fostering

____ Ministering ____ Granting ____ Providing

HUMOR

____ Laughter ____ Telling jokes ____ Wit ____ Fun ____ Jollity

CREATIVITY

____ Designing ____ Inventing ____ Synthesizing ____ Imagining

____ Ingenuity ____ Originality ____ Conceiving ____ Planning

____ Building ____ Perfecting ____ Assembling ____ Inspiring

LEARNING

____ Growing ____ Detecting ____ Perceiving ____ Realizing

____ Uncovering ____ Discerning ____ Distinguishing

____ Observing ____ Learning ____ Studying

TO FEEL

____ To experience ____ To sense ____ To emote

____ To feel good ____ To glow ____ Being with the energy flow

____ Being in touch
with sensations

Consider This

A small business owner will want his personal values to guide the company's values. This puts a burden on the owner to ensure that his values are the right ones to achieve the vision. It also puts an appropriate requirement on the owner to walk his talk.

LEADERSHIP

____ Guiding ____ Inspiring ____ Influencing ____ Causing

____ Arousing ____ Enrolling ____ Reigning ____ Governing

____ Ruling ____ Persuading ____ Cajoling ____ Coaching

MASTERY

____Being an expert ____Dominating a field ____Superiority ____Primacy

____Preeminence ____Greatness ____Out-doing ____Setting standards

____Excellence ____Self-control ____Justice ____Fulfillment

____Trust

FINANCIAL

____Financial independence ____Reserves ___Investing

____Reliable income ____Net worth growth ___Active management

PLEASURE

____Being hedonistic ____Sex ____Sensual Bliss

____Being amused ____Being entertained ____Playing games

____Sports

RELATING

____Being connected ____Being part of a community ____Family

____To unite ____To nurture ____Being linked

____Being bonded ____Being integrated ____Being with

SENSITIVITY

____Tenderness ____Support ____Wisdom

____To empathize ____To see ____Being present

____Responding ____Perceiving

____Touch ____Showing compassion

SPIRITUALITY

____Being aware ____Being accepting ____Being awake ____Holiness

____Relating with God ____Being devoted ____Honoring ____Meditation

____Being passionate ____Being religious ____Ritual

____Gratitude ____Love for all that is ____Peace

TEACHING

____To educate ____To instruct ____To enlighten ____Informing

____Preparing ____Edifying ____Priming ____Uplifting

____Explaining

WINNING

____Prevailing   ____Accomplishing   ____Attaining   ____Scoring

____Acquiring   ____Triumph   ____Predominating   ____Attracting

____Persistence   ____Competition   ____Cooperation

Consider This

Values can be subtle. They guide what you do, but you may not recognize them. You take them for granted; yet, they are often the most powerful forces in your life. Recognize and honor your values.

Add up how many "1"s you have. If there are more than ten, put a star next to the ten individual values you consider most important. This may be difficult since you already deem these values to be "exceptionally important." To make it easier, ask yourself the following question: "If I lived by only one value, which one would it be?" Then ask the same question for two values, then three values, and so on until you've reached ten. Let your heart guide you in making these selections. After you have the top ten, use the same process to put another star next to the top five within the top ten. If you think carefully, you may be surprised to find that first choice didn't make it into to the top five; or maybe your first choice is still your most important value. The important thing is too follow your heart and not judge your choices.

You now know what your most important values are. Reflect on your top five. See how they interact and where they appear to be independent of the other values in your top five. It is this combination of values that makes you unique. Savor this insight.

Next, bring the words to life. For each value, write down how you see that value at work in your life. Then, identify how that value would affect your life if you were more consistent in its use or used it all the time to guide your life. The goal here is to see how increasing the quantity and quality of each value in your life would affect you. How do you feel about that?

Examine opportunities to have the values work more in combination with each other. Often, there is power in using a combination of important values in a situation. This power is worth discovering.

Examine Your Roots

Organizations also benefit greatly from a focus on values. In fact, it is as important for an organization to identify its values as it is for it to define its vision and mission.

A systematic process to identify the core values of an organization usually involves examining an organization's history. Values that guide a company do not appear on your doorstep one morning. They usually have been there for a long time, guiding day-to-day actions.

All the people involved in the value identification process benefit from looking back in time at what values guided the company. Interview old-timers and review previous company publications for great clues.

Nine Steps to Identifying Organizational Values

Done right, identifying company values involves every level of the company. Like the vision and mission process, it also takes quality time.

Companies frequently use the following nine steps:

Step 1: Top management agrees to begin the process. It is critical that this process has their support. Their support needs to identify the process to the rest of the company as a number one priority.

Step 2: The top manager, owner, chairman, or CEO identifies what he or she thinks the company's top three to five values are. This must not be an off-the-top-of-the-head exercise. The top person needs to conduct the historical review, reflect on current operational values, and assess which values are supportive of the vision and mission.

Step 3: The management team goes through a similar process, independently of the top manager. Membership on the team is critical. Be sure to include all functions. If there are some very new employees on the team, consider adding a few "wild card" veterans to the process. It is best if the managers work independently first and then meet to compare notes. A trained group facilitator is critical to a smooth process. Personal and business coaches can also be a great resource to help guide this process. Often, the challenging part of this process is agreeing on the top three to five values. Before embarking on the process, the team, with the facilitator or coach's help, should agree on ground rules about how to develop consensus.

Step 4: The top manager and the management team meet and compare results. When there are differences, explore why they exist. It may be that the team's #6 was the top manager's #5, so they are not far apart. Sometimes, what appears to be a difference between the two is resolved with a third word that captures the essence of the both words. Again, a facilitator or coach can help resolve differences.

Step 5: Solicit employee reaction and input. Gather together, by function or in cross-functional meetings, small groups of people who really care about the company. In some instances, add newer and less committed people for diversity.

Share with these groups the tentative working list developed in the previous step. It is very important that these be zero-risk meetings and that people understand their importance.

Step 6: Seek key customer input and reaction. Because most successful companies are customer-driven, the company's values need to be important to them also. Often the coach or facilitator, in conjunction with sales, can reach important and respected customers. You need the input of key decision-makers.

Step 7: The management team reviews all the work and agrees in principle to the three to five values. They then recruit a good writer from within the group, if possible, to create an inspiring and clear statement of the values. After a final review, they are ready to recommend values to the top manager.

Step 8: The top manager reviews and ultimately agrees to the values. Upon receiving the team's recommendation, this manager should reflect on it for several days. This is one of the most important decisions a top manager can make.

Step 9: When a list of values has been approved, announce them company-wide. This needs to be a special process. Do not only announce the values; also discuss how to use them every day in the company.

Personal Coaching

Organizations can learn from parents. Parents are constantly teaching values, so many that the values can become a blur. As a family, spend an evening identifying the three values that your family agrees are most important. Write them down and post them on the refrigerator or in another prominent spot. Hold each other accountable to them. If organizations focused this much on values they would be more productive and aligned.

Everyday Values Brought to Life

Values on a piece of paper are not valuable. Values need to live and breathe as a part of the everyday life of an organization.

Ingram Micro, a company whose vision and mission statements were discussed briefly in the previous chapter, took several bold moves to establish a strong sense of values in the company. Jerre Stead joined the company as the new chairman when the company went public. When he joined this international company, he called all the top managers together to identify their values. Some managers did not believe the wording of the message, since the previous management would never called a meting of all top managers. Some concluded that there must be a misunderstanding. Their confusion quickly cleared when they checked. Jerre had said "all."

To call all the top managers together in a multi-billion dollar, international company as one of the first orders of business was unprecedented. This is just the type of message the top manager wants to communicate about the importance of values.

Sage Advice

Values are tapes we play on the Walkman of the mind: any tune we choose so long as it does not disturb others.
—Jonathan Sacks, British Chief Rabbi in "The Persistence of Faith," 1990 Reith Lecture

Speed Bump

When your values are in a state of change, confusion can exist. Activities you loved now wane in interest. People you shared these activities with can be confused and take the change personally. Be alert to changes and signal to others that you are changing, and that it is not them in whom you are losing interest.

What came out of this effort was the following statement of values:

Our Values—We commit to these values to guide our decisions and our behaviors.

➤ Teamwork: We promote and support a diverse, yet unified, team.

➤ Respect: We honor the rights and beliefs of our fellow associates, our customers, our shareowners, our suppliers, and our community. We treat others with the highest degree of dignity, equality, and trust.

➤ Accountability: We accept our individual and team responsibilities, and we meet our commitments. We take responsibility for our performance in all our decisions and actions.

➤ Integrity: We employ the highest ethical standards, demonstrating honesty and fairness in every action that we take.

➤ Innovation: We are creative in delivering value to our fellow associates, customers, shareowners, suppliers, and community. We anticipate change and capitalize on the many opportunities that arise.

To bring the values to life, Jerre took several high profile actions, including the establishment of an 800 number directly to him. He invited anyone in the company to call him if they felt the company was not acting in accordance with its values. This got attention. It is the rather bold action that underscores the importance of values.

Today, Ingram Micro has moved from being the second largest to the largest distributor in America. Over the last two years, it has been one of the fastest growing companies in an industry that does not normally see double-digit growth rates. Values play a key role in this upward trend.

The key to bringing values to life is having them be a part of everyday decision making. When determining what to do, ask yourself what your values would lead you to do.

The Personal Way

Identifying and using a values approach to personal life utilizes the same principles that work in an organization. Once identified, they need to become a part of every moment of your life. At first, this can feel like a strain. If the values are right for you, they quickly become the easy and welcomed paths to follow.

Ryan's Evolution

When Ryan went through the process of identifying his values, he found one that puzzled him. Whereas he highly valued "adventure," he sensed this value was fading. His marriage a couple of years ago and newborn child seemed to be changing his outlook. As he went through the process, he began to have mixed feelings about "adventure." The value had led to some great times—climbing mountains and going to remote, exotic places, but his heart was telling him he now wanted more family-oriented values.

So "bonding with his family" replaced adventure on his list of top three values. Along with integrity and leadership, his values felt right. As he explored them further, he found different dimensions that intrigued him.

Leadership had a wider range of meanings and applications than he had at first thought. It had the traditional meaning of getting out in front and showing the way. This worked at his job and at his church. Sometimes, he knew he was a leader when he lined up behind someone else who had a great idea. Knowing when to get out of the way was a leadership quality of which he was proud. Leadership also meant sharing the lead. He reflected on his co-chairperson position with a major local charity. Working cooperatively was a dimension of leadership that he really enjoyed. He felt good knowing that leadership was a value that had multiple dimensions.

Integrity raised different issues for him. He discovered times when he did not tell the whole truth, so as not to hurt others. As he reflected on these times, he discovered that most of the time it only delayed the inevitable. He realized that when people did learn the whole truth, it was usually under less than ideal conditions, making things that much worse. The few instances when he had not told the whole truth lingered over him like a dark cloud. He could only wonder when it would come out and under what conditions.

Personal Coaching

Take stock of your values every year. They change and you need to keep pace with them. It is much easier if you do this consciously. Awareness of goals enables you to make them active guides in your journey through life.

Although it was going to be tough, Ryan realized the value of total truth all the time. He developed an affirmation with which he started each day. This affirmation reminded him of the importance of integrity. He also disciplined himself to pause before reacting to situations. He used the pause to connect with his integrity value. Instead of reacting from old habit, he trained himself to connect with and follow his heart, which knew his values.

After only three months of concentrated effort, Ryan looked back and saw that the focus had paid big dividends. Living by his values had significantly increased the happiness and joy in his life. People who saw him infrequently thought he was a changed person.

The Least You Need to Know

➤ In conjunction with the vision and mission, values powerfully guide an individual or organization.

➤ In an organization, broad involvement in the identification process is critical to the organization's acceptance and use of values.

➤ Values need to be more than words on paper. Bold, strong actions make them powerful tools.

➤ Values are dynamic, especially on a personal level. Live by today's values. What you value today may be different than a year ago.

Chapter 4

Trust: Without It You Are a Five-Hour Manager

In This Chapter

➤ Learn the two ingredients to being trusted by others

➤ Build trust five minutes at a time

➤ Turn goofs into proof you are trustworthy

➤ Learn how much you trust yourself

Trust is a simple word. You all know its power. You love it when there is trust in a relationship with a person or a company. It hurts when the trust is violated, because whatever good was present when there was trust tends to vanish.

In this chapter, you learn about how to build and nurture trust in an organization and in your life. Trust is something you consciously build every day, five minutes at a time. When you goof, and everyone does, you can take action to ensure trust is actually strengthened.

Trust—It Is Like Glue

Management gurus talk about trust as the glue that holds everything together in business. It is critical to your success as a Five-Minute Manager.

Without two-way trust, you will never be a Five-Minute Manager. You will be a five-hour manager because if you do not trust people, you will be constantly checking on others and often feel compelled to take on every task yourself. If others do not trust you, rework will be high and people will work with hidden agendas, which ultimately undermine making progress. Most importantly, without trust doing what is right becomes a monumental task.

Once you have secured the trust of others, ensure that you maintain it. What took years to build can be lost in less than five minutes; and rebuilding can take months, if not years, if it can be rebuilt at all.

Sage Advice

"Trust is the highest form of human motivation. It brings out the very best in people."
—Stephen R. Covey, *The 7 Habits of Highly Effective People*

Knowing yourself and trusting yourself go hand in hand. Self-trust is the starting point on the journey towards achieving trust in relationships.

There are two fundamental requirements for trust to exist. First, there needs to be integrity. If you want others' trust, you need to be truthful all the time. It is not good enough that you know you are truthful. Other people need to know as well. The second requirement is competency in your work. People need to know that you have the skills to do what you say you are going to do.

Both requirements need to be fulfilled. If you are only competent but not truthful, you will not be trusted. If you tell the truth all the time, but you are not competent, people will not trust you to do a job.

Trust Recipe Ingredient Number One: Integrity

Living with integrity is critical to being trusted by others.

To have integrity simply, "Tell the truth, the whole truth, so help you God." To maintain integrity, truth cannot be a "fair weather" trait. Integrity means the truth is your constant companion. If you make a mistake, you admit it. If you are confused, admit it. Pride and the desire to look good are not your friends when they block the truth. It does not mean that you have to tell everyone everything about yourself. The focus here is on telling the truth on subjects before you.

Another dimension of integrity is doing what you say you are going to do. When you keep commitments, people learn to trust you. If you cannot keep a commitment, you still build trust by admitting the truth before people expect you to deliver on your commitment.

Speed Bump

When asked if you can do something, pause and reflect. When committing, confirm what you have agreed to do.

How you manage the commitments you make is the most powerful indicator of your integrity. Be careful of the commitments you make. Do not make casual commitments. When you make one, record it, track it, and deliver it. If you really want to build trust, under-promise and over-deliver.

Openness is an important dimension of maintaining integrity, and it relates to telling "the whole truth." If everything you say is the truth, but you withhold critical parts of the truth, then you are not acting with integrity. Telling a partial truth, especially when the withheld parts make you look bad, is anti-integrity. You need to trust that the "truth will set you free."

Another aspect of integrity is active truth-seeking. For example, when analyzing a test market, evaluate all aspects. The spirit of seeking the truth and doing what is right should guide your investigations. When you discover glitches and unexpected events, view them as lessons that will lead you in a better direction. When mistakes and the unexpected become friends, projects and people prosper.

Start Now to Repair Your Integrity

Integrity can be repaired. You can decide from this moment forward you to live with integrity and to repair any lack of integrity with which you are currently living. The following steps will help you do it:

1. List five actions in the last week where you were not 100 percent honest.

2. For each one, list what caused your actions.

3. Say with passion each morning, "I tell the whole truth all the time." Say it quietly or loudly, but with energy.

4. Stop associating with people who do not tell the truth all the time.

5. When asked for an opinion, whisper "truth" to yourself before replying.

Personal Coaching

Be committed to a lifelong effort to build personal awareness. Life is a journey, and you need to be more aware each step of the way. Personal growth makes each step more joyful. Integrity plays an important role in this growth. If we are not honest with ourselves, the road will be filled with bumps and detours.

Trust Recipe Ingredient Number Two: Competency

You can be completely truthful, all the time, and still not be trusted to do your job. You also need to be skilled and knowledgeable at what you do or people will not trust you.

Competency has a couple of dimensions. First, you need to have the complete set of core competencies expected of someone in your job. Education and experience build skills, and these often become necessary hiring or promotion credentials. Without them, you will repeatedly fail to complete successfully the assignments you agree to do.

The second dimension of competency is the level of each skill you possess. Whereas there is a certain minimal expectation for each skill, each person tends to be better at some skills than others. For example, a marketing manger is expected to be analytical and creative but it is unlikely that these skills are equally as strong in all marketing managers. Thus, it is important that self-knowledge be strong so that you do not commit to doing something that requires a higher skill level than you possess.

Building Trust Five Minutes at a Time

You build trust by addressing the opportunities that are before you with truthfulness and competency. By doing this, people will gradually come to trust you.

Because trust is critical to being an effective Five-Minute Manager, proactively demonstrate your trustworthiness. A proactive plan spotlights your integrity and competency.

Step 1: Turn Goofs into Proof You Are Trustworthy

When you discover that something you expected to happen did not happen or that something you did caused an unexpected result, be forthright and constructive. Come forward with the truth, even if looked at one way it does not reflect positively on you. Use the truth to learn and demonstrate how to do something better the next time.

> ### Personal Coaching
>
> When you make a mistake, do not hide or feel ashamed. If you had to join a support group for people who made mistakes in their life, everyone on the planet would be a member. "Admit and Grow" is not a bad life slogan.

When you proactively do this, people's trust in you rises dramatically. This is what happened in the following example at a large consumer products company.

Callie's Story

Callie, an associate marketing manager on a cake mix brand, discovered that her January couponing produced far lower results than she and others expected. Coupon redemption was 30 percent lower than estimated and shipments were 6 percent lower.

She was the first person to analyze the couponing; when she discovered the results, she quickly moved to discover the reasons for the lower than predicted redemption. She quickly discovered the mistake and developed a new way to do it. The mistake was that two major newspapers delivering the coupon had printing errors. These errors delayed coupon delivery into a far less desirable week—there was less store volume that week and the paper delivered a competitive coupon that week.

Callie learned that other company brands often pre-print coupons and deliver them to the papers for them to insert into the Sunday edition.

With this information, she became a proactive Five-Minute Manager. She presented to her brand manager a five-minute overview that outlined results, lessons, and how to do it better. She backed it up with a one-page report her manager could read in five minutes. The report highlighted that her coupon promotion had not achieved the objectives she had promised. She outlined the reason and her recommendation for the next time to prevent the mistake from happening again. In case her manager wanted more information, she held in reserve several exhibits that provided details on sales and costs. As a Five-Minute Manager, she impressed her manager with her ability to concisely focus on critical elements in both her oral presentation and written report. In doing so, she made it easy for the manager to see her good work.

She impressed her manager. Callie was the first to report the shortfall of her project. She turned a potential negative into a positive because she spoke the truth: Results were not as good as expected. She demonstrated the ability to turn a mistake into a constructive learning experience. Some managers confronted with this situation try to call attention to noncritical factors, such as an increase in retailer displays and ads. This is only an attempt to cloud the truth that the coupon event did not deliver the promised sales. No matter how good retailer support was, if sales were below predictions for the event, it was not the expected immediate success. This cannot be sugar coated, but in situations where goals are not reached there are usually great learning opportunities. Thus, an apparent lack of success can be turned into the springboard for future success.

Speed Bump

When you experience what some regard as failure, pause and reframe the experience. History is full of "failures" that people learned from and turned into later triumphs. Abraham Lincoln ran for and lost eight straight elections for a variety of offices before winning the presidential election on his first try.

Step 2: I Am Good and You Should Know It

Proactively demonstrating your competency is a great way to build trust. This is not showboating or bragging but honest sharing that also turns into a learning opportunity.

One way is to share some of your work with others. For example, a sales manager conducts an analysis of a potential, untargeted customer. She gathers all the publicly available information and conducts inspections of several of the customer's stores. With this information, she formulates a plan to sell her products to the customer.

She now has the opportunity to demonstrate her competency and to learn. She goes to her manager and shares her plan as a Five-Minute Manager. Her purposes are to demonstrate skill at analyzing a new business opportunity and to gather the benefits of her manager's more extensive experience and skills. Demonstrating skill and openness to learning more are powerful trust builders.

Another situation is one in which you have an unexpectedly strong skill. Take the case of Brad, a junior travel agent at a local agency. He has one of the highest accuracy and customer satisfaction

Personal Coaching

When you forget to take care of yourself, you are not helpful to others. You are frustrated, tired, and irritable. Take care, even extreme self-care, of yourself. Being trustworthy is aided by ensuring your self-esteem is high.

ratings in the office. His managers expect him to solve customer problems creatively, and based on his customer ratings, he does this well.

Brad identifies an opportunity to make a greater contribution. He prides himself on being knowledgeable about computers and a variety of software. He develops the idea of high impact, low cost travel brochures as a way to communicate better the romantic vacations in which the agency specializes. Brad shows how desktop publishing software produces high quality, customized, timely, and very low cost flyers complete with stunning photographs. Over two weeks, he develops several samples in his spare time on the job. When he presents his brochures, his manager quickly agrees and moves to implement Brad's recommendations.

Brad impresses his manager with his initiative, creativity, special computer skills, and resourcefulness. In so doing, his manager's view of Brad's competency increases significantly. He knows he can trust Brad to fulfill his basic responsibilities and to bring important added value to the job.

Step 3: Multidirectional Trust

So far, you have explored only one dimension of trust in business—that of associates with their managers. Trust building also works both laterally and down the management hierarchy. Both are critical dimensions of trust, and again you need both elements—integrity and competency.

Trust is important to every person with whom you interact. With your secretary or administrative assistant, two-way trust is essential. For example, if you trust your secretary to send an important letter to the head of a department with little direction, it frees you up to work on critical objectives that need to be completed today. If the trust is mutual, your assistant can make commitments in your name without fear of embarrassment that you will not live up to them.

When you experience a senior manager's trust, you know how much more you can accomplish. It can be a subtle feeling, but it generates an inner confidence that propels you forward. If you are a manager, you know how empowering it is to trust a manager that works for you. You do not live in fear of a mistake erupting. You know a trusted manager brings up issues and seeks win-win solutions with you before these issues become major problems.

Personal Coaching

When you experience trust in all areas of your life, it is synergistic. Learning how to trust and being trustworthy with friends and family members provides more opportunities to make trust a keynote in your life.

As a Five-Minute Manager, you develop trust among the people you are responsible for by

➤ Being open about not having all the answers. People do not trust a know-it-all manager. A manager who can say, "Together we can discover the answers," will engender trust, as long as actions are consistent with the statement.

➤ Sharing work with your associates. A great way to engender trust is to share with some of your associates a draft of a memo you are writing to their management. Sharing a memo with the request to "make sure it is right and please point out how to improve it" builds trust. Associates know what management is told. They are shaping what thoughts are shared, and they respect the collaborative approach. An additional benefit is demonstrating your competency through analysis, recommendations, and the reasoning you use to support your recommendations.

➤ Becoming engaged in a search for truth. Employees do not trust the manager who only wants to hear good news that supports previously articulated recommendations. They trust and respect the manager who searches for truth, for the best way, even if it turns out to be counter to their previous views. Doing this requires looking at all the facts and searching for meaning and suggestions of better ways to do something.

The Five-Minute Manager develops trust with people in other functions and departments, but it is more difficult. The increased difficulty comes from a lower appreciation for and less understanding of the competencies of people in different departments and functions. In addition, fewer interactions produce fewer opportunities to develop knowledge of each other, including how trustworthy each person is. Without knowing, many people adopt what they consider to be a healthy dose of skepticism. Unfortunately, there is nothing healthy about it.

Given the greater difficulty, it is important that additional effort be made to build bridges of knowledge about integrity and competency. The ways a manager develops trust with associates also work with people in other departments and functions, but more slowly. Address another function's lack of understanding about the skills required in your function by proactively making presentations about what you do.

Consider This

When you experience a violation of trust with someone, it often seriously damages the relationship. The pain is great, especially in a close, long-term relationship. The damage is often ultimately fatal for a relationship, even if it continues for a period after the violation of trust.

Other functional managers often are curious about what you do. Engage them in a discussion about what you do, and be sure to speak their language. For example, a bridging subject in a marketing manager's discussion with a finance manager can be about how the marketing manager sets and manages budgets. In discussing the creative process, the marketing manager can discuss the cost of producing a commercial, in addition to sharing with the finance manager how an agency produces a commercial.

Make similar efforts to build trust with other functional managers. You might try the following:

➤ Share a draft of your memo to your management that involves their function in some direct or even indirect way. Ask for their perspective and improvement thoughts. After you have revised the memo, share the final version with them, as a blind copy, if necessary. This is an opportunity to demonstrate your competency and integrity.

➤ Keeping your commitments is a powerful way to build trust with other departments. Be on time for meetings. Look for opportunities to help other functional managers. When you tell them that the help will be there tomorrow, make sure it is there early. Under-promise what you can really do and over-deliver. It makes the small commitment more visible to the recipient.

Personal Coaching

Sharing and openness work at home too. Unpleasant surprises undermine, even destroy trust, with friends and family. Take the time each week to catch up on life's events. In a busy life, it is too easy to forget personal relationships. Do not let forgetfulness undermine trust.

If you are new to a job, make building the trust of others your number one priority. Building trust takes time, so start right away. Be consistent in everything you do. The smallest violation of trust can be a big setback. In five minutes, you can wipe out five months of effort to build trust.

When trust is not present or is weak, it handicaps the Five-Minute Manager. Everything takes longer, requires more effort, and even a completed task has lower quality and quantity than expected. Trust is that important.

An Oft Forgotten Dimension of Trust

Most people usually think of trust as outwardly directed. You either trust or do not trust other people or institutions.

Maybe the most important dimension of trust is self-trust. Do you trust yourself?

Answering this question requires addressing the same issues you use to determine if you trust someone else. Doing this requires self-awareness. You need to look candidly at yourself. Without candor, your false assessments come back to haunt you. Perhaps the biggest damage is to self-esteem, which you should treat as a crown jewel. When you address the issues of your integrity and competency, be totally honest.

Assess your integrity. How honest are you with yourself? You like to think you are honest with yourself, but often your assessments are more wishful than honest. Do an inventory and be honest—it is for your benefit.

Use the same spirit when you evaluate your competencies. Know what you can and cannot do, not what you wish you could do or what you think you could do if you tried. Humility and honesty are crucial to trusting yourself. Bragging only ends up teaching you that you are not as good as you think you are.

The power of honest self-understanding is almost impossible to overestimate. When you act with high quality self-understanding, your confidence and self-esteem are high. Your humility is also high because a part of self-understanding is knowing what you do not know or do well.

When you know yourself, others can sense it. You interact with others in a calmly confident manner that inspires trust and confidence in you. Reflect on people who have this quality. Doesn't it feel good to be with them? You trust them completely.

Personal Coaching

Self-awareness is the key to self-trust. Being self-aware requires an inward journey. The inward journey is best done quietly. Meditation and contemplation are great guides along this path.

The Least You Need to Know

➤ Trust is the glue that holds organizations together.

➤ To be trusted by others, you need to have integrity and competency.

➤ Integrity requires total honesty, all the time.

➤ It takes five minutes to violate trust, and it can take years to rebuild.

➤ Be competent, build skills, and show them off.

➤ Trusting yourself starts with knowing yourself.

Chapter 5

Just Listen

In This Chapter

➤ Learn just what poor listeners we are

➤ Learn how to prepare to listen

➤ Loving to learn aids listening

➤ The three responses that dramatically improve your comprehension

---

We are remarkably poor listeners; and there is almost no training available on how to be an effective listener. There are, however, some simple steps you can take right now to become a better listener. Although the steps are simple, the lifelong habits you need to change can not be disposed of overnight.

A company of good listeners is critically important to the success of a Five-Minute Manager. As a result, good listening ranks, like vision and values, among the most important foundation elements of Five-Minute Management. A company of great listeners is on the threshold of being an optimally performing company.

Gosh! We're Not Good Listeners

Research has repeatedly demonstrated that we are not good listeners. According to these tests, we remember only 25 to 45 percent of what we heard just a few minutes before. Put another way, we forget or never hear 55 to 75 percent of what is said.

Research further suggests that our poor listening skills develop at a very early age. In one study, first graders recalled 90 percent, second graders 80 percent, junior high school students 44 percent. By graduation from high school, it was only 28 percent.

Consider This

A survey of all major companies showed that two-thirds of their 50–billion-dollar training budgets are spent on improving communication skills.

We are not poor listeners because of a lack of practice. Studies suggest we spend 80 percent of our time in some form of communication. Of that, we spend 45 percent of the time listening, 30 percent speaking, 16 percent reading, and 9 percent writing.

Personal Coaching

Children are great listening teachers. Their language is simple and their agendas uncomplicated. Their communication is also loaded with energy. Listen closely and you will smile.

If Five-Minute Managers work in poor listening environments, they will never be effective managers. They pack their communications with information. If listening skills are not sharp, the Five-Minute Manager becomes at least the ten- or fifteen-minute manager.

How Difficult Can It Be?

Learning how to be a better listener is not difficult. This chapter shares several tips on how to be a better listener. With commitment and conscious effort, listening becomes a powerful skill.

If this is the case, why aren't we better listeners? First, listening skills are not usually taught. Information and training can fix this.

Second, and most importantly, we do not recognize or reward good listeners. We reward great speakers—actors and politicians, for example. Within business, we reward the person demonstrating meeting leadership. This leadership ability usually involves great verbal and interpersonal skills. The person who listens well often goes unnoticed. If a person listens well and uses what they have heard in their verbal communication, we credit their interpersonal skills more than their listening skills. In addition, not many personnel reviews make great listening skills a priority.

With all this said, it should be no surprise that we are not good listeners. If we closely watch great business leaders, we discover most are above average listeners. Without watching and listening closely to these leaders, we only see the results of their good listening—an insightful addition or penetrating question, for example.

Listening Made Easy

Listening is easy. Sit or stand still. Rest your jaw muscles. It is the easiest part of the communication process.

Because it is so easy, enjoy it. This attitude is critical. If you do not enjoy listening, you will never be a good listener.

The two major benefits of being a great listener are learning and greatly improved results you will read more on this later.

Second, all of your communication is dramatically more effective when you are a great listener. Your questions are on target, and your responses go to the heart of every issue. You make better decisions. There is less rework, and higher quality abounds. Now you can be a Five-Minute Manager.

Personal Coaching

Friends can be great teachers. They care about and know you. Reflect back to them what you hear. Then, encourage them to tell you the rest of the story—the unsaid, the emotions, and the confusion. You both will be better listeners.

Create an Open Space in Which to Listen

The most important step toward becoming a great listener happens before you have heard one word. Clear your mind to create the space for new information to enter.

One of the biggest impediments to great listening is the expectation you have before someone begins talking to you. When you know someone is going to talk to you, your mind begins whirring with a variety of thoughts and feelings. You recall the last time you talked to this person and begin wondering what they want to talk about this time. You start guessing, and those guesses turn into strong expectations in which you believe. By the time the person shows up, you have it all figured out.

Sage Advice

It is the province of knowledge to speak, and it is the privilege of wisdom to listen.
—Oliver Wendell Holmes

When the person actually begins talking, you are focused on your own expectations, and not what they are saying. As a result of your focus, you hear mostly what you expected the person to say. You do not hear and comprehend what they are really saying.

With No Expectations, Expect Success

Janice recognized the importance of clearing her mind in her job as a negotiator for her car parts company. There had been several unsuccessful sessions with a potential supplier who had products that would help her company. This was to be their last session, and she really wanted to find a way to make a deal.

She remembered a lesson from an earlier training session and felt it was her one hope to change the outcome of the upcoming negotiating session. Thirty minutes before the session, Janice went back to her hotel. In the quiet of her room, she started to review the expectations she had for the meeting. She knew the other company would insist on certain conditions and terms, because it had done so in the two previous sessions.

With some effort, she let go of the expectations. She knew they might change; maybe she was missing something they were proposing. She imagined her expectations leaving her mind. In their place, she imagined clear, calm, and open space. She released all tension and thoughts.

When she met with the other company, she felt physically different. She was more peaceful and alert. As negotiations progressed, she heard most of the same words again, but now she also noticed their tonality. She noticed the body language of the representatives of the other company. Because she was calm, she listened with her heart as well as her mind. She sensed they were passionate about certain parts of their proposal, and any suggestion that these parts be changed would likely derail the negotiations. She intuitively sensed also, however, that they were less passionate about one particular part of their proposal. This prompted several thoughts. When she suggested trading it for something that was important to her company, they agreed after a brief discussion.

They shook hands and closed a win-win deal. Janice reflected on how this time had been different. Both sides asked for the same terms, so there was no change. In previous sessions, Janice had challenged each of their terms. Because in this session she had been calmer and sensitive to everything they said, including tonality and body language, she was able to hear points she had not before. Because she did not challenge any of their passionate points, they did not feel threatened when Janice asked for concessions on less important points.

You too can experience benefits like this; clearing your mind of expectations before listening works. When you replace the expectations with a calm and receptive mind, you hear about twice as much. This simple step we can all take provides major benefits.

Personal Coaching

Maybe the toughest place to let go of expectations is with someone we have known for years—a spouse or best friend, for example. On a quiet morning listen to your inner chatter and examine your feelings every time this person talks. See how often you prefilter what is said. Now you know how high a mountain you must climb.

Speed Bump

Clearing your mind before communicating is not easy. We are creatures of habit and charge into a conversation believing we know what to do and how to do it. To learn how to clear your mind and become centered usually requires stomping on your brakes and stopping to develop the new habit.

Listening to Learn

When listening to learn replaces listening to reply, your listening skills take another big step forward.

Most of us today listen to reply. That is, as someone talks we are formulating a reply in our head. We register the first few words, quickly determine where the speaker is going, and start determining how to respond. While we are formulating a reply, our listening effectiveness approaches nil. If we recognize that the other person is doing the same thing when we are talking, we begin to see how ineffective many conversations are.

Replace listening to reply with listening to learn. It is not easy for most people to make this change; we have spent our whole life listening to reply. It is one of our strongest, most ingrained habits.

The elements necessary to change this strong habit are

➤ Let go of the need to win or be right. Replace it with the need to seek win-win solutions.

➤ Understand that the Universe delivers gifts to us in all kinds of packages. If we judge gifts by their wrapping, we reject many of them.

➤ Know the thrill and excitement of learning. For some people, learning is a threat to the status quo. Change may be theoretically good, but usually for other people, not themselves. Reconnect with the thrill of a time when learning made a very positive contribution to your life. Reconnect with that energy every day. This motivating energy will lead you forward.

➤ Use the discipline and structures necessary to transform intent to change into actual change. Some people use affirmations each morning and before important communicational opportunities to bring about change. If you use affirmations, make them unconditional. "I will be a good listener," feels very different from "I am a good listener," or "I love listening to learn." The former says you are not there yet, but will be sometime in the future. The latter says you are now a good listener. The difference may be subtle until you tune into how different they feel to your heart and mind.

Personal Coaching

Try this at home. Without telling someone you are close to, commit yourself to learning something from regular conversation you do not now know. It is often toughest to learn from people about whom we think we know everything. Savor your surprise when you do learn, because it will happen.

Validate and Mirror

We make a listening error when we assume we have heard and understood everything. It is one of the more common listening mistakes. When we make it, we base all of our subsequent thinking on an assumption that might be slightly or totally wrong.

Personal Coaching

Try this at home as well. Listen to your spouse or a good friend, and mirror back what you think you have heard. Then listen very closely to their reply. You may be shocked by what you missed. It may not be exact words you missed, but missed emotions are critical content in any conversation.

Jettison this now. In its place needs to be an assumption that we did not accurately hear what a person said. A variety of responses help us validate what we think we heard and make the necessary corrections.

Response 1: "I heard you say … "

Using this response, you simply mirror back what you think you heard. It is a simple, yet powerful, listening technique. Using this one technique all the time improves your listening. When using it, have an attitude that welcomes the response, "No. What I said was … "

If you resent, instead of welcome this response, two problems occur. First, the other person senses this, thus minimizing the openness this technique can create. Second, the "not welcome here attitude" limits your comprehension because a part of your brain is spinning around negative energy.

Response 2: "By … do you mean … "

This response helps you take what you think you heard and add an interpretation that you want the other person to verify. It is a step up from just mirroring back to a person. It is valuable when you think a person means more than they have just said or that they have not been completely forthcoming. If this is the case, it is an invitation to the other person to address potentially new issues. When this happens, the communication is well focused and productive. Again, as the listener, you need to be equally receptive to a negative as well as a positive response. If not, you may be manipulating instead of honestly seeking the truth.

Response 3: "If … then … "

This response helps you take what you think you heard and add a proposal of your own. For example, "If you believe there is more than enough water for the project, then the excess can be used for my agricultural needs." This is usually a statement, rather than a question.

The first part is an invitation for the speaker to validate what you think you heard. Making the connection between what you think you heard and your own message is a great method of creating an easy flow of communication. Each party feels the other is listening and using that information accurately and productively.

There are numerous books and teachers of better listening skills. This section touches on the specific skills that help the Five-Minute Manager be effective and efficient. When learned and embraced, these skills elevate the listening comprehension in any organization or relationship.

The Least You Need to Know

➤ You are not as good a listener as you think you are.

➤ Before listening to someone, clear out expectations and become calm and centered.

➤ Listening to learn instead of listening to reply requires an attitude adjustment.

➤ Validate what you think you heard, and discover the rest of the story.

➤ Interpret what you think you heard to bring added value to a conversation.

➤ Validating what you think you heard and adding your thoughts create an easy flow of conversation.

Chapter 6

Cooperate, Don't Compete

In This Chapter

➤ Learn the pitfalls of competition

➤ Understand the research results of cooperation versus competition

➤ Discover the myths of competition

➤ See how cooperation creates win-win solutions

Five-Minute Managers greatly appreciate the value of cooperation. They have seen how competition within a company shuts down lines of communication and virtually prevents optimal results. When the spirit of cooperation pervades a company, magic is possible.

To help people appreciate this power, Five-Minute Managers teach about the pitfalls of competition. Their message makes common sense to most people, even those who have elevated competition to the status of a virtue.

Cooperation Is a Necessity

Cooperation is the last, but very important foundation element for the Five-Minute Manager. If an organization has competing divisions or functions, they minimize the effectiveness of the Five-Minute Manager.

If the Five-Minute Manager operates in an environment where competition thrives between groups, the following conditions hinder effectiveness:

➤ Competing groups see the world as a zero sum equation. In this worldview, if one group gets what it wants, another group must lose something of equal value. This view triggers other actions that inhibit an organization's success.

➤ Competitors do not give information or resources to each other. This withholding is the crux of the problem with competition. Without the information to make the most informed decisions, organizations struggle. Decisions are made and remade as they encounter errors caused by lack of the right facts.

➤ A competitor often tries to make a fellow competitor fail. In addition to limited sharing, a competitor can knowingly mislead another competitor in a number of ways. For example, they can tell the truth, but only part of the truth. What is left out could be critical to success. The goal is to make the other group look bad. When competition escalates to this level, it is a disease that weakens the competitors and all others in the organization.

The Science Against Competition

Researchers have studied the differences in groups working cooperatively and groups working competitively to complete the same task. The results overwhelmingly favor cooperation. In almost all cases where differences arose, the group working cooperatively to complete tasks performed better. When quality becomes an important ingredient to success, the benefits of cooperation are accentuated.

It is my opinion that cooperation is better than competition within an organization and between different organizations. I know this idea is tough for Adam Smith devotees to swallow. For those of you who believe strongly in competition, try to focus only on the strengths and benefits of cooperation. For you, both cooperation and competition can help you achieve success. Try to cooperate more than you have in the past. As you do, focus both on how people feel about the process and on the results they achieve. Proof of the benefits of cooperation is likely to come from this experience.

Speed Bump

We assume that competition is good because that is what we have always been told. Few of us have actually paused to consider if competition is the best way.

A 1981 study by two researchers reviewed all the academic research done on competition and cooperation—122 research projects—between 1924 and 1980. In 65 of the projects, cooperation promoted higher achievement, and in only 8 of the projects did competition outperform cooperation. There was no statistical difference in the balance of the studies. Subsequent studies have shown even greater advantages to cooperation.

Some Myths About Competition

In our culture, competition has been elevated to the status of a virtue. The demise of communism and the triumph of capitalism with its free-market framework probably have enhanced this view.

A suggestion to ban competition within an organization would do much more than raise eyebrows. Over the years we have come to believe that at least some degree of competition is healthy, if not necessary to organizational success.

In my experience it is not. In most situations, competition produces stress, anxiety, and fear. Although some proponents say these conditions are positive, most mental health experts agree that fear and its related emotions are the most negative forces that affect a person.

On the other hand, a person's best performance is seen when "in the zone" or flow. This peak performance time is associated with fun and a range of positive emotions. Being in the zone produces excellent results in short periods. Others, like Abraham Maslow, associate peak performance with self-actualization. Self-actualization is also a period almost devoid of negativity. If some exists, it is handled with ease.

The sales function is one of the most competitive of a company. It is customary to have people compete against each other for sales and for the highest achievement versus meeting only individual sales quotas.

Personal Coaching

Competition at home? Your initial answer may be "No." But look closer and you will find at least five things over which you compete with family members. One easy example is the television remote. How quickly can you find four more?

Early in my business career, I was a member of the sales force of a large, successful company. The monthly rankings were closely watched, because they influenced career and salary progress. The competition to be Number One was intense and produced very little cooperation between sales representatives. The bonds were minimal, fun virtually nonexistent, and success met minimal standards.

Later in my career, when I ran a large sales organization, we abolished individual goals and set company-wide goals and quotas. Formal competition between individuals was nonexistent. This spawned terrific cooperation, friendlier interpersonal relationships, and business results that led the nation in that field.

The following sections list some of the myths that surround competition. Thinkers and researchers are increasingly challenging these myths with interesting results.

Competition Is Part of Human Nature

The pioneering work of Margaret Mead showed that humans are not innately competitive. She concluded from her research of many cultures that whether a culture values cooperation or competition is dependent on the "total social emphasis of that society."

For most of us, this passes the test of our experience. We all know people who avoid competition whenever possible. They do not enjoy competitive sports or the negative feelings that mar a competitive relationship.

Consider This

Cooperation outperforms competition because trying to beat another person or group is different from trying to do well. When you compete, the primary focus is winning. When you cooperate, the focus is performing the task well.

Competition Is Fun!

Supporters of this myth point to sports to support their case. Almost all of our games are competitive games, and we play games to have fun, don't we?

To test this hypothesis, watch a competitive sport and keep your focus on the faces of the players. You might want to keep a little scorecard of your own. Record how many smiles and grimaces you see. If the score is not ten to one in favor of negative reactions, then it is an unusually positive game.

In competitive sports, there are many more losers than winners. In leagues from Little League to the NBA, there is ultimately only one winner at the end of the season, and a large group of those who are losers in their last game.

Within business, we often see the same dynamics. We also see the pain caused by competition. With competition comes the possibility and fear of failure. Although competition's proponents often point to this fear as a positive force, virtually every psychologist will tell you that fear is the single most negative force in most people. This is especially true over long periods of time. The fear of losing is a powerful distracter and inhibitor.

A first step for many businesses is eliminating individual competition and installing group competition. This encourages cooperation to achieve results within the group. Unfortunately, it still invites stress and fear, which are success inhibitors. The next step is to expand the size of the groups until ultimately the entire company is a group working to achieve common goals.

This is where the visioning process can be especially effective. When an entire company enthusiastically embraces a vision, mission, and shared values, you are sure to find high levels of cooperation and, associated with it, superior results. One of the unintended benefits in many cases of the visioning process is that it pulls a company together under a common umbrella to become more open and united. When this happens, cooperation is a natural consequence.

In my experience, morale improves and turnover decreases under these circumstances. In one major company that tracked among other things how much fun people had on the job, the fun rating soared when they went to a more cooperative approach. Again, more fun was directly associated with record results—far better than the company division experienced under an intensely competitive system.

Competition Creates Greater Innovation

This myth is a function of our economic culture and not of our common sense. Supporters of this myth point to technological innovation in the United States as proof that a competitive culture produces superior ideas and products.

This makes sense only because we have not experienced the full power of cooperation. Consider the following propositions.

The best way to cure cancer is to …

> ➤ have all drug companies cooperate by sharing all they know, including all their patents and proprietary research.

> ➤ have all the drug companies compete as they do now. They work independently and keep their findings and patents to themselves.

In a similar manner, would we have better performing and safer cars if all the manufacturers shared their technology, knowledge, and patents?

Within particular circumstances, all the evidence suggests that the sharing and mixing of diverse perspectives that comes from cooperation produces better results. We saw earlier how competitors do not share all they know and can even mislead in their effort to win. Clearly these actions are not conducive to optimal innovation.

Personal Coaching

Do you have a smile on your face and joy in your heart when you compete with friends and family? Think about this and do not be surprised if you realize these are some of your less positive times.

Cooperation and the Five-Minute Manager

When the spirit of cooperation pervades an organization, communication and productivity flourish. People working together for a common goal are a powerful force. When harnessed internally within an organization, they can make that company a winner with its customers and consumers and suppliers.

Developing the spirit of cooperation is a matter of recognition and rewards. If a company rewards winners when there are losers, it will encourage a competitive environment. If it nurtures sharing and learning from others and recognizes the efforts of all, the spirit of cooperation will take root.

Consider This

Studies show that competition produces especially poor results when creativity is an important and required skill. Separate studies confirm the value of group stimulation and encouragement in creatively focused tasks.

Making Cooperation Stronger at My Company

If cooperation is so important how can I make it stronger at my company?

That is a good question!

There are two simple yet powerful keys to increasing the level of cooperation in your business.

Share and Learn

First, the company needs to encourage and reward sharing and learning from each other. Some companies become a "learning company," where new structures and processes facilitate sharing and learning from each other. For example, General Electric divisions meet on a regular basis; the only purpose of these meetings is to share what they have learned since the last meeting.

Personal Coaching

Try the cooperation principles out at home. Talk them over (it is a form of cooperation!) and determine how you can pick one area of your life in which to cooperate. Try it for a week with no competition allowed.

The Five-Minute Manager routinely asks people making a recommendation what they have learned on the subject from others in the company. If the response is that they have not asked or they asked and they did not learn anything, then the Five-Minute Manager asks them to go back and dig deeper and harder. They always come back with nuggets of learning that produce a stronger recommendation.

Technology is a great facilitator of sharing and learning. E-mail facilitates the rapid exchange of information. For example, a person in Bombay, India can scan a picture in about a minute and send it to a person in New York in less than thirty seconds. Newsletters are a common method of sharing, and they are rapidly increasing because of the ease of developing and distributing via e-mail.

Win-Win

The second key to creating a spirit of cooperation in your business and life is to always seek win-win solutions.

For many people this is an incredibly difficult challenge. When the root of their challenge is discovered, it traces back to their view of the world. Changing someone's view of the world is never easy, but in a few paragraphs your understanding will take big strides forward.

There are two key assumptions that many people hold. First, they view the world from a "Darwinian" perspective—only the tough survive. Second, they believe they live in a zero-sum world. You can challenge these two assumptions, or you can ignore them. The Five-Minute Manager chooses the latter. Taking these two assumptions head-on guarantees a protracted debate and not much else.

The Five-Minute Manager ignores the underlying beliefs in favor of demonstrating the power of win-win. The Five-Minute Manager does not agree to any proposal unless it is win-win. The standard is not just any win-win solution, but the best win-win solution.

Initially, managers that work for the Five-Minute Manager fear they will get less than their optimal solution when they agree to a win-win solution. They think of it as compromise, which they believe is something you do only when you have to.

At the prodding of the Five-Minute Manager, they gradually discover that win-win solutions are what the person who invented the word synergy really had in mind.

Win-win solutions are always stronger than win-lose solutions. ALWAYS. You become a believer when you learn how to always seek them out. You become as good at win-win as you were at win-lose. When that happens, watch out! Whatever goals you have set, increase them, because you now know the magic spell for truly optimal performance.

Sharing, learning, and win-win are the powerful combination that powers up the spirit of cooperation in any company.

Personal Coaching

The next time there is a difference over what to do in your family, stop the discussion. Ask everyone involved to agree that they will do nothing until they have a win-win solution. Agreement to this should be relatively easy. Seeking the first win-win solution will take a few tries. When you have it, observe the sense of surprise and smiles.

The Least You Need to Know

➤ Competition tends to create a lack of sharing and even some misleading of one group when it competes with another group.

➤ When researchers study projects done cooperatively and competitively, in the majority of cases, the cooperatively completed projects generate better results.

➤ Human beings are not innately competitive.

➤ For most competitors, competition is not fun. There are more losers than winners.

➤ Greater innovation occurs with the sharing and interactive characteristics of a cooperative approach to a project.

➤ Sharing and win–win solutions are the keys to increasing the spirit of cooperation in your company.

Part 2
Five-Minute Goals

Goals are common to all businesses. Often they serve as focal points. There can be daily sales goals, cash flow goals, shipment goals, and other goals in every function, at every level of the company.

Careers and compensation are often linked to the level of goal achievement. Setting goals, planning and executing plans to achieve goals, and planning evaluations can consume significant parts of every person's business day.

As important and central as goals are to a business, many managers do not know how to effectively set goals, a critical stage in the life of a goal. Mistakes made in goal setting can undermine the best companies.

In this part, you learn the care Five-Minute Managers take in setting goals that can inspire. Inspiring goals enable a business to take a big leap towards achieving its vision.

Chapter 7

Key Data First, and Maybe Only

> ### In This Chapter
>
> ➤ Learn about the vast data available to most manufacturers of products
>
> ➤ Discover how to identify the very few key data points the Five-Minute Manager needs to know how their business is performing
>
> ➤ Learn about the vast resources on the Internet that help you run your business

Before setting goals, the collection and analysis of key data is critical. There are two important elements here. First, the Five-Minute Manager collects and analyzes only key data. What is key data? Simply defined, it is data that relates directly to the behavior of our customers and consumers.

In many cases, there is a difference between customers and consumers. For example, a manufacturer who uses retailers to sell its products has customers (retailers) and consumers (people purchasing the product in the store).

There is considerable data available for a consumer products company selling its products through grocery stores. The following is only a partial list of the types of data available from suppliers like A. C. Nielsen, who collect the data from grocery and drug stores and sell it to manufacturers:

➤ Retail price

➤ Promotion price

➤ Difference in price versus key competitor

➤ Display size

➤ Market share

➤ Share of category segments

➤ Number of displays

➤ Display location

➤ Retailer ad or no ad

➤ Size of retailer ad

➤ Position on the shelf

➤ Promotion volume

➤ Regular price volume

For many products, most of the listed data is not critical to understanding consumer behavior. For example, only the "Difference in price versus key competitor" data may be predictive of consumer behavior. That is, as the relationship changes to favor your brand, you sell more product, and you sell less when it goes in the opposite direction. You determine this through rigorous statistical analysis that demonstrates a strong correlation between changes in this factor and changes in your business.

When using the same statistical analysis on the number of displays and the size of a retailer ad, there may not be a relationship between changes in the factors and changes in your business. Before concluding this, any business should conduct several tests using the data. The key factors vary for different types of businesses and for brands with large and small market share.

The important point is that the Five-Minute Manager focuses on the data that directly affects business results. The result is that, in most cases, the Five-Minute Manager automatically excludes over 90 percent of the data from consideration. Thus, in a world of data-overload, the Five-Minute Manager knows what factors really matter.

Second, the data collection and analysis are broader than most managers may think necessary. That is because the Five-Minute Manager has broad vision.

This seems to counter the key data point, but it is not. For example, the person who is not a Five-Minute Manager may focus only on the data coming from retailers of the product. This is dangerous. There are additional quantitative data sources that can directly influence business results. For example, quantitative consumer research often provides critical answers to business problems and presents new growth opportunities. In addition, qualitative sources bring valuable perspectives.

Speed Bump

For each business there are unique and critical data points. Do not assume that what is important for one business is important for your business.

Personal Coaching

The data you have at home and how easy it is to analyze may surprise you. If you use software like Quicken or Money, you can analyze income and expenses in many ways for multiple time periods. Spend ten minutes this week learning how to put this power to work for you.

The Five-Minute Manager reviews all of these key sources before drawing conclusions about needs and possible goals to address those needs. In this chapter, we will discuss some of these broader sources.

Consider This

Databases first appeared in the 1960s, and by 1980 there was an information science. In the mid-1980s, experts in this science started the first attempts at artificial intelligence in an attempt to mimic intelligent human behavior.

Get the Shovels Out

Many companies take time once a year to conduct an extensive review of their operations. They identify how the current plan worked and did not work, and what changes occurred among retailers, consumers, products, competitors, and within their own company. After arriving at this understanding, you have the groundwork for constructing next year's plan. Often this review is part of the process of agreeing on volume and profit forecasts for the next year.

Customer Data—Usually There Is More Than Enough Data

For manufacturers who sell through retailers, there usually is an abundance of data; in fact, the information can be overwhelming at times. Often you can get data by year, month, week, and even the day. There is data for every size, flavor, scent, and taste that you sell. The data can tell you how much you sold at a special price and how much at regular prices. If you want to know how much you sold from an in-store display and how much from the shelf, the information is available. You can determine how much was sold through grocery stores, drug stores, and mass-merchandisers, such as Wal-Mart and K-Mart. You can even determine how much volume was sold through which major chains, all broken out in the detail just described. Alcoholic beverage sellers can determine volume through liquor stores in many states.

Personal Coaching

You work hard to save money. Step one is defining your investment objectives. Then seek and read advice. Invest the time necessary to become a personal expert. You can do it. Use Internet resources and the local library to discover the investment opportunities that will work hardest for you. It is almost that easy.

WHEW! In some cases, this is only the beginning.

All of this data costs money, and there are additional costs associated with the hardware and software needed to manipulate the data. Companies need to examine closely these cost versus the value received. If they do not have the in-house resources and talent to manage the data, they should not buy it. If management does not understand and use the conclusions drawn to help improve the business, they should not buy it. If the senior management is not comfortable with statistical analysis of data, it might be a waste of time and money to buy all the available data, until you have educated them on its benefits.

Consider This

Local area networks (LANs) are the key to efficient data sharing. Computers linked together help users easily and quickly share critical information. In larger computer networks, a bridge passes information between LANs. A router connects a LAN to a larger network. A gateway connects networks that use different languages. This hierarchy is the backbone of companies that are good at sharing information.

I Have the Data. Now What Do I Do?

For many managers, just getting data is the tough part. After receiving it, they may only do a cursory examination of it.

Five-Minute Managers know the challenges involved in gaining crucial insights that will propel their businesses to new heights. Their experience teaches them that it often takes considerable digging through a variety of data sources to gleam the few insights that make a difference. They are adept with the tools that enable them to gain these insights quickly and with minimum effort. Each time they work to solve a problem; they use new skills and sources. Over time, they have a portfolio of tools to use on future challenges.

The basic tool is statistical analysis, which determines if there is a positive or negative correlation between two or more sets of data. For example, if a manager suspects there is a relationship between volume changes and changes in the price difference between his or her company's product and a competitor's, he or she would subject that data to analysis. For the purposes of this discussion, assume the following data:

Product Data

Date	Price Diff: A vs. B	Volume
2/10	$.23	153
2/11	.26	147
2/12	.27	145
2/13	.12	167
2/14	-.10	183
2/15	-.10	187
2/16	-.12	192
2/17	-.05	175
2/18	+.05	170
2/19	+.06	169
2/20	+.10	163
2/21	+.10	162
2/22	+.20	155

Just looking over this data, the Five-Minute Manager can see a possible strong relationship between changes in the price difference and volume. When conducting this type of analysis, it is usually desirable to receive daily data. Key data points, like prices, tend to remain the same in a day. Weekly data represents an average of seven days, which can mask the true dynamics at work.

It is also very helpful to use data from one retailer. If not, you receive the daily data as an average price for all the chains for that day. In truth, that average price may not have been used by any of the chains. Making decisions using prices that consumers never actually see can weaken the analysis.

In matters of such importance, use a good statistical software package to analyze the data. A. C. Nielsen and others can supply them. You can conduct a simple correlation analysis using Microsoft's Excel software. The more complex software packages provide warnings about where the data is weak. They also suggest about how much of the change in day to day volume is due to the variable, the price difference in this case.

Excel is also good for charting data. Charts are pictures that can be very helpful. In this case, the Excel chart of our data looks like this:

Speed Bump

Do not let statistical analysis over-whelm your common sense. Use all input, including your personal observations, to make decisions.

Chart of Price and Volume Changes

Day	Price Difference	Volume
10-Feb	$0.23	153
11-Feb	$0.26	147
12-Feb	$0.27	145
13-Feb	$0.12	167
14-Feb	-$0.10	183
15-Feb	-$0.10	187
16-Feb	-$0.12	192
17-Feb	-$0.05	175
18-Feb	$0.05	170
19-Feb	$0.06	169
20-Feb	$0.10	163
21-Feb	$0.10	162
22-Feb	$0.20	155

After a thorough analysis, the Five-Minute Manager finds about one piece of key datum for every fifty pieces of data. Again, key data is that data that demonstrates a strong relationship between changes in that data and changes in volume or market share. Therefore, if you want to improve business results, improve the key data relationships.

That is not to say that all the other data is worthless. For example, there might not be a relationship between display data (number of displays and average size of a display) and volume. Although not key in this regard, the data does help to evaluate sales execution of a promotion event. Did sales persuade retailers to support the promotion event, a couponing promotion, for example, with special in-store locations separate from the shelf location?

Let the Consumer's Voice Be Heard

Going directly to consumers and listening to them is typically the most valuable type of research. However, although it is typically the most valuable, it is still fallible.

There are several types of consumer research that can produce key data points depending on the category of product and its sales dynamics. For example, researching taste differences between products is a critical measure for some and not for others. Even with those products where taste is important, the best method of researching those differences can vary.

In-Home Consumer Research

When done right, this is one of the most reliable forms of consumer research. In this research, consumers are recruited by an independent research company to use one or more products in their homes. In most cases, the products arrive without any brand identification. Consumers use the products as they normally would. The consumers recruited to use the products are usually already users of a product of this type. When they are not users, they may be people a company believes are potential users. The independent research company monitors usage through follow-up calls and by asking questions at the conclusion of the consumer testing.

In many cases, two or more products are tested. Sometimes the same consumer uses all the products in sequence, or they may use only one. The choice of procedure depends on the test objectives and the necessary sensitivity of the test.

After using the products, the consumers respond to a series of questions, including an overall rating and their purchase intent. How we ask the questions is critical.

Consider This

For a company just beginning to use consumer research, the transition can be difficult. When you are accustomed to relying on personal evaluation, it can be difficult relying on the opinion of many anonymous consumers.

For example, if sweetness of the product is an important evaluation point, there are at least two ways to ask the question. First, "Is the product you tasted too sweet? Yes or No." Second, "Is the sweetness of the product you tasted too sweet, just right, or not sweet enough?" In the first question, we raise an issue—the product may be too sweet. In the second, there is no such issue. The second way of asking about sweetness is more objective and likely to produce answers that reflect consumer real-world reactions.

In the vast majority of these tests, the overall rating of the products is equal. Sometimes there are internal differences, "fresher fruit taste," for example. These differences may be meaningful to some subgroups of consumers. For example, if you tested two bars of leading deodorant soaps, they have differences like aroma and amount of lather, but your overall rating is likely to be the same since they both seem to get you equally clean.

Consumers' preference for one product over another is potentially very important news. The company may be in the position to tell all consumers through advertising they will prefer the testing company's product to a competitive product. Often the reason for the preference is a key product benefit, cleaning tough grease, for example. When this is the case, a company may tout this advantage in its advertising.

When a product is not a winner in these consumer tests, it becomes Research and Development's challenge to make the product a winner. To make the product perform better in certain situations, they will focus on the key benefit that leads a consumer to prefer one product to another.

Slice (a former Pepsi lemon and lime–flavored product) is an example of why caution is necessary in this kind of research. Before the introduction of Slice's 10 percent real juice product, another soft drink manufacturer did research on an orange flavored product with 10 percent juice. It did in-home research pairing the juice-added product with a product without added juice. During the test, consumers were not told about the presence or absence of juice. The test came back saying that consumers did not prefer one product to another.

Slice, with its 10 percent real juice, was a big success a few months later. This surprised the other company. They were curious, so they redid the test. This time they told people one of the products had 10 percent juice. Although they tested the same products as before, the results were dramatically different. When consumers knew one product contained real juice, they overwhelming preferred it to the other product. In the real world, they decided to tell people the product had real juice, so the second test was a better indication of consumer reaction.

Speed Bump

In consumer research, some products can be preferred on benefits that are difficult to explain to consumers. For example, it may be "richer lather." If a win in consumer research is not easy to understand and explain, you may not be able to leverage it for business growth. Describing "richer lather" is a challenge since there are several product components that contribute to richer lather—amount of air and feel, for example.

When a company has a preferred product, it is a key data point that makes a significant difference in the marketplace. The Five-Minute Manager pays close attention to this data. If a competitor changes its product, the Five-Minute Manager wants to know immediately if it has maintained or lost its preference.

A note of caution—this research is best when tangible benefits, such as taste or cleaning ability, are the reason consumers buy a product. When style, or simply how it looks, are the primary reasons for purchase, in-home testing may not be the best research technique. Research often struggles when it tries to measure non-tangible benefits, like style, which are very personal and not subject to easy descriptions.

If you are a medium or small manufacturer, do not quickly conclude that you cannot afford in-home research. This kind of research can cost as little as $30,000, exclusive of product costs.

Other Consumer Voices

Other forms of consumer research can be valuable to the Five-Minute Manager.

Habits and Practices Research

This research determines how, when, and where consumers use a product. It is often most useful when it tracks changes in these conditions over time. If a cleaning product, for example, is used increasingly on windows and less on kitchen counters, it may require a reformulation to make it work better on windows, making it leave less residue or film, for example.

Focus Groups

in a focus group a moderator questions prescreened consumers (consumers who use a particular type of product, for example) at a site while people from the manufacturer watch from behind a one-way mirror. This is the only type of research many companies do. When this is the only type of research used, it probably does more harm than good. Whereas the two previous types of research use balanced, nationally representative panels of consumers, focus groups do not. This is purely qualitative research that can provide clues, but not conclusions. Never use what you hear in a focus group to make important decisions.

The Internet—A Gold Mine for Many

When casting a wider net, the Internet is often a valuable research source. A variety of information is available, often at little or no cost. The search engines are usually impressive and quickly bring you to the information you seek.

For example, if learning as much as you can about a competitor is important, you can search many business magazines, newspapers, and news sites. If information on a category of products is important, such as soft drinks, it can also be very helpful.

The following is a listing of some useful Web sites:

➤ **Business Week (www.businessweek.com)** Here you can search back issues with a powerful search engine. The catch is that you have to pay for the articles you want to retrieve and save.

➤ **Time-Life Publications (cgi.pathfinder.com)** This site includes magazines such as Fortune, Money, Time, Life, and People. This is a great search location with a powerful, flexible search engine. The articles you retrieve here are free.

Personal Coaching

Manufacturers are frequently surprised by how people use their products. When they find many people not using a product optimally, they will put much better instructions on their package. Try reading the labels of the products in your home. Guaranteed, you will find at least one product you can use better or for something of which you were not aware.

➤ **Leader to Leader (www.pfdf.org/leaderbooks)** At this site you will find a great list of articles by authors like Warren Bennis and Peter Drucker.

➤ **Working Mother Magazine (www.workingmother.com)** Look up this site to find good articles about working mothers. Unfortunately, the search engine is cumbersome and difficult with which to work.

➤ **Edgar On-line (www.edgar-online.com)** If you want SEC data on a company, this is a very good site.

➤ **Library of Congress (lcweb.loc.gov/homepage)** You can spend the better part of a morning exploring what is available at this site. This site is resource rich. You can connect with many university research facilities, obtain details on current and past legislative issues, and address a wide range of copyright topics. The site is easy to navigate and fast loading so exploring is fun.

➤ **Franklin Covey (www.covey.com)** This site is resource-rich. It includes a series of articles written by Covey and others that are available only here. You can also create your personal mission statement here.

➤ **Sample Business Plans (www.bplans.com/index1.html)** Wonderful tips and samples of business plans are available at this popular site.

➤ **CNNfn (cnnfn.com)** This powerful site allows you to search. The stories are usually not as comprehensive as the magazine articles, but they still can be valuable.

➤ **MSNBC (www.msnbc.com)** This powerful news site has very good search capability. As with the CNN site, you can customize the news you see daily. Check the "Find" and "Index" functions to search for what you need.

➤ **Entrepreneur Magazine (www.entrepreneurmag.com)** This magazine provides excellent help for entrepreneurs.

➤ **Virtual Reference Desk (www.refdesk.com/facts)** Search for area codes, quotations, newspapers, the Old Farmer's Almanac, statistics, and about twenty other subjects.

➤ **Information Please (www.infoplease.com)** This site helps find the answers to your questions with almanacs, dictionaries, and encyclopedias. There are more than 30,000 searchable biographies and even help for kids.

➤ **Discovery Channel (www.discovery.com)** With this site's great search function, you can search previous Discovery programs plus TLC, Travel, Animal Planet, Health, and Wings channel programs.

➤ **USA Today (www.usatoday.com)** Search USA Today's archives and retrieve articles for one dollar each.

➤ **ABC News (abcnews.go.com)** Access a very good search engine from ABC's homepage. There is no cost for retrieved news stories.

➤ **CBS News (www.cbs.com)** Like the other news sites, this one has a good search function and provides you with the ability to customize your daily news.

➤ **New York Times (www.nytimes.com)** You can search previous stories, but you must pay for the articles you retrieve. Look for the "Search the Site" location on the homepage.

➤ **Medical Journals (www.webmedlit.com)** this is a wonderful site if you want to search for medical topics. Again, this is a site where you must pay for the articles you retrieve.

➤ **Inc. Magazine (www.inc.com)** This is a research site on AOL and the Web. It includes a powerful search engine, and the articles do not cost extra.

➤ **Electric Library (www.elibrary.com)** This is a monthly subscription site where you can search hundreds of magazines, books, transcripts, and newspapers. The search engine is very powerful.

➤ **Iquest** This CompuServe-only service allows you to search hundreds of magazines and newspapers. This has a flexible and power search engine.

Personal Coaching

You can connect to the Internet through an Internet Service Provider (ISP) or an online service, such as AOL or CompuServe. The amount you pay may actually be less with an online provider, depending on how many hours you use it each month. With an online provider, you get all the access of an ISP, plus numerous exclusive services. Online providers also provide free trial service.

Search Engines

Most of the Internet resources discussed so far search news sources. When you want a broader search, search engines enable you to access the entire Internet. To the surprise of some, there are significant differences between search engines. The following list of search engines details some of these differences:

➤ **Northern Light (www.northernlight.com)** This site is recommended by most magazines as the best on the net. You can search not only the Web, but you also search over one hundred magazines and newspapers. This site is so good because it groups all the finds into folders. In my search of the term "business management," it found 140,852 sites and grouped them into thirteen folders. The number of sites found on any given search might vary daily.

➤ **Alta Vista (www.altavista.com)** This popular site offers many services besides searching. In my search of the term "business management," it found 129,905 sites.

➤ **Excite (www.excite.com)** This is one of the multi-service portal sites. In my search of the term "business management," it found 42,970 sites.

➤ **HotBot (www.hotbot.com)** Like Excite, this is a portal site with a good search engine. In my search of the term "business management," it found 2,960 sites.

➤ **Infoseek (www.infoseek.com)** Like others, this is a portal site. As a portal site, it offers links to a wide variety of services. In my search of the term "business management," it found 55,724 sites.

Consider This

Ross Perot's first primary business was Electronic Data Systems, which he founded in 1962. Twenty-two years later, he sold it to General Motors for $2.5 billion. He renewed his commitment to data processing four years later when, in 1988, he founded Perot Systems Corporation.

The Internet and Internet service providers such as AOL and CompuServe provide powerful ways of staying current with important subjects. None of us, including the Five-Minute Manager, has the time to read every important magazine and newspaper. Despite this, the Internet provides resources from which, in as little as five minutes, you can collect all the information you need.

The Least You Need to Know

➤ There is abundant data about customers and consumers available to most manufacturers that sell through retailers.

➤ With all the available data, the challenge is to identify the key data points that routinely make a difference in your business. These factors can differ for various categories of products and brands within a category.

➤ Consumer research is essential to any company. It enables the company to know how consumers rate its product versus competitors' products and how they use them.

➤ Discover on the Internet what all the major magazines and newspapers have said about various companies, brands, and categories of product over the last several years.

➤ Some search engines are better than others at quickly delivering the results you want. The Five-Minute Manager knows how to use the best engines to the company's advantage.

WHICH ONE?

Chapter 8

Whatever You Do, Be Sure You Have the Right Strategy

In This Chapter

➤ Strategy is not what many people think it is

➤ Three elements of every strategy statement

➤ Competitors are great teachers

➤ Get intimate with your consumers

➤ Know that you can do exceptionally well

Strategy is one of the most misused words in business. The most frequent mistake people make is to describe tactics and goals and not true strategy.

So what is strategy? Dictionaries provide limited help when it comes to defining strategy. Webster's defines strategy as, "A plan of action intended to accomplish a specific goal." This suggests that strategy plays a role in guiding how we accomplish a goal.

That is helpful, but for many people that help can mean tactics. Strategy is not tactics.

Strategy defines the essence of a business, as well as why and how the business will succeed. It serves as the guiding force for all the goals and actions taken in a business. All goals need to be consistent with the strategy. Any tactics used to achieve the goals need to be consistent with the strategy. Tactics are the daily and weekly actions which translate the spirit of the strategy into concrete business results.

A properly constructed strategy includes three critical perspectives:

➤ It starts with what we do better than others, the unique combination of assets and competencies that make us who we are as a business.

➤ An in-depth understanding of our competitors is critical.

➤ The consumer tells us what is important to them, and we become intimate with the consumer.

Personal Coaching

Inventory all of your prior work experiences and skills you have developed in your current business. You will be surprised what you have done in your life. How can you use these to implement a new idea?

Sage Advice

"Knowing what you cannot do is more important than knowing what you can do."
—Lucille Ball

What Makes Us So Good?

We need to understand our strengths. As a corollary to this, we also understand our shortcomings.

The reason for this is obvious to most, but it is worth saying. Whatever strategy we adopt must reflect our very best capabilities. In today's competitive world, using our second or third best competencies is a recipe for failure.

How do we determine our strengths? This requires a thorough, objective evaluation. As such, it is not an easy undertaking.

The team approach works best. A business unit assembles qualified people from every key function. The first step is benchmarking superior performance. The benchmarks define what superior performance and results are. For example, in manufacturing benchmarks define line speeds and production rates by the best in the business. In each area, we need to know what truly outstanding competencies look like.

The following is only a partial list of questions we can ask:

➤ Marketing

1. Research—How good is our consumer research capability? What is the size of the department? What skills and experience do we have? Can we conduct all major forms of research? Do we have any proprietary forms of research? How extensive is our research library? Is there any national organization ranking or evaluation of our research organization?

2. Advertising—Can we produce world class advertising? What is the record of accomplishment of our agencies on our brands and other businesses? Are they strongest on established businesses or in new products? Can they attract the best people in the industry? How knowledgeable are the agency people about our business?

➤ **Research and Development**

1. Patents—What patents do we have that relate to our business? Are we applying for more in the next year? What are the prospects for additional patents in the next five years?

2. Staffing—In what skills do we specialize? Which ones are weaknesses today? What direction is future staffing going to take? Are we attracting the top Ph.D. graduates?

3. Supplier Relationships—How strong are our relationships with key suppliers? Do we have any exclusivity of use agreements with them? Are there any joint research efforts? If so, in what areas?

The inquiry is extensive; this is just a sample beginning. It is critical for the evaluation to seek objectivity at every stage. Sometimes this is difficult for people within the organization. When facing this, a consultant who can help gauge the competencies may be critical. Often several consultants with skills in the specific functions are required. For the purposes of providing benchmarks, make their assignments very focused and, thus, relatively inexpensive. Before hiring a consultant, check extensively the written record on the functional and skill areas under study. Often you can narrow the scope of a consultant's assignment, and save money doing it, by reviewing the available literature already written on the subject. With the Internet and access to university and government libraries you can often obtain as much as half of the information you need.

At the conclusion of this step, draw up a concise statement of what the organization's strengths and weaknesses are. It should highlight one to three truly superior strengths. Do not focus only on measurable and tangible competencies. There are many important potential strengths that are difficult to measure, but are nonetheless very powerful. For example, the esprit de corps of an organization and its enthusiastic commitment to the vision and mission of a business can be powerful success drivers. Conversely, if morale is low and turnover is high, note this.

Once completed, update it annually. At the five-year mark, consider redoing the evaluation. A fresh look with many new faces can discover previously unseen strengths.

Personal Coaching

How do you stack up? How does your training compare to others at your level in business? How does the performance of your investments compare to the averages and to the best?

73

What Are Your Competitors Good at and Likely to Do?

Understanding your company's strengths is not enough; you also need to know your competitors' strengths. The idea of doing a in-depth study of a competitor is new for many people.

Personal Coaching

Do business with a competitor. Call up and order something. See how they treat their customers and keep their promises.

To lead the study, use someone with a broad perspective and assign that person the task of becoming the competitor. The person chosen to head the effort should be someone who fills a function driving business success. For example, in the computer business, it might be someone from production or research and development. In a company that sells high volume products through large retailers, it might be someone from marketing or sales.

It becomes that person's objective to learn everything about the key competitor they already know about their company. This is an achievable objective, although at first it may not seem so. A team of people may be assembled to help accomplish this.

We can learn about competitors from many sources. The following is a partial list:

➤ **Published materials**—There is a wealth of information in magazines, newspapers, network and online news groups, and books. Fortunately, the Five-Minute Manager can search almost all of these resources on the Internet—with both search engines for the entire Internet and at magazine, newspaper, and network news group sites like CNN and MSNBC. The previous chapter provided a list of some of these resources.

➤ **Suppliers**—Within the limitations of any existing confidentiality agreements, suppliers of both your company and competitors are a valuable resource. In the Pepsi and Coke cola wars, packaging suppliers were a resource for both sides. Both companies often learned about new products and reformulations from these sources.

➤ **Recruiters**—Within their confidentiality agreements, executive recruiters can often provide useful information about the type and number of people hired by a competitor.

➤ **Current employees**—Often current employees have worked for a competitor in the past.

➤ **Tours**—One of the best data-collection methods is touring competitive facilities that are open to the public. In tours of production facilities, you can discover manufacturing processes, age of equipment, volume estimates, and gain a sense of employee morale. If the site is unionized, this last item can be an important piece of information in estimating competitor costs.

➤ **Store visits**—You can visit a competitor's store. See how they display their products. If it differs from your way, figure out their reasoning for doing it that way. Would this work for you?

➤ **Competitor materials**—Collect all available materials from competitors. This includes annual reports, press releases, and recruiting materials available on college campuses. It also includes the not-so-public information, such as special filings with the SEC and patents granted and applied for by the company.

➤ **Data services**—One service tracks radio and television advertising spending by brands; you can purchase this data. When you buy this data, determine what they estimate your spending to be, and see if it is accurate. This will tell you how reliable the data is for the competitors listed.

The purpose in collecting the information is to construct a profile of the competitors' strengths and weaknesses, plus their vision, mission, values, strategies, and key goals. You want to know what they are likely to do and what skills they have and do not have to accomplish their objectives.

After collecting information, one of the first tasks is estimating the economics of a company. We want to know their product cost and for how much they sell it. Imagine your company making the product, and ask how much would it cost. Modify this information according to what you have learned about how the competitor differs from your company.

Examine every initiative the competitor has taken in the last three years. Seek to understand the thinking behind the initiative. What strengths did they have that enabled them to do it? Why did they choose one specific initiative over other options? How did they financially support the effort and what did they achieve? This is only a sampling of the types of questions you can ask.

The result of your efforts should be a one-page description for each competitor that outlines their strengths and weaknesses. It should also detail the company's objectives and its ability to achieve these objectives over the next several years. The report can also discuss the implications for your company.

Personal Coaching

If yours is a service business, make a point of asking five customers a day why they bought from you. You will get the best information if you ask after they have made their purchase.

Crawl in Bed with the Consumer

The third perspective necessary to create a strategy is that of the consumer or user of your products. The goal is to become nothing less than intimate with the consumer.

You want to know everything possible about the consumer. This includes conducting the traditional research discussed in the previous chapter. This is a very valuable place to start, but as extensive as it may be, it is only a start. The pages and pages of numbers in this research provide only clues to the feelings, emotions, rewards, and frustrations a consumer has with your product.

The starting place is you. If you are not a user of your product, become one immediately. Pay close attention to every aspect of your product. How easy is it to open? What do the instructions tell you? How easy are they to follow? Stop after each step and write down how you feel about the product. Use it every day, if possible, and note how your feelings change. How do your usage patterns change over time? Do you like the product more or less as you use it more? What is the best thing about your product?

Once you are intimate with the product, see how other consumers feel about it. If possible, go where consumers are using your product. If you do not think this is possible, challenge your assumptions and find a way to do it.

Focus groups or one-on-one discussions with consumers at a research facility will suffice if you cannot go where consumers use your product. You need to recognize that intimacy is more difficult away from the place people use the product.

Personal Coaching

Take one of your best customers to lunch every week. Develop an in-depth series of questions and track each person's answers. Look for patterns in their answers. Why did they switch their patronage to your business? Have they been tempted recently to switch to another business?

When you are with consumers, note their language very closely. What consumer language is associated with your product? How do consumers feel about using your product? Are there any moments of joy? What is the best part of the experience with your product? Probe carefully; you do not want consumers inventing language for the first time to answer your questions. You want their real language.

When they share their thoughts, watch and listen closely. Examine their faces and body language. What emotions are there? How intense are their feelings? In what circumstances is the product most appreciated?

This process takes time. It is very difficult to develop insights that are real and intimate. Done well, the benefits are often extraordinary and long-lasting.

Crawling in Bed with the Consumer—a True Story

The Folgers Coffee Company started as a family business and became well established in the central and western United States before its purchase by Procter & Gamble. It remained at its Kansas City headquarters for several years before moving to the head-quarters of Proctor & Gamble in Cincinnati.

The business grew steadily under P&G's management. Its growth accelerated with the development of the "Mrs. Olsen" advertising campaign. This campaign featured a friendly, older lady who talked about why she loved Folgers Coffee. Her credibility propelled the brand to the number two market share position.

After becoming number two in market share, Folgers found its growth gradually slowed and then stabilized. General Foods' Maxwell House brand held the number one position. Although there were actually some differences between the products, there was not an overall consumer preference for either brand. For most consumers these two products are indistinguishable from each other in a blind tasting situation.

Folgers undertook an effort to replace the "Mrs. Olsen" advertising campaign. The advertising agency and brand management group at P&G knew this was a risk because of how long the "Mrs. Olsen" campaign had been successful. They knew the campaign had made the brand number two, but there were no indications that it could drive the brand to share leadership.

Consider This

As successful as Folgers has been, many other Procter & Gamble brands have tried and not achieved the same success. Soap brands have tried to find the defining moment for their products with little success. Gaining powerful insights is a challenging quantitative and qualitative process.

Through extensive consumer research, both formal and informal, the agency and brand developed new insights into how consumers used and appreciated coffee. It was not, however, until they "crawled into bed" with consumers that they found the insight to drive Folgers to the number one share position.

They discovered the most powerful, though fleeting, moment in the coffee experience is when a person is lying in bed in the morning. As they begin to wake up, the aroma of brewing coffee wafts into the room. Research showed this moment to be the high-light of the coffee experience for many people.

The agency and brand manger used this insight to develop advertising that linked Folgers to this moment in a powerful way. Most of the ads feature someone lying in bed and waking up to the aroma of fresh-brewed coffee. With a smiling face, the person heads to the kitchen to have a cup of Folgers. The ads feature memorable music and lyrics that link Folgers to the moment—"The best part of waking up is Folgers in your cup."

These ads immediately reinstated Folgers share growth. Folgers eventually dethroned Maxwell House from the number one position. For over 10 years, that original consumer insight, a result of people becoming intimate with the consumer, has been associated with business success. The product taste, price, and packaging did not change. Maxwell House did not lose the number one position; Folgers won it by winning consumers' hearts.

Pull It Together

You have collected all this information; now the tough work can begin. Using the information productively can be a roller coaster ride, as the following business discovered.

A beverage brand thought it had developed some breakthrough understandings that would shape their business strategy. They learned the following:

➤ Their main competitor had cut back on staffing in several areas of the business. There was only one junior person in marketing, for example.

➤ Their main competitor had shifted its corporate focus to an entirely nonbeverage business. All its press releases were about this new business area. It was clear that the competitor was not going to give much emphasis to the brand with which they competed.

➤ Their company had a patent on a production process that produced fresher tasting fruit products. In addition, a new research facility had promising leads that might lead to additional patents.

➤ Their research showed customers wanted new flavors. These customers tended to be the largest volume purchasers.

➤ Their customers had very positive feelings about the brand. They were proud of it and enjoyed recommending it to friends.

Personal Coaching

What is your strategy to realize your vision? Adapt this process to develop a personal strategy. It increases self-esteem and confidence even when your vision is not realized.

With this information, the brand recommended taking a more aggressive strategy. They wanted to take advantage of the cut backs and shift in business focus at their competitor and to use their proprietary strengths in fresh fruit products to introduce several new products over the next several years.

From their perspective, there seemed to be a strong case for an aggressive strategy. When they discussed their plans with finance, they discovered it was a positive profit picture.

What they had not discovered was that their company was also making a strategic shift. In companies that do not openly share broader strategic thinking this creates consider wasted effort. Often senior management purposely does not share this broader thinking because they do not want to stifle new thinking by their business groups.

Although its brand was the largest volume brand at the company, the company had decided to shift its focus to compete in new segments of the beverage business. This meant backing off the business. Thus, whereas their strategy to use their increased advantages made sense to those working on the specific brand, it did not fit into the broader changing corporate strategy.

They then developed an alternative strategy that still allowed them to use their advantages on a lower scale. In addition, they adopted a more aggressive cost reduction and price increase program. This helped fund the company's new business focus.

The Least You Need to Know

➤ Strategy does not mean tactics and goals. Strategy guides both of these.

➤ You can know your competitors as well as you know your own company.

➤ Know all your company's strengths, especially what you do exceptionally well. Then make sure you know what you are not good at doing.

➤ To know intimately your consumers, you need to know their feelings, including the most positive moments in which they use your product or service.

➤ Using all the information you have collected can be a challenge and a continuation of the learning process.

Chapter 9

Goal of a Goal

In This Chapter

➤ Identify needs before setting goals

➤ Learn the pitfalls of not making a goal specific enough

➤ Know if your goals are measurable or not

➤ Learn how important an achievable goal is

➤ Learn the difference between goals as a master and as a servant

Most people set personal and business goals. Most people intend to accomplish the goal when they set it. Some time after setting the goal, frustration sets in.

There are many reasons for the frustration, but a key reason is lack of clarity and accuracy when setting the goal. When that occurs, the goal becomes foggy. What did you really want to accomplish? When this happens, intent slackens and the goal ceases to be something you want to accomplish. Maybe you will try again, but often you just drop the idea.

This is unfortunate because the need and idea that prompted setting the original goal may be very important. When you do not meet the minimal requirements of goal setting, you almost guarantee frustration. This frustration sometimes leads to the conclusion that the goal is not achievable; that may not be the case. A better statement of the goal may make the path to achieving it clearer.

The Five-Minute Manager's Data Summary

Before moving to set goals, summarize all the relevant findings and needs. Typically, this means a one-page summary that captures key insights, your current needs, and what business factors drive success.

For example, Mike was the brand manager on a beverage brand with only one major competitor. With the help of his assistants, he analyzed over thirty business factors, trying to determine whether they were key drivers of volume and market share.

After this effort, he found only three factors that made a difference. First, changes in the price difference between the two brands correlated with changes in market share. This relationship was consistent over three years.

Second, he found that when consumers preferred a flavor of their product in an in-home consumer test, it always achieved share leadership of that flavor segment. When consumers did not prefer a flavor, the flavor achieved close to parity share of the flavor segment.

Third, when he did not have a flavor that their competitor had, it caused share to erode. For example, when the competitor introduced a new tropical flavor, it immediately increased its share and decreased the share of his brand.

This was a little tricky because the evidence suggested that minor flavors were not worth pursuing; they had difficulty identifying the threshold where it became big enough to respond to with a product of their own. For example, a competitor's new lime flavor generated a small business increase that quickly declined. This demonstrated the need to closely watch for the longer term viability of a new flavor before deciding to respond with their own flavor.

Speed Bump

When drawing conclusions about what the key drivers in your business are, remaining calm and focused is very important. Do not begin this activity during a flurry of activity. Do it when other issues are blocked out, interruptions stopped, and you are calm and centered.

Consider This

Sometimes those running a small business convince themselves that they do not need to do the things a big company does. They are right, of course, except for when it comes to setting goals. To avoid frustration, follow the same rules no matter what size company you run.

Mike took the Five-Minute Manager approach to summarizing the three findings. The following are his summaries:

➤ **Finding 1**—Changes in the price difference between our brand and the key competitive brand explain about 80 percent of the share changes between the brands over the last 12 months. This is down from 83 percent in the previous 12 months and 86 percent in the 12 months before that. This suggested a strong cause and effect relationship that was consistent over time.

➤ **Need**—We need a stronger brand equity that offers either new benefits or stronger existing benefits. Relying on price differences to differentiate the brands puts constant pressure on profits and sacrifices brand equity. Practically, this can lead to distinctive new products or added value or services that are proprietary.

➤ **Finding 2**—The berry and tropical flavored products are our only products preferred versus our key competitor's same flavors by consumers in blind in-home consumer testing. Both flavors enjoy over a 65 percent share of their flavor segments, whereas our products that are equally preferred to the key competitor have an average of a 49 percent share. By having products consumers prefer over the competition, major share advantages are gained and held.

➤ **Need**—Using four preferred flavors instead of parity products would generate an average of a 16 share point gain in these flavor segments.

➤ **Finding 3**—Our key competitor has three flavors we do not. Two of these are a declining 2 percent of the category and one is a growing $4^1/_2$ percent of the category.

➤ **Need**—Although the data is not definitive on this subject, if we developed a product consumers preferred to their flavor with $4^1/_2$ percent of market share and this flavor continued to grow, we should introduce the new product.

From Findings and Needs to More Help

Before setting goals, you need additional input, often from a variety of functions. In the example, Mike needed input from research and development before setting goals. Do they have research leads that give them confidence to make a new consumer-preferred product? For example, are there emerging technologies that allow the economical use of real fruit juice? Are there new product ideas that would give the brand a competitive product advantage? This could be the

Speed Bump

When you get input from others, it may require learning new terminology and processes. Be prepared to invest the necessary time.

answer to decreasing the brand's price sensitivity and increasing its brand equity. He also needed finance's input on the profit implications of the marketing and volume plans. Sales should review how the plans fit into their calendar. Other functions need to review the preliminary plans before setting goals.

You Better Be Specific

There are four requirements for every goal statement. You can remember them with the acronym SMAC, which stands for Specific, Measurable, Achievable, and Compatible. There are other versions of this, but most address the same points.

The first requirement is that the goal needs to be specific. This may seem obvious, but it is surprising how often managers violate this rule.

For example, is this goal specific? "We will sell one million cases of our new flavor, starting on December 3rd, to all major grocery and drug store customers." It certainly includes many details. It is missing, however, at least one key specific. Over what period of time will the one million cases be sold? Is this the goal for the first three months, six months, or the first year? This detail makes a very big difference in later determining success.

Personal Coaching

Be precise when setting personal goals. The power in personal goals comes from knowing what you want. Not putting start and completion dates on your goals can result in your efforts being unfocused and ultimately dying a slow death. Assigning dates emphasizes urgency and commitment, two important success drivers.

Sometimes you leave out details like this because you assume that everyone knows what you mean. Everyone has had painful experiences with assumptions. "Do not assume" is one of the few fixed rules the Five-Minute Manager follows.

In setting a specific goal, you need to define

➤ what you want to achieve.

➤ within what time frame you want to achieve it.

➤ how you are going to achieve it.

➤ who is going to do what.

The What Needs to Be Crystal Clear

Details define what you want. This can be a quantity of a product. If it comes in more than one size, define if your goal concerns one specific size or all sizes. Do the same for flavors or other variables affecting your specific business.

Not all cases are equal. Sometimes there is a physical case and a statistical case. The latter is a way of defining all cases in terms of equal volume per case. For example, a 50-pack of a 5-ounce product is half of a statistical case, whereas a 100-pack of the 5-ounce product is full statistical case.

When using percentage changes to state the goal, the baseline needs to be clear. To avoid ambiguity and confusion, it is usually best to avoid stating goals in terms of percentage.

Where Is the Start and Finish Line?

If a goal defines an ending date but not a start date, it can make a big difference in the outcome. If you expect to sell a certain amount of volume, usually a certain number of months is required to achieve that goal. Again, be careful that an end date does not assume the beginning date. Also, be careful about saying things like "over the first six months." If those six months are in peak or low seasonality for your target product or products, there will be a significant difference in how much volume you sell. Seasonality refers to how much product sells at different times of the year. For example, summer is peak seasonality for soft drinks because it is hotter (the need for refreshment is higher) and kids (the prime consumer) are out of school.

How Are You Going to Do That?

If you set a goal to sell two million physical cases between March and June 2000, it may not be specific enough. For example, it may require television advertising to sell that much volume. Thus, the goal needs to reflect that advertising is necessary to achieve the goal. The volume goal without advertising might be only one million cases.

Personal Coaching

When you set personal goals, do not stop when you have a clear statement of what you want to do. Think of the immediate next steps that you will take, including what you will do today. Actions trigger momentum.

In stating a goal, define the crucial elements necessary to achieve it. The goal does not need many details to accomplish this. Only use short crucial descriptions. The example goal would be better stated, "The goal is to sell two million physical cases between March and June 2000 as part of the management-approved Heavy-Up Television Program."

Who Is Really Going to Do What?

This is another place where ambiguity can sabotage a goal. For example, if a business team says its goal is to sell one million cases, then the goal does not accurately reflect who is expected to sell the one million cases. The person on the team from research and development certainly is not going to call on any customers to make a sale. Thus, this is a goal for the sales department, not the team. The team might have an associated goal of achieving a certain profit target that every team member contributes to achieving. For example, if the goal is a specific increase in profit for the fiscal year, research and development will find and use lower cost ingredients, marketing will reduce coupon spending, and sales will sell the agreed upon volume.

The sales member of the team might have a goal like this—"Sales will sell one million physical cases of new berry flavor between March and June 2000 using the management-approved Heavy-Up Television Program."

Bring Your Measuring Tape

If the Five-Minute Manager sets a specific goal, the specifics must be measurable. For example, the Five-Minute Manager may agree with an associate that this associate will reduce his angry outbursts by 50 percent in the next month. What is the baseline and how is it accurately measured? How do you measure outbursts in the next month? These are very challenging questions that probably do not have perfect answers. Although reducing the outbursts is highly desirable, it is very difficult to measure. As a result, an angry outburst could occur when the Five-Minute Manager and associate meet at the end of the month to discuss whether they achieved the goal. Without easy, agreed-to measurements, you invite ambiguity and confusion. In this case, the Five-Minute Manager probably should focus on an objective that is results-oriented.

> **Speed Bump**
>
> When setting personal goals it is often tempting to say you want more or less of something. Resist this temptation. Both one hundred and one million are more. Less or more goals often lead to quitting when you make a little progress, even when much more progress is achievable.

Can We Do This?

For a variety of reasons, "Dilbert"-type companies routinely set goals they cannot meet. Some companies set sales quotas knowing that the vast majority of sales managers will not reach the goal.

This goal-setting philosophy emphasizes setting stretch goals. This approach assumes that if people achieve goals, they will slack off. So, they set unachievable goals in the hope that people keep striving to achieve them. In some cases, so they think, people will strive so hard that they actually achieve the goal.

> **Consider This**
>
> When setting personal goals, make sure they are achievable. A goal that states, "I will achieve enlightenment by two o'clock in the afternoon next Sunday" is not achievable for most of us. Although this point is exaggerated, if your personal goals are desirable but not achievable in the time period you set, this is a recipe for frustration and lost self-esteem when you fail.

Most of the time, however, people disregard these goals. They know the goals are not achievable; therefore, they do not take them seriously. If a manager tries to hold them accountable, they either try to get through the conversation or, in rare cases, they counter with the unreasonableness of the goal. Then they may even offer an alternative, a more reasonable goal. Eventually, however, even managers tend to give up trying to inspire people to achieve unreachable goals. At this point, the quotas merely take up space on a piece of paper.

The alternative is to set goals that are achievable. Doing this often requires assembling building blocks that have a basis in previous experience. For example, if a manager is proposing an associate achieve a 1,000 case volume increase, the increase might be divided into the following building blocks:

➤ Selling a new size to 80 percent of the associate's customers will increase volume by 550 cases. The basis for this is the last two new size introductions on similar products produced volume gains of 525 and 550 cases.

➤ Selling two major customers two more in-store display programs over the next three months will sell an incremental 450 cases. The previous three display programs have averaged 220 incremental cases per program.

When establishing goals with this approach, people not only learn the goal is achievable, but what they need to do to achieve it becomes clear.

Does This Goal Match My Other Goals?

One of the most frustrating things people face is having multiple goals, some of which conflict or appear to conflict with each other. The usual culprit is time. You find yourself with one goal that requires 100 percent of your time over the next month and another goal that requires twenty hours in the same month. Unless a person decides to increase work hours and sacrifice home, personal, and community time, both goals cannot be accomplished. Even with these sacrifices, accomplishing both goals in one month may be impossible if they take longer than originally estimated.

In this situation a person experiences pressure and fear of failure. Both factors limit effectiveness when you most need it.

It is a common situation for goals to be incompatible with each other. In other situations, you commit to goals where there are enough resources, such as money, to accomplish each goal separately, but not together. In such a case, the goal maker needs to make sure before they committing to a goal that it is compatible with all the resources necessary to achieve it.

Another way a goal can be incompatible is when it is not consistent with the vision, mission, and

Personal Coaching

When examining other goals for possible conflicts, some may be hard to detect. Some very important goals may be unstated. Examine your actions and you will discover them.

values of a company or division. The primary goals of each function and department need to be in support of and compatible with the company's vision, mission, and values.

Goals—Masters or Servants

You invest effort to review and prepare to establish a goal; then you go through the process of writing and selling the goal to the management. This often requires tremendous energy and time. The investment in creating and agreeing to a goal can also involve people strongly aligning themselves with the goal. In some cases, career and salary progress may be closely linked to the achievement of the goal. When a goal is critical to a company's overall success, the board of directors may agree to it and publish it in the annual report for everyone to see.

Consider This

In your personal life, it can be tempting to set many goals. There are fitness, reading, diet, family, vacation, and community goals, for example. Individually they are achievable, but collectively you do not stand a chance. Lay all of them out on one page; collect the information you need to set priorities; and set and act on your priorities.

Goals as Master

At whatever level of commitment there is when people agree to a goal, people decide to make the goal their master or servant. For many people, when a goal is set, options are not an option.

When this occurs, the goal becomes your master. You said you are going to do it, so you are going to do it, no matter what obstacles you face. A theoretical option at this point is not accomplishing the goal, but this is clearly unacceptable when a goal is your master.

When a goal is your master, you organize single-mindedly around the task of achieving it. As the saying goes, "You have your marching orders." You draw timelines, assign responsibilities, and marshal resources. You establish checkpoints, hold meetings, and issue reports. You are on the way to achieving the goal.

When you encounter the unexpected, which is usually the norm, you pause to assess the situation. The question is "How do we overcome this obstacle to achieving the goal?" You spare no effort, including securing new resources and making sacrifices. Perseverance is your ally. You do not allow any doubt. Allegiance to the goal (strategy) is unwavering.

Depending on the nature of the obstacle, you may need to make changes in everything other than the goal itself. It remains intact, while organization, staffing, and plans may change, dramatically if necessary.

You repeat the process whenever you encounter an obstacle. Stress can be high when encountering obstacles because a goal usually includes a completion time. Obstacles only serve to delay; therefore, from this perspective, obstacles are only enemies.

When you discover many unexpected obstacles, the pursuit of the goal becomes a struggle. Whatever sense of exhilaration or inspiration you experienced in the beginning dissipates, and pursuit of the goal becomes dogged.

When you finally achieve the goal, there is more a sense of relief than celebration. Fatigue and stress diminish whatever sense of accomplishment you may have.

If you only partially achieve the goal, or do not achieve it at all, there is a sense of failure. If lessons are there, you may want nothing to do with them. You only want to disassociate yourselves with the goal. The effects of this failure can linger as you approach the task of accomplishing the next goal, reducing enthusiasm and ownership of the next goal. This only has the effect of making accomplishment of the next goal tougher from the beginning.

Speed Bump

When your goal includes an element of "I should do this," watch out. This type of goal is about doing something for other people, for example, doing something they expect of you. In many cases, it is not something you choose, nor does it fit your vision. "Should goals" seldom have the energy behind them to succeed.

The Stress-Free Way—Goals as Servants

You need two key changes to convert a goal from a master to a servant. First, obstacles need to become friends and teachers. Second, a goal's dynamic needs to be understood, which means that it can change as you learn more than you knew at the time of setting the goal.

When a goal is a servant, you go through the same rigorous preparation to set a goal, but in gaining agreement to the goal, you use different language. You tell management that you view the goal dynamically. You expect learning will be a major benefit of working to achieve the goal. As you gain new information, you make the right midcourse changes. The potential changes might include increasing or decreasing the quantity or quality measures stated in the goal, completely redefining all key elements of the goal, or even recommending no further pursuit of the goal.

If you announce the goal broadly, you include language that reflects the expectation that learning will occur. Stated from the "master" perspective such a goal might read:

"By July 1, 2000, the aircraft division of XYZ Company will assemble and sell the first 100 A6 model aircraft."

From the "servant" perspective it might read:

"By mid-summer 2000, the aircraft division of the XYZ Company will learn how to produce its new A6 model plane at an efficient rate."

This example highlights a situation where the servant perspective is critical. When a company learns how to do something for the first time, produce a new aircraft model in this example, it is important that the goal be a servant and not a master. Encountering the unknown is expected in these situations, and, you must expect to learn.

In almost all situations, it is better for a goal be a servant than a master. For many managers this is scary. They like having goals engraved in stone and are accustomed to using this to spur their employees on to achieving the goal. The fear is that if a goal is renegotiable, then people will always opt for a lesser version of the original goal. Certainly, where there is a lack of alignment around a vision and mission and low morale, this is a risk. In these situations, however, attainment of most goals is likely to be low, regardless of how high you set them.

In most situations, including the one just described, the end result is likely to be better when a goal is a servant. You see the goal as more honest and fair. For those managers involved in the setting of the goal, there is less fear that the unknown will make achieving the goal a struggle. You see obstacles as opportunities to learn and to design a better goal. By converting threats to friends, you reduce fear, anxiety, and stress. When these negative factors are not present, you are more creative, and you interact with each other in a spirit of cooperation. Both factors greatly improve the outcome.

Personal Coaching

When life is viewed as a journey and goals as steps along the way, learning becomes fun. On any journey you see new sites and meet new people. They can all be your teachers, if you only let them.

Officially changing a goal should not be easy, but neither should it be too tough. The spirit guiding the process should be one of doing your best work. You do that when the right minds engage the apparent learnings and create a new direction. The learnings need to be reliable and significant enough to warrant a change. The spirit guiding the creation of new direction should be doing what is right for everyone, not just a key manager with a vested interest.

Everyone involved needs to have an understanding of the key assumptions and benchmarks necessary to achieve the goal. This understanding promotes sincere and informed commitment. It also operates according to one of Abraham Maslow's assumptions of enlightened management policy, which simply states, "Assume in all your people the impulse to achieve."

The Least You Need to Know

➤ Before considering your goals, know your needs.

➤ Make goals very clear by being specific. Goals should operate in an ambiguity-free zone.

➤ When you have a specific goal, make sure it is measurable. It is nice to know when you have crossed the finish line.

➤ Unachievable goals cease to be goals.

➤ Rigorously examine a goal to see if it is compatible with other goals that you have already agreed to.

➤ Make goals your servant, not your master. Welcome obstacles as opportunities to learn.

Chapter 10

Score with Your Goals

In This Chapter

➤ How to make sure you are ready to start

➤ Getting off to a fast start

➤ The power of action

➤ Expecting and wanting to learn

➤ Persevering for success

➤ Celebrating for success

To get to this point, you have done lots of good work. You have analyzed your business, developed a strategy, and know the requirements for outstanding goal statements. When you set out to set goals recognize that in the same period of time you can set lofty, inspiring goals or rather pedestrian ones. It is not the amount of time spent on setting a goal that determines its quality. Rather, it is the spirit of aspiring to your very best that makes the difference. When this spirit guides goal setting, the process can be effortless.

Starting Line Preparation

You have set your goals. You are ready to start. Pause.

Review all of your goals one more time. Do you really have enough resources, especially time, to accomplish all that you have promised?

This question is critical when different goals share the same resources. Many resources can serve only one purpose at a time. Some resources, such as machines, require change time before converting to another use. In calculating required time for a resource, be sure to include change over time and consider planned maintenance times. The routine can sometimes become the unexpected, even when we could have planned for scheduled down times very easily in advance.

Speed Bump

To formalize your agreement, have your manager initial your one-page goal statement. Without clear and acknowledged agreement, you often waste good work done by busy people.

Are You Sure People Agree?

Before starting, check your agreements. Do not assume that just because you told someone your goal that your co-worker agrees with it. Maybe the individual wanted to think about it or was too busy with another topic to give you full attention. Do not mistake a casual "OK" for agreement.

Sometimes managers agree, developing questions only afterwards. Unfortunately, they sometimes forget to ask these questions. The considerable effort and enthusiasm generated to start working on a goal quickly halts when the questions finally surface. Then you enter a period of responding and changing as necessary. After a positive resolution, you can restart, but the second beginning is seldom as strong as the original one. This only serves to make more difficult the achievement of an already challenging goal.

To avoid stopping and restarting and manage your managers, send them a signal before you start that you want to do the right thing the right way—a Total Quality way of looking at it. It can be a short note that invites them to or notifies them of a kick-off meeting. If you do not wish to hold a meeting, the note can simply remind them that you will begin your project on a certain date. Be sure to give them at least a day's notice.

Personal Coaching

Every business should have a broadly accepted and understood process for gaining agreement to proposals. When adhered to, this process actually speeds resolution and results in solid agreements that are difficult to challenge.

Be sure your goal is written. It should be no more than one page. The Five-Minute Manager includes all necessary information on this page. It includes all the elements of the goal—specifics, the measure of success, and attainability. It also addresses any compatibility issues. Also, list key elements of the plan to achieve the goal on this page.

When you are ready to go, visualize the desired result. Have it very clear in your mind. You want to know what success looks like. The visualization process is very powerful. Let it work for you.

Rally Around

When you are ready to begin, start with a bang, not a whimper. Even if you are the only one working towards the goal, make the beginning of your effort an important event.

If you work with others, hold a kick-off meeting. It can be as simple as a breakfast or as elaborate as a full audiovisual extravaganza. Large companies often hold multimedia meetings to launch new products, a new size of existing product, or some other significant goal. They know that they want a inspiring beginning. In a world crowded with goals, an important one needs a memorable launching.

The meetings generate enthusiasm and convey important information. When words, pictures, and sounds all work together, the results can be impressive.

For example, when a large international company bought a small Coca-Cola bottler, it quickly found itself needing to introduce Diet Coke. As the managers examined their situation, they noted several challenges. There was mistrust among the bottler employees of the large company that had acquired them. The new managers observed the bottler's track record of being consistently number two to Pepsi. New product launches had typically fizzled quickly, and the bottler's results ranked in the lower half of all bottlers in the United States.

Sage Advice

"Nothing great was ever achieved without enthusiasm."
—Ralph Waldo Emerson

The management concluded they needed a fast and enthusiastic beginning. Their experience with the parent company told them that a multimedia kick-off meeting could address all their needs.

To prepare for the meeting, their meeting production crew visited every department at the bottler. With cameras rolling, the people in each department sang an energetic rock and roll song that supported the theme of the meeting. They included all 600 people employed with the bottler.

They also included several impressive flourishes in the meeting, including fireworks and waiters in tuxedos who served samples of the new product. Clearly, the hit of the meeting was the portion in which the employees saw themselves on a big screen having fun singing the theme song for the meeting. The enthusiasm was contagious and overwhelming.

The managers accomplished the objective of letting each person in the acquired company know that he or she was important. Their enthusiasm got the Diet Coke introduction off to such a fast start that the bottler rocketed past its goal and achieved the highest introductory market share out of the more than 500 bottlers that introduced Diet Coke. It also propelled the bottler's total market share to number one in one key market and to parity in its other key market.

Act!

Do not make the mistake of relying on the meeting to inspire people to accomplish the goal. That is the easy part.

There has been enough talking. Now it is time to act.

Those first actions taken toward the goal are the most important. Whether it is a personal goal or one for an entire company, people form opinions during those first steps. You do not want people to believe that accomplishing the goal is much more difficult than anticipated. This belief can drain the enthusiasm of a group in much less time than it takes to create the enthusiasm.

Sage Advice

"An ounce of action is worth a ton of theory."
—Friedrich Engels (1820–95), German social philosopher

How do you avoid this problem? There are a couple of keys. The first is having a plan to accomplish the goal. Know your first step. What "tools" will you have with you? Have confidence that your skill with those tools is at the expert, not rookie, level.

The first step toward achieving your goal seldom involves taking on your biggest, most challenging situation. If it is a sales goal, you gain experience with smaller customers before tackling your largest volume customer. There are exceptions. For example, if the product or program that you are introducing is one that a particular customer has asked for or played a key role in developing, make them the first you tell about the product or program.

By trying out your "tools" on less challenging situations at first, you gain experience and confidence. Both of these are critical to long-term success.

Personal Coaching

Some leading companies have customer advisory panels. These panels make proposals and help the company understand the implications of their ideas. When these work well, major new ideas are virtually pre-sold.

As a manager, be sure to be there when people take those first steps. Your purposes are to help and to learn. You help by adding your skills to overcome the early challenges. You learn because you see the plan in action. The plan and reality are seldom identical. There is always something to learn. As a manager, you can transmit lessons throughout the organization quickly. You can also share those early successes to help build momentum.

Learn and Then Learn Some More

Expect success, but also expect to learn.

Even when you only experience success, you have a wonderful opportunity to learn. In this case, learning can propel you well over the goal. Learning always takes you higher when you let it.

As we learned in the discussion about goals as masters or servants, we can experience obstacles in two ways. They can be negative or positive. You see them positively when you make the learning, no matter how painful at the time, an opportunity to improve.

Because working to achieve a goal always presents lessons, how do you make best use of them? The best way is sharing them immediately with others. With e-mail and conference calling, share what you learn when you learn it. A manager traveling with a laptop computer can plug into a local phone and transmit an e-mail within a few minutes. They can place cell phone calls to other managers and associates to pass along the new information.

Good plans usually have contingent plans. Trigger these plans when you learn something you thought might happen. In this situation, lessons immediately become new "tools" to help in the achievement of the goal. When you have learned enough as a manager to trigger the use of contingency plans, you have multiple communication devices that can quickly spread the word.

Maybe the most important aspect of learning is the desire to learn. A Five-Minute Manager always asks, "What am I learning right now?" The desire to learn produces much faster and deeper understanding. When you approach learning this way, you learn when not already under stress, such as during a crisis. What you learn in a stress-free environment is often broader and longer lasting.

Sage Advice

"In a time of drastic change it is the learners who inherit the future." —Eric Hoffer (1902–83), U.S. philosopher

Persist

Perseverance is a key ingredient in accomplishing goals. Important goals usually take more time to accomplish than less important goals. You need to start with the expectation that you will have to persist at some point. Having that expectation makes it easier when you discover the need.

When you are several weeks or months into working toward a goal, you may discover diminished enthusiasm and fatigue. You have learned much. Your new information has helped, but it requires constant focus and effort to maintain progress. Persistence and a steady, comfortable pace are good companions at this point. With this approach, you will have the reserves necessary to sprint when needed.

Sage Advice

"Patience and tenacity of purpose are worth more than twice their weight of cleverness." —Thomas Henry Huxley (1825–95), English biologist

Do not persist blindly. The attitude cannot be "If I just keep plugging away, I will get there." This attitude shuts down learning and creativity.

Without these, just continuing doggedly can be a recipe for problems. When coming across those problems, you will be ill equipped to address them with vigor and imagination.

Each day as you persist, review your one-page goal statement. Visualize achievement of the goal. Keep it fresh and alive.

Celebrate!

Celebrate the first day, the last day, and every day in-between. Celebrate steps toward the goal, great efforts that did not end in success, and the learning that all this engenders.

Celebrations play a major role in achieving a goal. Plan to celebrate and you will celebrate.

It is crucial to recognize the role encouragement plays in motivation. You only need to reflect on a situation where someone celebrated something you did. You remember it felt good. Perhaps more importantly, it unlocked more creativity and energy that took you to an even higher level.

A celebration is not saying, "Good job." A celebration says, "Good job," and then shares the good job with others. It is positive, upbeat, and very public. People seldom celebrate in closets.

Personal Coaching

When opening a new retail outlet, celebrate by giving prizes to every tenth customer for a week or the first 20 customers in the store on the first day, for example.

Thankfully, there are more ways to celebrate than could be covered in another 50 pages. Seeing your name in print is one of the best ways to celebrate. It enables the person whose actions you are celebrating to share the good news with family and friends. This can be especially helpful if a person has reduced family time to help accomplish a goal. Putting something in print is more lasting than the spoken word. Pre-planning celebrations helps make them true celebrations. For example, choose the special paper and special certificates you plan to use and order them in quantity. Plan to use all of it.

Consider This

Small offices are a great place to immediately reward good effort and results. Each day, recognize the star of the day by measures that are fair and understood. Take the person to lunch the next day to make the reward immediate.

Be sure to find reasons to celebrate on the first day. In fact, plan first day activities that are very likely to produce celebration-worthy results. Celebrate on the second day and every day thereafter.

Put special emphasis on celebrating lessons that become creative solutions or tools. This sends the message to the organization that learning is good. If the lessons are good, then lessons converted into new ideas are even better.

Celebrate great efforts that were not successful or as successful as hoped. Maybe the effort got the company closer to making the sale than any previous effort. Perhaps someone used an especially creative approach that can help in other situations. Maybe a person's efforts were well above the normal in resourcefulness, planning, and persistence. These are all worthy of celebrating. This also sends the message that you can dare to do great things and do not fear failure. That message is worth celebrating.

The Least you Need to Know

➤ Pause before you start. Do you have all the necessary agreements? Is your goal clearly stated on one page?

➤ Take the first steps with enthusiasm and inspiration.

➤ Now is the time to act. The Five-Minute Manager is on the front line helping from the start.

➤ A desire and expectation that you will learn produces faster and better results.

➤ There will be times when you need to persist. Be ready for those times by reminding yourself of the goal and visualizing its achievement.

➤ Celebrate achievements and lessons from day one.

Part 3
Feedback

In the business communication process, nothing is more difficult than providing feedback, praise, or criticism. Most managers are fairly good at telling and explaining. They can share the details of a new project and talk about their function's achievements.

Yet, when managers knows that they need to deliver criticism or praise, lumps develop in their throats. If it is criticism, they have mixed feelings about possibly hurting another person's feelings or dealing with the reaction. If it is praise, they become cautious. They do not want to be too positive because then, they fear, the person will slack off.

In this part, you learn how the Five-Minute Manager confidently and effectively uses praise and criticism. They use it to inspire and guide a business to achieve its vision.

Chapter 11

The Answers to "When?" and "Where?" Are Easy

In This Chapter

➤ How the Five-Minute Manager alerts people to high praise levels

➤ The best time to deliver positive feedback

➤ Expand the opportunities to praise

➤ When to praise in public and when to praise in private

➤ Learn a great management technique for delivering praise

If you just read one sentence in this chapter, read the next one.

The answer to when to give praise is whenever there is the slightest provocation.

Alert—It Is Coming

Five-Minute Managers recognize and appreciate the value of positive feedback. For them positive feedback represents their most powerful and most frequent communication.

Because it is so powerful, Five-Minute Managers alert people that positive feedback is coming. They do not want it to be a surprise. Most people do not expect frequent positive feedback.

During their childhood, some employees' parents doled out praise in small infrequent doses. Their teachers certainly were not effusive with praise. Although there may have been some, the majority of praise occurred at graduation ceremonies—a once in a lifetime event. If they went on to college, they received even less praise. The connection to instructors and professors seemed even more remote than in high school. If they went to work after high school graduation, they may never have heard a positive comment. When was the last time you heard a McDonald's supervisor compliment a counter person about the speed with which they filled your order? In the Army or the other armed services, drill instructors rarely say, "Great sit-ups, Jones."

Consider This

Studies suggest a minimum of a four to one positive to negative feedback ratio is necessary to optimize results. Although counting may not be practical, it should make yourself and others feel that your feedback is overwhelmingly positive.

The Five-Minute Manager recognizes this prior history, and therefore the need to alert people that they are going to hear positive feedback. The Five-Minute Manager wants people to expect positive feedback. When people know it is possible, they can seek it. A poor manager makes praise a rarity, and people who work for this person know better than to expect or seek praise.

The Five-Minute Manager does not want people to believe that the frequent praise is hiding some dark, mysterious agenda. For the Five-Minute Manager, praise is simply the right way to treat others. Praising says, "Thank you for doing good work. Keep it up!" The Five-Minute Manager knows a positive response to good work is contagious. It reinforces good deeds and makes work fun. When people have fun, they do better work. Therefore, the Five-Minute Manager is a praise-aholic.

Speed Bump

Many of us are strangely reluctant to praise others. If it feels strange to you, look inward and connect with your feelings. Do not ignore them or you will find it very difficult to praise others.

The Five-Minute Manager alerts people to imminent praise in several ways. As a part of every new employee's orientation there is a portion of the first hour detailing when a person can expect to receive positive feedback. A person transferring from another company or division, where there might not be a Five-Minute Manager, should receive a similar orientation.

Five-Minute Managers also alert their own managers. Most managers become a bit befuddled when they observe the Five-Minute Manager praising people. They wonder if it is for the manager's benefit, asking: Is this manager trying to impress *me*? Five-Minute Managers do not praise to advance their own careers; so they share with their manager why they praise as they do.

When the Five-Minute Manager is finished informing people, there is a clear expectation that positive feedback will be a frequent occurrence. The frequency does not make it less special. Rather, the frequency reflects employee performance. The Five-Minute Manager recognizes that most people do many good things every hour they are at work. For the Five-Minute Manager, there is no shortage of good news to recognize. The Five-Minute Manager does not need a "once in a career" achievement to have a reason to praise someone. The major reason for organizational success is the sum of many little things done well and consistently.

Consider This

Opinion surveys indicate that about half of all people say they are holding back their best effort on the job. One of the key reasons is a lack of trust, which often leads to lesser commitment.

As Soon as You See or Hear It

Now is a good time to praise someone. Why now?—because there is something good happening in your organization right now. The Five-Minute Manager's job is to see it or hear it and then praise it.

To fulfill this responsibility, the Five-Minute Manager tends to be a walkabout manager, to be out where people are working. Five-Minute Managers want to lend help wherever they can and know that helping includes getting out of the way. They observe and engage people in conversations as part of their personal learning efforts.

The Five-Minute Manager recognizes that positive feedback is most powerful when given immediately after the good performance.

The person receiving the praise forms an immediate connection between the good deed and the praise. Five-Minute Managers do not make them wait for the department's annual awards banquet. Because Five-Minute Managers praise when good deeds happen; they are always on the lookout for good deeds to praise.

Personal Coaching

When you observe a person in a group doing a good job in a tough situation, you can give them praise while they are working. A smile with eye contact and a thumbs up can be a big boost.

Customer Service Examples

While monitoring an interaction between a service agent and a customer, a Five-Minute Manager observes the friendly and positive nature of the conversation. Although it does not result in a sale, the Five-Minute Manager compliments the agent's positive attitude and treatment of the customer. The Five-Minute Manager rewards good skills, even though no sale is made.

Later, a Five-Minute Manager observes a conversation between an angry customer and a sales clerk. The customer wants to return a product under circumstances that fall outside the company's return policy. The sales clerk is calm and attentive, but the customer increases his or her decibel level to get his way. The sales clerk, sensing that ordinary negotiation is not working, offers to make the person's case to the supervisor. The sales clerk leaves and returns after a brief conversation with the supervisor. They offer to meet the customer half-way and calmly and objectively point out that the customer's actions contributed to the problem. After a pause, the customer agrees. After processing the paperwork, the clerk thanks the customer for his patience and understanding. The Five-Minute Manager unobtrusively observes this interplay. As soon as the customer leaves, the Five-Minute Manager quietly and calmly praises the clerk for remaining calm in the eye of the storm and for thinking quickly.

Two such situations are hourly occurrences in any business driven by customer service. Almost every interaction with a customer is an opportunity to deliver praise. The Five-Minute Manager has abundant opportunities to praise.

Personal Coaching

If you run a small business, you are in the best position to provide positive feedback that makes a difference. Usually, most people in a small business are working together in a relatively small space. The owner can easily and frequently highlight good deeds in a way that uplifts the entire company. This is something managers in bigger companies find more difficult to do.

Sales Representative Example

A Five-Minute Manager works with a sales representative calling on grocery stores that sell their company's products. When they enter the store, their first priority is to check the shelving and display of their product. While the representative does this, the Five-Minute Manager asks him or her several questions. The sales representative answers each question positively. The Five-Minute Manager's response to each answer always includes some praise. One time she compliments the representative's product and customer knowledge. After another answer, there is an opportunity to praise the representative's knowledge of the store. While the representative makes a presentation to the store manager, the Five-Minute Manager makes mental notes. As soon as the presentation is completed, the Five-Minute Manager notes the representative's good use of facts and his or her creative responses to questions. In this case, the Five-Minute Manager slightly delays the feedback so that it does not interrupt the presentation. The key is to time the positive feedback to be as close to the event as possible, being careful to not interrupt important, on-going effort.

Celebrate the Celebrations

Whereas the Five-Minute Manager is committed to providing positive feedback when good deeds are seen or heard, they do not limit their praise to these times. These times are merely starting points.

The Five-Minute Manager creatively seeks opportunities to build on positive feedback. They may celebrate the employee of the month as a way of summarizing work done well. To avoid a competitive situation in which one person wins and all others lose, make multiple awards with different and creative names.

Some examples are

➤ "The Cuddly Bear," for the person who consistently has the best rapport with the toughest of the company's customers.

➤ "The Beaming Light," for the biggest and brightest smiles.

➤ "The Two Foot Pencil," for the person exhibiting the most mental sharpness to carve out creative deals.

Personal Coaching

As a small business owner, you are often the primary sales person. When you complete a sales presentation, reflect positively on what you have just done. Note the good skills you used and what you learned. Determine how to use these lessons and pat yourself on the back for being able to see that.

With today's desktop publishing software, the Five-Minute Manager can spend thirty minutes a month developing personalized awards to recognize good work. When you make good news fun, it is like putting a turbo booster on your team's engine.

The Public Wanderer

Holland is a manager who believes in Managing By Wandering Around (MBWA). She knows that MBWA works best when its purpose is to deliver positive feedback.

Holland plans to visit different workspaces at least twice a day. She is on the prowl to find good deeds done well.

When she arrives in a place, she pauses to get a sense of what is going on right now. Before coming to the place, she reviews what the department does and who are the key people. Because she visits each space frequently, she knows most of the people in each department by name.

She knows when new people join the company, and she makes a point of visiting with them first when she arrives in a department. She is quick to get new people talking about themselves, the subject they know best. She asks about their families, what is important in their lives, and what they did before joining the company. As she learns

Personal Coaching

If you have not been a wanderer, do not begin without telling people why you are wandering. If you do not, people tend to fear the worst. They feel threatened and put themselves on guard. Tension and anxiety go up and productivity and work quality go down. Be honest. Say, "I am observing the good things you are doing." Then do what you say you are going to do.

strong character traits or accomplishments, she is quick to provide a pat on the back or a positive comment.

When she meets Austin on his second day at work, she notes several good things about him. His reasons for joining the company are particularly encouraging. She responds, "That is really good. You have thought this out. You should be proud of the effort you put into making an important decision." When he talks about some of his extracurricular accomplishments in college, she notes he has filled several strong leadership roles. She replies, "You led some important organizations in college. People seem to see you as a leader. That is a great strength that you will find ways to use here."

Later, she observes Mason discussing something with John who is from another department. She wanders over and sits on a nearby chair to observe. People in the department know of her visits and her observing is not uncomfortable for Mason or John.

When they seemed to have solved the problem, she adds a few thoughts. To Mason she says, "Your use of key facts and an objective viewpoint work well. Although the facts do not reflect well on John's department, you shared them in a way that did not make him wrong. That's a great skill to have." To John she says, "You did a wonderful job of calmly listening. It was clear that you learned something new. Your first response to Mason was very positive and constructive. That quickly set the tone. From there you quickly arrived at a win-win solution. Both of you should remember how you did this, because it will help you throughout your careers."

She moves on and observes Mike engrossed in a spreadsheet on his computer screen. She walks into his cubicle and sits. They briefly discuss what he is doing and the challenge he faces at the moment. As he is describing it to her, he gains insight. He pauses for a moment, changes a couple of formulas, and checks the results. A smile appears on his face. He has solved the problem that has bedeviled him for twenty minutes.

Holland is pleased for him. She says, "Congratulations. Your sharing the problem with me and listening to yourself talking seemed to trigger new thinking. Remember that in the future, and visit one of your associates when you get stuck. Often, you gain fresh perspective. The second thing I liked was your quick thinking. I saw you leap from one conclusion to another and quickly use them to make changes that worked. You are good at this. Take confidence from what you have done. It will help you as you tackle that new project we start on next week."

"Where?" Where It Is Right

Holland's example does two things to help us learn about where is the best place to praise people. First, she goes into the place in which people work to give praise. She does not take notes, retreat to her office, and then call or write a memo. Whereas both of those techniques are also effective, Holland knows that face-to-face when a good deed happens is the best place to give positive feedback. People are always more comfortable in their own space. It is the home game versus away game phenomena.

Second, she gives both private and public feed-back. To Austin and Mike, she provides the feedback so that only they could hear it. That is not because there is anything personal or confi-dential, but because it was the right way. Imagine how Austin would feel if Holland invited other people in the department over to hear about his college accomplishments. As a new hire, it might have been uncomfortable for him.

To Mason and John, she provides feedback to their group of two. She notes individual skills and interpersonal skills. When providing feedback to two or more people, look for this combination of positive individual and interpersonal qualities.

Speed Bump

The same style of delivering feed-back is not best for everyone. Some like to receive praise quietly, whereas others love a loud high five. Because the praise is given for the benefit of the individual, tailor it to each situation.

Doing It in Public

When delivering praise to a large group of people, it is best to focus on group accom-plishments. If you single out only one or two people, it makes others uncomfortable.

This should not deter you from delivering positive feedback to a large group. In fact, this can be one of the most powerful forms of praise. This form of praise usually addresses accomplishments made over a preceding period, but not necessarily the immediately preceding period. For example, an awards dinner may recognize the accomplishments of the last month.

The Least You Need to Know

➤ As a Five-Minute Manager inform people that you love to praise. People learn to expect and seek praise.

➤ Provide praise as soon as you can after the good deed. Make a strong connec-tion between the praise and the deed.

➤ Start with immediate praise and look for opportunities to give weekly, monthly, and annual praise.

➤ Praise in pubic or private, whichever is appropriate to the situation.

➤ Management By Wandering Around (MBWA) is a tool the Five-Minute Manager uses to deliver praise.

➤ Public praise should focus on group accomplishments and interpersonal dynamics.

Chapter 12

Positive Feedback: Having Fun Doing It

In This Chapter

➤ Discover your praise style's strengths and pitfalls

➤ How to be a multi-skilled praiser

➤ The seven elements of great positive feedback

➤ The benefits of positive feedback

➤ Praise for the boss

➤ An abundance of opportunities to deliver positive feedback

Most people need lessons to become better at delivering positive feedback. Most who are not Five-Minute Managers do not give praise frequently, and have never had a lesson. "Why would I?" you may ask, "Isn't it something that comes naturally?"

You have a point. When you are centered in and focused on your heart, you let good news flow, and it is natural. Unfortunately, most people are not centered in their hearts, which is their intuitive connection. Intuition is a function of the higher mind, and is highly reliable. Most people use logic and emotions to guide them. Even when you are heart-centered, it is helpful to know some skills that make positive feedback stronger.

How Most of Us Give One-Dimensional Praise

There are many ways to give praise, but most people rely on one or two types to deliver good news. The following are six of the most popular:

➤ The Politician

➤ The Whisperer

➤ The Rare Find

➤ The Exclaimer

➤ The Writer

➤ The Body

In the following sections, examine each way; then explore how to expand your personal repertoire. As you examine each style, you will see that each one has its shortcomings. Later, we examine if there is an ideal style.

The Politician

Everyone is familiar with this method. You see it on television all the time.

A manager sweeps into a room, shaking hands (kissing babies, if they have the misfortune to be around), and slapping people on the backs. He says close to the same thing to each person. He smiles and is positive in his comments. Often, he thanks people for helping him or the company. He touches almost everyone in the room, addresses a few brief parting comments to everyone, and then moves on.

Personal Coaching

Be careful not to be a "Home Politician." Family members who expect more personal interaction often are alienated by this style.

He feels he has made his presence felt and 100 percent positive. He does not concentrate on any one person; therefore, he does not play favorites. His energy is upbeat, and he hopes this is contagious.

The problem with this approach is that though you attempt to touch everyone, you touch no one. There is nothing personal and unique about the feedback. The feedback is not for the benefit of the employees. It is for the benefit of the manager who is trying to appear efficient and caring. It provides no opportunity for people to improve their understanding of each other.

The Whisperer

Managers who use this approach share their positive comments in very soft voices. They want the comments to appear personal and confidential, even if there is nothing in them that warrants sensitive treatment. The person who praises this way may also want their praise to appear to be heartfelt.

In wanting to make it personal, they may also convey a feeling of secrecy. This can create mistrust among those who see the exchange but do not hear it. The feeling is what we experience when two people whisper as they tell each other a secret from which we are excluded. This is not a good feeling. We wonder what they have to hide.

The Rare Find

This person treats good news as a rare event. There is a sense of surprise. Sometimes the manager seems overwhelmed by the good news and good deeds. The intent is good. The manager wants to demonstrate a high level of pleasure.

The person receiving this type of praise becomes overwhelmed. The accomplishment being praised may be an everyday occurrence. When a manager reacts so strongly, confusion and embarrassment often result. The recipient of the praise knows co-workers understand the accomplishment is routine and is embarrassed the manager seems to think it is so rare. The manager who praises this way risks looking like a fool who does not understand the business. Using this method can hurt both the manager and the associate.

The Exclaimer

This style shares some similarities with the previous style; however, it has an important difference. The Exclaimer knows what he is talking about in most cases. He approaches giving praise as an opportunity for loud celebration. He delivers praise loudly. He uses decibels as punctuation. He delivers back slaps and talks loudly enough for everyone to hear him. He also will call others over to hear what they have to say.

The enthusiasm of the Exclaimer is good, but it can embarrass the person receiving the praise. The employee appreciates that the manager knows the importance of what they are praising, but the loud volume is unsettling. Just as the Whisperer creates problems sometimes by being too soft, the Exclaimer creates a different set of problems by being too loud.

Speed Bump

The Exclaimer style, although driven by positive intent, can be too much about the person delivering the praise and not enough about the person who has earned it. If you like this style, make sure the focus is really on the person who earned the praise.

The Writer

The writer is uncomfortable delivering praise in person. Maybe he is shy or introverted. He does, however, believe strongly in the importance of praising; so, he does it in the one way in which he is comfortable. He wanders about, engages in brief discussions when needed, and then returns to his office. He writes a note of praise and sends it by e-mail or within the company's mail system.

The person receiving the note is usually appreciative but often a little perplexed trying to recall the

Personal Coaching

The Exclaimer style can be fun with kids when it is combined with some levity and humor. For kids (and adults who enjoy being kids at times), this makes positive feedback especially welcome and memorable. Try including a healthy dose of fun the next time your praise a child.

113

specific situation. The memory is a little foggy. It is clear that the manager observed part of the situation but did not get the whole story, as he would have if there had been a discussion at the time. A note lacks the energy of a person-to-person exchange. It also lacks the depth of good feeling we feel when a manager delivers it in person.

The Body

Managers who use this method use their bodies to communicate praise. While observing an exchange between two people, they give an energetic thumbs up to signal their pleasure with how things are going, or they make eye contact with a person, flash a big smile, and nod approval.

People receiving this kind of praise feel good, but they are not always sure what the praise is for. They are deep in conversation when they receive the positive feedback, and they need to stay engaged in the conversation. Consequently, they welcome the positive feedback, but the specifics of the reward are vague.

Sage Advice

"Man consists of two parts, his mind and his body, only the body has more fun."
—Woody Allen, in the film *Love and Death*

Is There an Ideal Style?

Yes, the ideal style is the one that is right for the situation and the person. All styles, with the exception of the Rare Find, will assist the Five-Minute Manager in delivering praise.

The Politician approach is not often useful, but it has its moments. For example, if a department just achieved its monthly goal, the Five-Minute Manager might leave the office and go to the department to deliver congratulations. In this case, shaking everyone's hand and delivering a short message of praise is the right way to deliver praise.

The Whisperer approach is right in rare situations in which the praise does involve something confidential. The subject most likely involves something personal about the person receiving the praise. Using this approach, the Five-Minute Manager speaks in a soft voice and seeks privacy to make the other person feel comfortable.

The loud praise of the Exclaimer also has its place. For example, when there is a breakthrough achievement, whooping it up is consistent with the work done well. This style should be used sparingly, just as exclamation marks are reserved for the exceptional situation in writing.

Personal Coaching

In a family, providing positive feedback may require all of these skills. Your sensitive teenager may be embarrassed by a parent, so whisper your praise. The energetic five-year-old may love the Exclaimer style. Your spouse may appreciate a variety of styles, including a nice note with a flower or small gift.

The Writer style also has some excellent uses. For example, it is the right approach to praise a person not in the same location as the Five-Minute Manager. It also has some benefits even when there is not a geographical separation. For example, a president of a company sends a personal note with everyone's annual bonus checks praising the wonderful accomplishments each person made during the year. Some recipients treasure the notes and keep them for years.

The Body approach also has benefits. When the Five-Minute Manager sees a good deed but does not want to interrupt the flow, pleasure is signaled with the hand or a smile. It should not stop there, however. There should be a follow-up conversation as soon as possible, in which the Five-Minute Manager provides the specific positives observed.

Two major elements are included in all of these methods of praise. First, the praise should occur as soon as possible after the accomplishment. Second, the praise should provide the specific details appreciated by the Five-Minute Manager. Do not make it a general, "Good job." You want to reinforce the use of specific skills. When you use general praise, the recipient is left to fill in their own specifics, and their list may not be the same as yours.

In addition to these two key elements, there are five other points you should make when delivering praise.

1. Tell a person how their good deed helps others in the company. Wherever possible, make it specific. For example, "That means that Sharon is going to receive quality input from you on time. You have just made her job easier."

2. Let the person savor the moment and enjoy the good feelings that inevitably come from well-given praise.

3. As the employee leaves, invite the person to do more good deeds. Reinforce your love of praising others. For example, "I hope to be back here in the next week, and I'd love to see more good work like this. Keep it up."

4. The intent of the praise must be a sincere recognition of good deeds done well. Your intent needs to be this pure. It cannot be manipulative. For example, you should not praise someone with the hope that you can then convince them to do something you know they might otherwise resist.

Personal Coaching

All the guidelines that are effective at work, also help at home. Kids are especially appreciative of praise, and when it is specific, it helps them learn. They know how what they have done helps others in the family.

5. A Five-Minute Manager is true to the title. Deliver your praise in about five minutes per person. You can easily meet all the suggested requirements for praise in five minutes. Limiting the praise to five minutes helps the person receiving the praise to comprehend your meaning. It is not so long and complicated that the important points get lost in a torrent of words.

Praise Those Benefits

Praise is one area in which the Five-Minute Manager spends more time than other managers. The Five-Minute Manager recognizes the value of praise. An organization in which praise, not criticism, dominates is more productive. Its employees consistently exceed goals and perform good deeds independent of prodding. They want to do well, not avoid doing poorly.

Positive feedback reinforces what you want people to do. They understand what you want them to do, not just what you do not want them to do, and they know why that is important to the company.

When there is a preponderance of positive feedback, there is fertile ground for inspiration. Inspiration does not flourish when a manager creates fear, anxiety, or avoidance with negative feedback. Positive feedback generates positive feelings in a person, which is the fertile ground for work done well to grow and prosper.

Consider This

In a small business in which people tend to work closely together all the time, positive feedback is critical. It not only rewards good deeds, it makes a major contribution to the overall work environment. Positive feedback contributes constructive, fun interpersonal communication.

The benefits of positive feedback are clear and easy to understand. Still, the vast majority of companies, including the biggest and those rated the best places to work, use negative feedback more than positive feedback. The belief in pushing people to improve whatever they do, including good work, blinds us to the benefits of positive feedback.

In the future, perhaps more people will see the benefits of positive feedback. The Five-Minute Manager is fond of a line in the song "Amazing Grace": "I once was blind, but now I see."

Who Should We Praise?

So far, the praise has been mostly between a traditional manager and their associate. Although this relationship provides the most obvious chance for positive feedback, the opportunities are much richer than that.

Broaden Your Vision

One morning, Kelly visits the shop for her morning wander, and she notices JD has crafted a particularly attractive coffee table. The style is new and it incorporates skills she has not known JD to use before.

Consider This

A small business has limited number of employees but an unlimited number of current and potential customers. Each of them is an opportunity to deliver positive feedback. When they tell you their business is growing, praise their results. When you hear or read a story about them or their business, praise them. Make it personal with a call or a handwritten note.

After observing JD for a few more minutes, Kelly approaches him and says, "That's some of your best work. I really like how you shaped the wood and the joints you used require some advanced skills. This type of custom project really helps the company build its reputation for fine work, and it opens a new market for us. This is an important project that you are working on. Good going."

JD replies that he has enjoyed working on the project. It is a special order for a customer. When the order came in, he says, he was a bit perplexed about how to handle it. Then, he adds, "When I shared the project with Bob, he said he could help, even though his project load was heavy at the moment. Bob stayed after work for three days in a row to teach me new wood shaping methods that I knew about but had never used. I couldn't have done this without his help."

Kelly acknowledges Bob's help and thanks JD for sharing that information with her. She then moves over to where Bob is working.

She says, "Bob, as I was admiring JD's good work on the coffee table, he told me about the help you gave him. He says it made it possible for him to do such a great job. I really appreciate your taking him under your wing and helping him develop those skills. You made a very important contribution to JD and to the company. As you know, work of this caliber builds our reputation and opens new markets for us. Thank you again for taking the initiative to help JD."

When she praises JD, Kelly learns of another good deed. It is not unusual for one good deed to have several parents or at least several helpers. In this case, the discussion with JD reveals there was a helper. In other cases, learning who else is involved may require

117

a question or two. It is not unusual for the Five-Minute Manager to discover three or four other opportunities to praise in one situation.

Praise Your Boss

The objective is not to be a sycophant or, in simpler terms, to "brown-nose." This is not an admirable trait or a particularly effective one. Nonetheless, praising a boss is the right thing to do in many situations.

The Five-Minute Manager praises the boss for the same reasons to praise their associates. The boss to know what has been particularly helpful. To do this, follow the same guidelines you use in praising others. Make the positive feedback specific and let the boss know its importance. Provide it as soon as the good deed occurs. The intent is to encourage the boss to keep doing what is helpful. Again, do this in five minutes or less.

For example, when Lauren is with Larry, her boss, they discuss the results of last month's sales and the plans for the next month. Larry shares some upcoming new product news he has just received. It will be introduced in two months, which was shorter than normal lead-time for a new product notification.

Lauren notes, "Larry, I really appreciate you sharing the new product news with me as soon as you receive it. It helps us plan for the event. For us a good pre-plan is crucial to achieving great results. Please keep that in mind when you receive other notifications. We can use every day of advance notice to ensure we accomplish the goals."

Personal Coaching

Praise your spouse today. It may be unexpected, but it will be welcome. You will not have to look long or hard to find something to praise. Merely open your ears and eyes and drop preconceived notions. Try it. You both will enjoy it.

Praise: It Is Right Anywhere

Some people treat praise as if it should be rationed. It should not. The good news is that for every job done well there is more than enough positive feedback available.

Within a business, look for opportunities to praise in what may appear to be nontraditional situations. The following are examples:

➤ When you are in a meeting with other departments, look for opportunities to praise people for good and helpful work. Maybe someone shared a report before the meeting that helped you prepare for the meeting. You can say, "Trudy, thank you for sending the report out yesterday. It allowed me to discover that I needed to prepare some data for the meeting. I would not have been able to do this without your advance notice. Thank you."

➤ As you walk in the building where you work, you see the security guard helping a person with a heavy load of papers. You stop to thank them for doing more than their normal job of watching people.

➤ You are in a large national meeting. At a break you seek out someone who works for the company in another state. Before now, you have only met over the phone. The person has provided help several times and you praised them on the phone. Now you want to make a stronger connection. When you find them, you again provide positive feedback on their most recent help.

This list could take up another fifty pages. There are that many opportunities. Discover your opportunities to praise and experience its magic and power.

Personal Coaching

The lawn or pool service people come every week. They are reliable, do good work, do not complain, and have been known to do something extra when it is needed. Sounds like they deserve your positive feedback.

The Least You Need to Know

➤ Know the best positive feedback style for each situation.

➤ Praise when the event happens, be specific, have the right intent, invite more good deeds, tell why it helps, and do all of this in five minutes.

➤ Praise encourages people to keep doing the good things that aid success.

➤ When you praise one person, you may discover several others also deserving of praise.

➤ Praise your boss to encourage him or her to keep doing what helps you.

➤ We see unlimited opportunities to praise others when we look for them.

Chapter 13

The When and Where of Criticism

In This Chapter

➤ The importance of timing when delivering negative feedback

➤ The importance of facts in criticism

➤ How to decide between public or private criticism

➤ Public criticism's special circumstances

The Five-Minute Manager loves delivering positive feedback, but there are times when criticizing is the correct action. What is right and in the best interests of the employee drives the Five-Minute Manager's actions.

When It Happens

The Five-Minute Manager wanders around. Although wandering sounds without purpose, you know from this book that wandering serves a great purpose. The Five-Minute manager wanders in search of good work and opportunities to deliver positive feedback.

While wandering, occasionally the Five-Minute Manager see something that warrants negative feedback. The first rule of negative feedback is the same as for praise. Deliver it directly after observing the activity or learning of it.

Make the Connection

Immediacy has benefits. First, there is immediate connection between the event and the feedback. There is no question what the Five-Minute Manager is criticizing. Feedback of any kind works best when there is no confusion about what the subject of the discussion.

The Trail Is Fresh

Second, because it is immediate, the facts are fresh; delivering feedback a day or even an hour later means having to rely on fading memories. Being clear on the facts is important to the sense of fairness the Five-Minute Manager wants associated with criticism. When it is immediate, the actual work may be present and used in the discussion. All of this helps the Five-Minute Manager achieve the objectives.

Sage Advice

"We learn more by welcoming criticism than rendering judgment."
—J. Jelinek

Put It Behind Everyone and Move On

Third, by providing the feedback immediately, you resolve the event quickly. Typically, if someone makes an error for which there will be criticism, that person knows the mistake. The gap between the error and the feedback is fertile ground for fear and anxiety to grow. Often a person imagines criticism far worse than what is actually given. This process is very detrimental to a person's performance in the interim period and can leave an unintended scar. This scar contributes to the impression that the work is not fun, which can, in time, contribute to turnover.

Personal Coaching

As parents know, getting facts straight in a sibling battle can be very difficult. You run the risk of believing one child and not the other, unless there is objective evidence supporting one view over the other. Respond in a way that does not take sides when the truth is not clear. Proceed with caution.

Make Sure You Have the Facts Right

There is one major caveat to the immediacy rule. The Five-Minute Manager must have the facts and an understanding of them before providing the negative feedback. Whereas, in most situations, the facts and their implications are clear at the time of the event, there are times when they are not. The Five-Minute Manager does not continue without understanding the facts.

Bill's Experience

Bill, a devoted Five-Minute Manager, is doing his afternoon wandering around. Today he is in the sales department.

He notes two good deeds by sales managers who creatively overcome some long-term obstacles with important customers. After praising them for their work, he is in a mood to celebrate.

He goes to Dick's office and asks how things are going. Dick shares with Bill the tough time he is having with an important customer. He has tried everything, even some of the creative approaches Bill has just witnessed.

The customer has been pressing for a better price and is open to creative methods of achieving this. Dick is working on a presentation in which he plans to promise the customer the ability to pay the promotion price for a product during the entire two-month promotion period. Dick has also talked to finance. He understands from the person he has talked to that there might be an opportunity to offer the customer payment in forty days instead of the normal thirty days. As a result, Dick has included this in his presentation, because he knows longer terms will address the customer's need to obtain a lower overall price. Dick has just finished preparing the presentation and is printing it out when Bill arrives.

Bill reviews it and quickly concludes that negative feedback is necessary here. Before doing so, he wants to make sure he has his facts straight. He asks about the extended promotion buying and learns that Dick had never done this before. Although he knows that the company usually only gives a customer one chance to buy at the promotion price, Dick thinks there is a loophole in the rather lengthy legal contract for the promotion. When pressed, he cannot find the section of the contract that would allow him to offer the extended buy.

When Bill asks Dick about the extended payment terms, he learns Dick has spoken to a new person in finance. This person is going to get back to Dick, and has not yet done so.

Once he has his facts straight, Bill says, "Dick, there are two mistakes in your presentation. Both are a result of not checking to make sure what you planned to say is accurate. The loophole you thought existed in the contract is not there, as we just discovered. The finance person has not gotten back to you, and you have not checked with them to see what they found. I can tell you what they will find. We do not offer any customer 40-day terms. The payment terms are the same for all customers."

Sage Advice

"Appreciate criticism since it reflects interest and often help. Give thanks and letting it go can be effective."
—Drs. Brinkman and Kirschner in *Deal With People You Can't Stand, How to Bring Out the Best in People at Their Worst*

Bill pauses, and then adds, "This is a serious error on your part. If you had made this presentation and the customer had bought because of these promises, our company would be in trouble. We would have to set the facts straight. We would lose the order and their trust. This is an important and tough customer. Without trust, we are not likely to sell to them for a long time."

Bill pauses again before concluding, "Dick, you are an important and respected sales manager. This company needs you doing the right thing all the time, especially when you are under intense pressure. By learning a lesson from this experience, I am sure you will become an even better sales manager." They shake hands and Bill moves on.

Speed Bump

Don't go overboard. Some advisers recommend pulling no punches in delivering negative feedback. This can easily lead to excessive emotion and inflammatory words. When this happens, the good will be lost.

Lessons Learned

As a good Five-Minute Manager, Bill knows to check his facts first. He does this and provides Dick immediate feedback on what could be a serious problem. Bill makes sure Dick understands the potential seriousness of his plan. In this case, Bill's wandering about may have prevented the mistake from escalating.

In Private or in Public? Yes

Many managers are uncomfortable delivering negative feedback. It makes them even more uncomfortable to deliver the news in a public area, because they risk an uncomfortable confrontation.

Yet delivering negative feedback in an open area has some advantages. First, being where the facts are and where an incident happens enables the Five-Minute Manager to use the facts and any samples of work to substantiate the feedback. If the Five-Minute Manager always calls a person to an office to give criticism, interruptions may be required to retrieve some data or samples. These kinds of interruptions can interfere with the feedback flow, which is so critical to the Five-Minute Manager.

Consider This

In a small business in which everyone works in the open and is close to one another, there are special challenges to delivering confidential criticism. The Five-Minute Manager makes special note of the circumstances and always respects feelings while delivering constructive negative feedback. Delaying the feedback slightly to gain confidentiality is usually a good tradeoff.

Second, the Five-Minute Manager can still maintain confidentiality and not embarrass the person receiving the negative feedback by using the Whisperer style mentioned in the previous chapter on praise. Delivering feedback this way is immediate and does not make the person receiving it unnecessarily uncomfortable.

The Whisperer style has another benefit. It softens the emotional impact and allows more focus on the substance of the criticism. This soft energy approach also minimizes the threatening aspect of the feedback. Many people receiving criticism have difficulty separating their feelings from their thoughts. Their feelings include fear, anxiety, and defensiveness, for example. Their minds evaluate the substance of the message—"Are the facts right and do I agree with the conclusions?", for example.

Delivering the criticism with soft quiet energy puts the focus where it needs to be. The Five-Minute Manager does not want to threaten. Instead, the person should process the substance, decide how to use it to improve, and then do better work.

Private Works

Delivering negative feedback in private has advantages and risks.

The main advantage is the ability to maintain privacy and confidentiality. Again, the Five-Minute Manager wants criticism to be constructive. Privacy eliminates factors that can threaten and embarrass a person.

Private negative feedback can also undermine your objective. A summons to the boss's office is seldom good news to most people. If it is so bad that they need to go there, so the thinking goes, it must be really bad. They feel threatened, and so do others who know of the summons. Thus, your good intentions of keeping the feedback confidential can produce more negative consequences than positive ones.

Obviously, keeping the summons confidential minimizes the negatives. Unfortunately, you probably still run the risk of causing the employee to feel threatened.

These feelings are minimized in a trusting environment. An earlier chapter discussed the value and importance of trust. When trust and openness exist, an invitation to the boss's office does not cause anxiety.

> **Sage Advice**
>
> "Every negative experience is a chance to heal something within yourself."
> —Tony Robbins in *Personal Power*

Out in the Open for Everyone

There are times that delivering criticism to a group is the right approach. This approach works best when the entire group has done something that requires criticism.

In these situations, it is especially important that the Five-Minute Manager see the activity that may be subject to criticism. Group dynamics can be tricky. Things said and unsaid are often equally important. Combinations of people also are an important dynamic. Finally, observing the body language and facial expressions of different people as they interact can be important.

Patricia's Experience

During one of her two wanderings a day, Patricia wanders into a meeting that appears to have begun a few minutes earlier. She quietly greets everyone and sits down at the table. She frequently joins their meetings, so they continue with their discussion.

Patricia observes that three people at one end of the table are quietly discussing something and not paying attention to Sam, the meeting leader. Sam continues talking about the objectives of the meeting and reviews the agreements reached at the last meeting. One person questions the prior agreement and a brief discussion follows. They quickly agree that the meeting notes are correct.

Sam then reviews the agenda. To accomplish the agenda, he has requested that every-one prepare before the meeting a one-page report presenting each function's view on the proposal they are discussing. He observes the sheepish looks on everyone's faces and says, "Based on the looks I am seeing, am I to assume that no one has prepared a report?" Knowing Patricia is there, they are reluctant to admit that they have not done as Sam requested.

Sam pauses for a minute to reflect. Looking at the agenda, he says, "The purpose of our meeting cannot be accomplished without that information. I suggest that we reschedule for next week." Everyone nods approval. As they begin to leave, Patricia asks, "Sam, when did your request for the one-page report go out?"

When Sam answers that he asked for this the day before the meeting, Patricia replies, "This meeting was a waste of everyone's time. The lack of preparation by everyone meant you did not have a productive meeting. The small group at the end of the table felt having their own discussion was more important than the group meeting. This group missed the discussion of the previous meeting's agreements because of their side discussion. Sam, when you need people to prepare a one-page report before a meeting, please give them more than one day's notice. Often busy schedules do not permit people to respond that quickly. For those of you who received the request, if you cannot complete the request, call Sam and tell him that. If enough of you had done that, Sam would have rescheduled the meeting."

She pauses for a moment before continuing, "All of you are talented and valuable people in this company. We all have busy schedules and cannot afford to waste time

Personal Coaching

It is often best to deliver negative feedback to each child privately, even when there are common elements in the wrongdoing. The personal dynamics and issues usually are different enough to warrant the individual attention.

Sage Advice

"Conventional people are roused to fury by departures from convention, largely because they regard such departures as a criticism of them-selves."
—Bertrand Russell (1872–1970), British philosopher, mathematician

like this. The time you spend in travel to and from the meeting and the time wasted here is all time you wish you had back. There is more than time at stake here. This meeting does not happen if there is a spirit of trust and cooperation driving you to achieve your important objectives. With this spirit you would have talked more before the meeting and seen the potential pitfalls, even those that you were personally responsible for. So, take a close look at your group dynamics and develop a plan to take a big step forward in your group effectiveness. You are all good people, and I look forward to visiting your regular meetings in the future. With the talent in this room, I am sure you will make rapid progress."

Group Criticism

When providing group criticism, make sure your comments include everyone in the group. It does not feel good to be criticized for something you did not do. If you are, you want to set your personal record straight, which can prompt an unproductive discussion in the group.

The Five-Minute Manager addresses this situation by discussing group dynamics. These dynamics encompass everyone in the group, including those who sit "innocently" on the sidelines. When delivering negative feedback to a group, address group issues. Address individual issues on a one-on-one basis.

The Least You Need to Know

➤ Whenever possible, deliver negative feedback immediately after an event occurs.

➤ Immediate criticism means the facts and details are clear in everyone's memory.

➤ Providing immediate negative feedback speeds the improvement process.

➤ Make sure you have the facts right before delivering criticism.

➤ You can deliver negative feedback in open areas with the right communication style.

➤ Public criticism works only when group dynamics are the issue.

Chapter 14

The Who and How of Criticism for the Five-Minute Manager

In This Chapter

➤ The conditions that determine if criticism is the right action

➤ Criticizing the boss

➤ What to do when someone in another function goofs

➤ Seven guidelines for delivering negative feedback

➤ The risks and signs of too much criticism

➤ The right mix of praise and criticism

➤ How to make performance reviews a powerful tool

The Five-Minute Manager discretely and carefully provides negative feedback when it is the correct thing to do. It is the correct option when work is below the standard for a task. The standard varies by task. It can be a quantitative measure, a legal requirement, a policy dictate, or a qualitative evaluation.

As you learned in the previous chapter, the Five-Minute Manager delivers criticism only after gathering all the facts and delivers it in private or public depending on the circumstances. The guiding light should always be what is most beneficial for the person receiving the criticism.

A Smaller Circle

The Five-Minute Manager definitely provides much less negative than positive feedback. If the work is of such poor quality that it warrants frequent criticism, then the Five-Minute Manager considers other responses.

When there is a consistent pattern of poor quality results, it suggests a need for additional and improved training. The Five-Minute Manager observes the patterns, identifies the skills needing improvement, and secures the help of quality teachers to conduct the necessary training. After a period of assimilation, the Five-Minute Manager again assesses results and skill levels. If there are still significant and consistent gaps, then additional training may be required.

Consider This

In a small business, managers may be reluctant to take someone off an assignment to attend training to address consistent performance problems. Losing one person for a few days can seem a big loss. The other options of firing the person or living with the poor performance should be carefully weighed. Training is usually the best option.

When the best training efforts do not produce the necessary results, the Five-Minute Manager considers the overall abilities of the person. For example, a department may have recently implemented a new software program that requires the ability to work with graphics and to think conceptually. Some individuals do not have the aptitude to master the new skills despite considerable quality training. The Five-Minute Manager then considers transferring such employees to other functions requiring the skills they do possess.

During this period, the Five-Minute Manager does not use increased levels of criticism to motivate people to improve. The Five-Minute Manager only uses criticism to infrequently address lower than necessary performance. When the frequency of criticism reaches a certain level, the Five-Minute Manager considers the solutions just discussed.

This is different from praise. Praise has no upper limit. For the Five-Minute Manager, the more praise the better.

Criticizing the Boss

Yes, it is OK to criticize your boss. The intention needs to be the same as with any other co-worker. The Five-Minute Manager wants to prompt the boss to more helpful behaviors.

When criticizing the boss, indicate what action or activity was not helpful from your perspective. Then, quickly point out an alternative approach that would be more helpful to you. This is a dynamic process, so expect some give and take while seeking an optimal solution. The Five-Minute Manager knows that the first suggestion may not be the best solution. The boss usually possesses greater experience and a different perspective. When you and your boss understand this, a better, more constructive action may emerge.

For example, when Brad is in a weekly meeting with his boss, he notes his boss has taken an important action without seeking Brad's input. Because his boss's actions seem counter to the best interests and needs of Brad's department, he shares his concerns. He says, "The decision you made last week raises some concerns. I have concerns about my department responding as quickly as it appears you need here. By seeking our input before making the decision, there may have been a better way to approach this. I promise to give the issues of this importance my undivided attention so you can get the information when you need it."

Brad's boss reflects for a moment. His reasons for not informing Brand included being pressed for time and thinking he understood all the issues. As they exchange thoughts, Brad's boss realizes he has forgotten an important project Brad's department has just begun working on. This project will take another two months to complete. The estimate is that the project consumes about 75 percent of the capacity in Brad's department.

This sharing helps the boss realize how he could have made a better decision. Brad and his boss quickly discuss how they will rescue the project the boss had agreed to. They work cooperatively and constructively.

This kind of discussion is not risk-free in all organizations, but it is possible in almost all organizations that possess the key foundation elements discussed in the first few chapters. Trust, a respect for listening, and a spirit of cooperation all aligned around a common vision open up powerful interpersonal dynamics.

Personal Coaching

Criticize our spouse or significant other? We do it, and sometimes all too often. We often think we have our facts straight, but we seldom fully understand the other person's perspective and experience. Couples often make great forward strides when they invest effort to do this.

Speed Bump

The primary challenge for a small business in which there are few separate functions is with suppliers. When there is a negative experience, you need to be careful to share with the supplier the impact on your company and search for understanding about the supplier's situation. Just making a supplier wrong can burn bridges and end what could be a productive long-term relationship.

131

Cross-Functional Criticism

Delivering negative feedback to those in other functions is challenging for all managers. The Five-Minute Manager recognizes where the challenges are. In most cases, it is difficult to have and understand all the facts because of lack of familiarity with the other function. For example, it is difficult for a marketing manager to appreciate and understand a finance manager's job. Thus, the marketing manager who observes a finance activity that is inconsistent with marketing's standards must acknowledge that it might not be an issue by finance's standards.

Despite this challenge, the marketing manager does not necessarily refrain from discussing concerns. Recognizing that she does not have all the facts, she shares the facts she does have. She shares the impact the finance manager's actions have on marketing and seeks to understand the issue from finance's perspective. When approached constructively, these discussions can be some of the most helpful for the Five-Minute Manager. There tends to be much greater gain in these discussions, in large part because there is so much opportunity to learn.

Seven Considerations for Criticism

The guidelines for providing negative feedback are essentially the same as those used for positive feedback. To review, they are

➤ Inform people that it is your practice to provide negative feedback and that you follow the other guidelines (listed below) when you deliver it.

➤ First ask questions and then criticize the action as soon as you understand the facts, unless unusual circumstances require you to wait to deliver criticism. This is consistent with Stephen Covey's habit to first seek to understand and then to be understood.

Sage Advice

"An artful critique focuses on what the person has done and can do rather than reading a mark of character into a job poorly done." —Daniel Goleman, *Emotional Intelligence*

➤ With the facts, the Five-Minute Manager provides specifics about how the actions were inconsistent with the appropriate standard. Part of the message is about the importance of the error and the impact it had or could have had. The message is clear and direct but not destructive to the person in tone or words.

➤ The Five-Minute Manager checks to make sure the criticism is understood. The check can be a visual one.

➤ Always confirm that the negative feedback is regarding an action, not the person.

➤ The Five-Minute Manager reaffirms the person's value to the company and the confidence and expectation that there will be good work in the future.

➤ The negative feedback conversation takes about five minutes. The Five-Minute Manager does not make a speech. The focus is on the future with clear, concise communication of specifics.

Warning!

For the Five-Minute Manager, criticism comes with a warning label. It reads, "Warning! Criticism may be hazardous to the health of your organization."

The Five-Minute Manager knows the warning signs of too much criticism in an organization. Negative feedback can, when carefully delivered, generate performance at a minimally acceptable level. Criticism cannot take an organization to optimal performance levels and sustain them.

The Five-Minute Manager knows that if negative feedback is too frequent, people slack off after achieving a goal. Their motivation is to reach the goal, largely to avoid the negative feedback generated when they do not reach a goal. The Five-Minute Manager also knows that in an environment where negative feedback is strong and prevalent people tend to work steadily towards a goal and then sprint at the end to finish it. There is no motivation, however, to get off to a fast start, maintain superior performance, and surpass the goal.

Where there is an excessively negative environment, negative attitudes and talk prevail among employees. The boss and the company are the targets of the negativity. The number of complaints about the amount of work and lack of help from others is high. It is also common to hear complaints about management not listening to the needs of employees.

Personal Coaching

To make the transition to a dramatic reduction in negative feedback and a significant increase in positive feedback, establish a daily positive "quota." Treat it as seriously as you treat a sales quota.

Finally, in companies where there is strong negative feedback, people's initiative and creativity tend to be low. If managers remove a performance requirement, productivity declines. Associates only want to do the minimum. In a strongly positive environment, some associates use the removal of a performance requirement to invent a new one. The loosening of requirements is an opportunity to take initiative and develop a creative idea.

It's in the Mix

The Five-Minute Manager knows the need to use both negative and positive feedback to create a top performing organization. If only one type of feedback is used, it should be the positive feedback. This is a rare, although highly desirable, situation.

When wandering, the Five-Minute Manager is primarily on the lookout for good work. The good manager personally enjoys delivering praise because it involves sharing positive thoughts that tend to uplift both the manager and the associate. Positive feedback generates smiles and a sense of fun. The Five-Minute Manager can immediately note the increase in energy. Over time that increase often leads to improvements, including a person's best work and highest creativity.

The immediate benefits of positive feedback to everyone involved are clear. The person receiving the feedback knows what good performance is and that it is important and appreciated. This produces even more quality work. Positive feedback often leads to high levels of contribution and good deeds.

There are also long-term benefits of positive feedback. Because people have more fun and experience more inspiration, turnover is lower. Lower turnover is a major benefit. Companies estimate that it costs six to twelve months salary to replace a person who leaves. That is expensive, but is only part of the loss. When a person leaves, the company loses experience and interpersonal relationships. It is often difficult to place a value on these, but those left behind feel the loss because they often have to pick up the slack.

Consider This

Do you know how much praise and criticism you deliver? Record how many times you praise and criticize. If praise is not at least four times as frequent, develop your plan to be at a ratio of four to one in two weeks and six to one in a month. Check your feelings throughout the weeks. This may the most fun you have ever had.

Whereas the Five-Minute Manager is not as enthusiastic about delivering negative feedback, it is clearly the right action in specific situations. It signals to a person that certain actions are inconsistent with the company achieving its vision, mission, and goals. In many cases, the noted actions are also inconsistent with the company's values. By providing negative feedback, the Five-Minute Manager stops a person from going in the wrong direction and helps that person to begin going in the right direction.

By stopping inappropriate actions, you stop and redirect activities that hold back an organization. Done well, the process of delivering criticism prompts right activities immediately.

The Five-Minute Manager takes pleasure from both negative and positive feedback. Positive feedback is immediately fun and upbeat. The reward of giving negative feedback comes from gaining alignment about what are good deeds and then seeing the person grow.

Performance Reviews

Performance reviews are how most people receive feedback. They can be once a year, every six months, or even once a quarter. Most employees do not look forward to them because they tend to consist of more negative feedback than positive feedback. Usually, they focus on areas to be improved, areas of below standard performance. When needed improvement is the focus, negative feedback is going to be the dominant theme.

The Five-Minute Manager recognizes this pitfall and focuses performance reviews predominantly on what a person has done well. If you look for work done well, it is usually easy to find. Five-Minute Managers performance reviews focus on these positives. For them, reviews are celebrations. They are also an important opportunity to focus on future opportunities. Positive feedback identifies skills the person enjoys doing and does well. These skills are natural areas to build on and with which to find new opportunities where they can contribute. Convincing a person to use these strengths in new situations is almost like convincing a chocaholic to eat a chocolate afternoon snack.

When appropriate, you should also discuss areas where performance is below standard. Look for patterns. Do not build performance objectives around a one-time shortfall. When there are patterns, training is the first response. Training can take many forms, from a formal class to on the job.

Speed Bump

Performance reviews should never be given to fill an administrative requirement. They are part of your investment in the most important asset any company has. As a manager, commit yourself to one review in the current period that takes the approach recommended here. On the next one, make it even better.

In these situations, it is helpful to take a long-term perspective. The setting of objectives should not stop with the completion of a training class. Rather, there should be steps detailed after the training. These steps can include manager reinforcement in the workplace and the achievement of specific performance and productivity levels.

In these situations, it is critical that there is a project in which the skills can be used. The Five-Minute Manager ensures that either there is a project on which to put the new skills to use or an appropriate project is assigned to the person.

Tricia faces this challenge when she conducts Mason's performance review. Mason is brand manger on a soap brand. Mason has recently completed an advertising development project on the brand in which he managed development and production of the television advertising.

Mason has done a good job working with the advertising agency on the project, but has encountered difficulty accepting breakthrough thinking from the agency. He had initially opposed the advertising that management ultimately agreed to produce. It involves new production techniques. Appreciating their value requires the ability to visualize the end product. Mason's difficulty in doing this has resulted in some pro-longed struggles and debates. Only when the agency produced a rough version of the ad was Mason able to see what others saw in the ad.

Tricia wants to give Mason another opportunity to work on his conceptual and visual-ization skills, but there are no advertising development projects on the brand's agenda for the next six months. Because Tricia is working on a new brand project in which they are just beginning to develop advertising, she invites Mason to participate in the agency meetings.

It is unusual to do this, but it presents Mason with an immediate opportunity to address a critical training need. It is this kind of resourceful thinking that is necessary when the important growth needs of people need immediate attention.

The Least You Need to Know

➤ Negative feedback is right when there is infrequent poor performance. Training is the right response when it is frequent.

➤ Negative feedback helps "train" the boss how to help you best.

➤ Criticizing another function requires learning about the function's environment before agreeing to win–win solutions.

➤ The seven guidelines for negative feedback are similar to the ones for praise.

➤ You need much more positive feedback than negative feedback for optimal results.

➤ Performance reviews are stronger when the dominant theme is positive.

Part 4
The Five-Minute Team

Teams are very popular and, managed correctly, are an effective method of managing a business. During the last two decades, teams have come to manage everything from single-purpose projects to the day-to-day operations of large businesses.

As important as teams have become, they represent a unique challenge for managers. In most cases, teams are cross-functional. Because direct management lines remain functional, managing in a team environment requires new management leverage points. Also, the types of management challenges differ on teams. Managers who are not sensitive and skilled in team dynamics face potentially disastrous results.

In this part, you learn how Five-Minute Managers use special skills to effectively develop and guide teams to the finish line. With these skills, Five-Minute Managers are as effective managing teams as they are in their functional roles.

Chapter 15

Why Is This Collection of People in This Room?

In This Chapter

➤ The importance of chartering a business team

➤ Creating a team mission before starting

➤ Team roles and their importance

➤ Creating a Five-Minute Agenda

➤ Writing a Five-Minute Meeting Summary

➤ The importance of the table's shape

The chapter title reflects how many people feel these days when they find themselves in a room with people they do not know or barely know. With the proliferation of business teams, this situation is quite common. The Five-Minute Manager believes in teams under the right conditions. Sometimes, for example, projects are executed better with one person providing leadership and coordination.

This chapter addresses some of the key elements of successful teams. Individually, each element ranges in importance. Collectively they form a strong foundation for the team to do its business.

The Person Who Started All This

If you trace the idea for a team back to its roots, you usually find one manager who first suggested the idea. Depending on the circumstances, this manager may become the chartering manager for the team.

Generally, there are two kinds of teams: on-going teams and single purpose teams. The on-going teams can meet regularly for years. A typical example is a brand team with responsibility for managing the delivery of an important objective, such as a profit forecast, for example. The team members come from all functions within the company. These can include finance, production, research and development, sales, marketing, logistics, and shipping. Usually the management level member of this team is a department head or important person in the function with responsibility for the brand's activities in the department.

The other type of team is a single purpose team that exists until it fulfills its purpose. For example, there may be a team assembled to manage the introduction of a new brand. Membership is usually from the same functions as the on-going team, but members work directly with the new brand. They begin work at an early stage in the new brand's life. They might begin to formulate a proposal for management or begin their work after management has agreed to introduce the new brand. They complete their work when the new brand moves into test market or expands nationally.

Sage Advice

"Surround yourself with a team of people you deeply care for, to whom you're inspired to contribute more and more, which causes you to demand more from yourself—this is true wealth!"
—Tony Robbins, *Personal Power*

In either case, the manager who initiates the team formulates a team charter. The team charter outlines management expectations and empowerment. It is the single most important document associated with the team. Without it, each person would define the team's purpose. When there is not a clear charter, teams usually spend a large portion of their time debating the basics of what they should or should not do.

Consider This

In small businesses in which everyone already feels part of a team, the company, teams also serve a function. Even though people work in the same space, when they become part of a formal team they communicate and cooperate in new ways. These new dimensions have benefits in day-to-day activities.

In most cases, the manager drafts the team charter in conjunction with some members of the team. The charter needs to define several aspects of the team, such as

➤ **Purpose**—Specifics are crucial because generalities only tend to confuse.

➤ **Measures**—The specifics need to be measurable. Without measures the team never knows when it has fulfilled the charter.

➤ **Time**—The charter defines how long the team will exist. Is it an on-going or single-purpose team? If it is a single-purpose team, the charter defines the completion date.

➤ **Membership**—The charter does not need to name names, it does need to define the functions and level of managers on the team.

➤ **Power**—The charter defines the powers of the team. There is a big difference between the power to recommend and the power to make decisions.

Here is an example of an effective team charter:

The Rejoice Team will execute the agreed-to management plan to begin test marketing Rejoice, a new brand. Team members are the Rejoice managers in sales, marketing, research and development, manufacturing, and shipping. The team will complete its work by March fifteenth, two weeks after the start of test market shipments.

The charter includes the key elements.

➤ **Purpose**—It is to "execute the agreed to management plan to begin test marketing Rejoice, a new brand." The team is not making recommendations or managing brand profits. It is executing the plans necessary to begin the test markets.

➤ **Measures**—The team "will be completed by March fifteenth, two weeks after the start of test market shipments." In other cases, the measure may be the achievement of a shipment objective or the formulation of a recommendation.

➤ **Time**—The team begins now that management has agreed to a test market plan and ends on March fifteenth.

➤ **Membership**—"Team members are the Rejoice managers in sales, marketing, research and development, manufacturing, and shipping."

➤ **Power**—They have the power to "execute the agreed-to management plan." They have the power to implement all the necessary steps leading to test market, including spending within the budgets agreed to in the plan. They also have the power to overcome obstacles as they appear.

Sage Advice

"Assume that everyone can enjoy good teamwork, friendship, good group spirit, good group homonomy, good belongingness, and group love."

—Abraham Maslow, *Maslow on Management*

The Team Has a Mission

When the team begins, it is helpful to define in detail what it wants to accomplish and how it will achieve this. The "how" includes such administrative agreements as meeting frequency, meeting locations, and important process elements. The process elements can include who will lead, how decisions will be made, and debate guidelines.

Although these details are important, a team's mission statement also includes words of inspiration and goals. For example, the team may want a "flawless introduction" or one that "begins on time and under budget."

Drafting a mission statement can be difficult, especially when the team first meets. Often, there are people who do not know each other and interpersonal dynamics are at the rudimentary stage.

The Five-Minute Manager asks the team to create a mission statement at the first meeting. Ideally, to overcome the challenges this represents, the Five-Minute Manager recommends two steps.

First, the team meets off-site for one or two days. They all arrive the evening before the meeting and go to dinner as a group. The group conducts warm-up exercises where people introduce themselves in a variety of ways. By the end of the evening, relationships are starting to build.

Second, the Five-Minute Manager requests that a trained meeting facilitator be a part of the first meeting. A trained facilitator assists the rapid development of an effective and efficient team. The facilitator leads a new group through several exercises that enable it to develop a mission statement that best fits the charter and unique group needs.

Consider This

Small businesses can access people experienced in business teams through their chamber of commerce. Also, the Small Business Administration (SBA) provides resources to help with team development.

The Five-Minute Manager knows these two steps usually result in an inspiring and practical mission statement for the group in the first meeting. The group is then ready to begin with a good map and compass to assist it.

Role Players

Teams usually start with the basic roles defined. Functional responsibilities tend to define the role each person plays on the team. These are important and respected roles.

When the person from manufacturing speaks, the team needs to recognize that person as the manufacturing expert. Teams break down quickly when other team members become "instant experts" in a function in which they do not work.

On the other hand, the person from manufacturing has the responsibility to represent the views of those in their function accurately and fully. Often, this requires them to consult with others performing their function if the required expertise is beyond their personal capabilities. If the team's rules permit, an additional expert may be invited to directly contribute expertise the team needs. Usually, the guest attends for one meeting.

Beyond these self-evident roles, other roles may develop in the team. For example, there can be a sub-group or a single team member to meet regularly with senior managers to update them on progress or to seek counsel.

Speed Bump

Make roles special and not routine and standard. If they become routine, there can be stigmas associated with some. Be creative with titles and make them fun.

Another obvious role is the team leader. Teams address this in several ways. First, there can be a rotating leader. The person representing each function at some point leads a team meeting. This option works best when there are irreconcilable differences between team members about who should lead.

Second, in some companies one person traditionally leads multi-function teams. For example, in many consumer products companies, the marketing or brand management representative leads the team. The rationale is that this is the function tasked with coordinating all the other functions' work on their brand or product.

A third option is that the team elects a leader. A fourth possibility is that the senior manager chartering the team designates a leader. Finally, the facilitator can continue to aid the team as its process leader. All these options have their place. A combination of chartering manager desires, cultural practices in the company, and the team's desires guide which option best serves the team.

The Five-Minute Agenda

Team meeting agendas are very important maps for a team. They indicate the specific plan to accomplish objectives in a meeting. With agreement by team members, an agenda outlines the step-by-step process for the meeting. It usually prevents confusion and detours, but sometimes both either of these can actually aid productivity of a meeting. The team can elect to follow the path of confusion and detours if developments warrant. Confusion and detours work best when there is a need for creative brainstorming.

A Homework Assignment

Besides outlining the path for the meeting, the agenda signals to all members what preparation each needs to make for the meeting. This is obvious if he or she is making a proposal. When they are not, members want to ensure the consideration of each function's perspective on the issues. They do not want the group making decisions without their informed consent.

As a result, the Five-Minute Manager knows to publish the agenda at least five days before the meeting. In fact, the team usually agrees to the rough outline of the agenda for the next meeting at the end of each meeting. On an efficient and effective team, team members are very prepared and responsive to agenda items.

Five Minutes Means Five Minutes

The Five-Minute Manager recognizes that people only require about five minutes to discuss most important subjects. There are exceptions, but a prepared team member can cover the critical points in this short amount of time. For the team member who wants to impress others with knowledge of a subject, this requirement is frustrating. Most team members, however, appreciate the concise, fact-filled, and clear presentations that result from this limit.

The following is an agenda for a Rejoice Team meeting:

Rejoice Team Meeting—February Twelfth

I.	Welcome and agenda review: Trudy	10:00–10:05
II.	Key developments in the last week	
	A. Manufacturing: Bill	10:05–10:10
	B. Marketing: Trudy	10:10–10:15
	C. Research and Development: Bob	10:15–10:20
III.	New shipping case proposal	
	A. Proposal: Bill	10:20–10:25
	B. Alternatives: Tricia (guest from shipping)	10:25–10:30
	C. Discussion	10:30–10:35
	D. Next steps and agreement	10:35–10:40
IV.	Sales request: Trudy	10:40–10:45
	A. Discussion	10:45–10:50
V.	Other business	10:50–10:55
VI.	Agree to next meeting's agenda	10:55–11:00
VII.	Adjourn	

The most important action item on the agenda has 20 minutes devoted to understanding and resolving the issue. By summarizing key inputs in five-minute presentations, the focus will remain clear. If a person feels more factual understanding is necessary, he can distribute materials to people before the meeting for their review. Assuming there are talented people on the team, there is no need to cover facts again. Thus, the focus is on what really is important. This, as we have learned, is a key operating principle for the Five-Minute Manager.

In some situations, five minutes is not sufficient. For example, a creative brainstorming session usually requires open-ended time commitments because it is impossible to predict when inspiration will strike. These situations should be exceptions. A team that can focus as a group of Five-Minute Managers is fun to watch and be part of.

Personal Coaching

Setting aside five minutes to address each important issue works. Instead of fighting this limit, have fun with it in your meetings. Set a timer and play "beat the clock."

Meeting Summaries—Write Them in Five Minutes

The summary of a meeting is important because it summarizes the agreements reached in a meeting. When the summary does this, it is a useful document to share with others who have an interest in the progress of a particular project.

As useful as it can be, the person from the team who writes the summary should write it in five minutes. It focuses on the essentials. Agreements and important milestones reached are two of the most useful elements of a summary.

Typically, who attended a meeting and who was absent, the time the meeting started and ended, and routine points made are not essential items. Once the meeting summary stops being a complete record of everything said at the meeting, it becomes a five-minute summary loaded with what you really need to know.

Personal Coaching

Try writing most memos in five minutes or less. Enjoy the surprise when you write what is important instead of all that there is to say.

And the Five-Minute Manager smiled.

The Round Table

Something as simple as the shape of a table can have surprising effect, especially when you include peers from different functions. Sometimes there are personal and functional jealousies on a team. One function can resent another function always appearing to be the leader. Personal dimensions, especially where some level of competition still exists, can create an undercurrent in team meetings that inhibits productivity.

Sage Advice

"Just to make sure we keep runaway egos in check, we regularly do teamwork exercises to illustrate the point that nobody has all the answers."

—Hal Rosenbluth and Diane McFerrin Peters, *The Customer Comes Second*

Meeting room designers tend to make rooms with four sides. As a result, they choose tables with four sides, usually rectangular in shape. These tables invite a person to be at the "head" of the table, which can exacerbate personal and functional sensitivities.

As a result, the Five-Minute Manager insists that all meeting tables are round. Although the primary intent is to address the potential personal and functional issues, there is another benefit. At a round table, everyone can see everyone else better than at a rectangular table. Thus, when people communicate there is eye contact and others can easily read body language.

Whereas a round table is not the optimal shape for space utilization, it is the best shape of optimizing interpersonal productivity.

The Least You Need to Know

➤ A team needs a charter, or it operates without a focus.

➤ Be sure your team develops its mission before any work is done. It is that important.

➤ Clear team member roles are critical to success.

➤ Take a team meeting five minutes at a time. Brevity and conciseness are powerful.

➤ Write a five-minute meeting summary by saying only what is important.

➤ A round meeting table addresses role issues and aids communication.

Chapter 16

The Team Stages for Success

In This Chapter

➤ Learn the four stages a team can go through

➤ Solving problems in a team

➤ How to restart a stalled team

➤ The benefits of a successful team

Most teams go through stages or cycles. If it is a short-term team, these cycles may not be as evident as they are with an on-going team.

At each stage the Five-Minute Manager knows there are specific steps that will help the team overcome the obstacles that occur. The Five-Minute Manager stays alert to the symptoms and is ready with a prescription.

Getting the Engine Started

On a cold morning, a car's engine can be hard to start. Likewise, a newly formed team with cold relationships starts slowly, if at all.

In the previous chapter you learned how the Five-Minute Manager asks the team to go off-site for the first meeting. There, team members develop a mission statement with the assistance of a skilled meeting facilitator. Although this helps, the team can stall after this meeting when the facilitator is no longer present. It can even happen when the facilitator remains with the team.

In the first few meetings, team members attend with a range of feelings. The Five-Minute Manager sees some of the following symptoms in the early stages of forming a team:

➤ **Why Me?**   People wonder why they have been assigned to the team. They are very busy with other responsibilities and feel that taking time off from these will only hurt their own high priority projects. In the team meetings they are quiet, even sullen. They think that if they are quiet and do not stir things up, the meeting will be over sooner. They do very little to build bridges to others on the team, including those they already know.

Speed Bump

A team has some similarities to a cold car engine. You do not want to rev everyone up too much at first, or damage is done. If the pace is too slow, however, you could stall.

➤ **I Don't Believe in This.**   You'll see this attitude when a person assigned to a project team does not believe the company should be working on that project. Warning signs of this problem are someone who argues against anything that would move the project forward. If the team is working on executing an already agreed-to plan, this person tries a variety of delaying tactics, such as arguing for additional study, revising the plan to make it better, and pointing out all possible problems. This team member never presents solutions, only problems and obstacles.

➤ **What's My Role?**   This person supports the project and knows why he is on the team, but is unclear as to his role on the team. The Five-Minute Manager usually sees these symptoms in someone who wants to be the leader and is not the leader. Consequently, he opposes most things that the formal leader says. The "I Don't Believe in This" person opposes the project, whereas the "What's My Role?" person opposes a person in the group. This person also tends to argue with others who support the group's leader.

Consider This

In a small business team, it is much more likely that problems from outside the team will appear between people on the team. Everyone knows each other in a small business. As a result, a small business manager needs to exercise greater caution about whom he or she puts on a team. Put people on the team who you know work well together.

The Five-Minute Manager knows that all of these types of people can be very destructive to a team. Not addressing the symptoms quickly cripples efforts, sometimes permanently. Therefore, the Five-Minute Manager is alert to the symptoms and works with team leaders to detect the early warning signs of each type.

The Five-Minute Manager is trained to be able to address each type of person, but even the least severe of each type is a challenge to turn around.

The Right Response to the "Why Me?" Type

The team's charter and mission are the Five-Minute Manager's best allies when dealing with this person. Turning this person around may require a double team. The team leader spots the symptoms quickly and within a week of the first meeting, the Five-Minute Manager schedules a private meeting, maybe lunch.

When Scott goes to lunch with Marilyn, he knows it will be a challenge to turn her around. At their first meeting, her body language is negative. She speaks in an angry tone, and she only speaks when necessary. Scott says, "You don't seem to be too happy to be part of the team. Am I imagining this or are you unhappy?"

Marilyn reflects before answering. She knows Scott and has worked with him in the past. She respects and likes Scott. She says, "You are right. I am upset that I am on the team. My favorite project is at a critical stage, and it demands the best I have in time and effort. I feel like every second I am away from this project only hurts its chances of succeeding. As you know, I have been working on this for about a year now."

Scott replies, "Thank you for sharing that with me. I do remember the project and how important it is to you. I also know how important our team's project is to the company." He then spends a few minutes reviewing the team's charter and mission. He adds some perspective from a senior manager about the importance of the project.

Marilyn replies, "That's helpful, but I simply cannot get my head into the team while the other project is so dependent on me to succeed. I promise to try to be as positive as I can, but I just can't take on a heavy load on the team."

Personal Coaching

Parents often hear, "Why me?" from their children Some of the same approaches that work on a business team work on the family "team." Helping kids understand their important roles and giving them help when they need it, reduces the frequency of "Why me?" at home.

Scott hears a possible way to resolve the problem. He has made progress, but he really needs her strong contributions for the team to succeed. It is time for a double team. Following their meeting, Scott goes to Marilyn's boss. He shares the problem and reiterates how important she is to the team. After some discussion, Marilyn's boss admitted she could use some help on her project. He assigns another talented person to work with her part-time on the project. Following the next team meeting, Marilyn pulls Scott aside and tells him the good news concerning her project. Scott asks if this will help her play a bigger role on the team. She agrees that it will.

149

Making a Believer of Mr. "I-Don't-Believe-in-This"

This person can be either the easiest for the Five-Minute Manager to turn around or the toughest. Again, the charter and mission statements are the Five-Minute Manager best allies. After noticing the symptoms, the manager meets privately with the person within a few days of the first meeting. The first objective is have the person verbalize the true feelings about the project. The key at this stage is determining the reasons for opposition to the team's project.

With this, the Five-Minute Manager uses personal knowledge to fill in gaps in understanding or to address issues the person raises. The Five-Minute Manager is not confrontational but instead conciliatory and compassionate. He discusses why the project is important in his view and shares his passion for the idea. He is sensitive throughout this discussion to avoid making the other person's feelings wrong.

The Five-Minute Manager also points out how much the team needs this reluctant member in order to succeed. Most teams only have one person representing a function, and it handicaps the team if that function is not effective.

Personal Coaching

In a small business, the I Don't Believe in This type can be so disruptive that it severely handicaps the team. Although it is unlikely that the attitude will surface for the first time on a team, the team setting magnifies the problem. The Five-Minute Manager needs to take quick action or it may discourage everyone in the small business.

After making these points, the Five-Minute Manager waits for a reaction. Most of the time, the person hears things not known before and the passion of the Five-Minute Manager starts to move the team member in a supportive direction. Often having time to think about the discussion for a day or so is helpful in changing the person's views.

If not, the Five-Minute Manager then approaches the person's functional boss for help. The first approach is to seek the supervisor's assistance by communicating another function's perspective about the importance of the project. At this stage, the Five-Minute Manager often discovers the boss merely asked the person to attend the team meeting without any briefing on the project's importance. In the rare situation that none of these efforts succeed, another functional representative should be named to the team.

Dealing with the "What's My Role?" Type

The first steps are the same with this person. Meet privately and draw out the person's concerns. Doing this requires a non-threatening environment. There should be no punishment if the person truly feels at odds with the team leader.

There are two directions the Five-Minute Manager takes in this situation. First, the manager shares the reasons for choosing the team leader. It can be the personal choice of the chartering manager or the leader's function's role in the project, for example. The leader's experiences as a manager in his or her function and with teams is also discussed.

Second, because the person clearly wants to play a leadership role, look for leadership opportunities within the team. There may be a subgroup of the team working on the most important part of the project. If it is right for the project, assign the person to be the subgroup's leader.

Usually, these steps are effective. When they are not, seek a replacement.

This Is Not What I Expected

When a team is inspired and cohesive from the start, it usually has high expectations. It writes into its mission statement that its execution will be "flawless and under budget," for example.

Three team meetings into the project, it is already clear that it is not going to be flawless. Unexpected challenges have surfaced and they are tough. The nature of the challenges suggests that it will require more money, not less, to complete the project. The two key elements of the mission are a shambles.

At the fourth meeting a series of symptoms emerge. More people are questioning the team leader's actions and plans. There is friction between people in the group that was not there before. Some who were enthusiastic supporters of the project are now questioning whether it is the right thing to do.

The Five-Minute Manager knows to address the situation quickly or it will deflate the team just when it needs to be kicking into the next gear to succeed.

The Five-Minute Manager invites people to constructively talk about what they are feeling. Ideally, the team leaves the meeting room and sits around a tree outside. What usually comes out is disillusionment and discouragement. It is proving to be tougher than thought. A few are anxious about being associated with a failure. It is not unusual to see people blaming others for their problems. The feelings can be intense.

With all the thoughts on the table, the Five-Minute Manager softly addresses concerns, going back to the brave words of the mission statement, "flawless and under budget." Everyone readily agrees that when they wrote this they knew very little about the challenges that lurked just around the corner.

Sage Advice

"He has achieved success who has lived well, laughed often and loved much; who has enjoyed the trust of pure women, the respect of intelligent men and the love of little children; who has filled his niche and accomplished his task; who has left the world better than he found it, whether by an improved poppy, a perfect poem, or a rescued soul; who has never lacked appreciation of Earth's beauty or failed to express it; who has always looked for the best in others and given them the best he had; whose life was an inspiration; whose memory a benediction."
—Betty Anderson Stanley, reprinted by the syndicated advice columnist Ann Landers, March 11, 1995

The expectation was really an uninformed wish rather than a fact-based goal. When everyone understand this, it is a good step forward.

The next step is to discuss the challenges the team faces. The leader plays a facilitating role, rather than a directing role. The team may even conduct a brainstorming session. This often reinvigorates the team and members become confident about overcoming the challenges they face. They may even want to divide into some subgroups to quickly develop the new ideas. It is powerful when an idea moves into action. The team resumes momentum and renews hope.

After these two steps, the leader determines if there are any issues with the leadership of the team. Often after discussing the challenges, the group determines the challenges, and not the leadership, were the real problem. If leadership is an issue, however, they discuss the points of friction one at a time.

Recall that earlier in this book the foundation elements of a strong company were discussed. If the foundation is strong, then a candid and productive discussion about team leadership can lead to positive new initiatives and understanding.

Typically this step-by-step discussion gets the team back on track. Not only is the business project moving forward again, the team's confidence is at a new high.

Consider This

It is not unheard of for a business team to turn into a new company or division. It possesses the essential ingredients—all important functions, management of a major project, and a strong sense of togetherness. In many cases, senior management has taken these ingredients to the next step by forming a stand-alone business unit.

Building Momentum

When a team successfully responds to a team crisis, it is ready to move to the next level.

Cooperation and sharing become powerful tools for the team. Members come to meetings prepared. Before meetings, they distribute valuable information another member may need for presentation. They resolve many potential issues before the meeting. The team members enjoy reporting their joint efforts and agreement.

This is the power stage for a team. Members do their best work. They do more than fill the minimum requirements. They seek additional resources to solve problems and develop new ideas. If they were behind schedule, they are now on schedule and seeking to finish ahead of schedule. They have the ideas to achieve this.

After completing the team's work, this is the period that sticks in their memories. Friendships and long-term alliances form at this stage. A trust develops that they rely on for years.

New challenges appear at this stage but are no longer the threat they were before. It is almost as if the team relishes the opportunity to take on new challenges.

Personal Coaching

When a small business has a high performing team, determine how to use the dynamics to benefit the entire business. Have team members share what is working in the team and brainstorm with others how that can work for the whole business.

Crossing the Finish Line

Whereas the business is better because of the team's efforts, the confidence of every member is also higher. Members have progressed from a group that hardly knew each other, to weathering a storm or two, to the finish line with work everyone is proud of.

The team leader makes sure everyone is recognized. Because most team members labored out of the sight of their functional bosses, the team leader writes a short note to each team member's supervisor. It thanks the supervisor for assigning the person to the team and outlines the team's and the individual's accomplishments.

Consider This

There is considerable research suggesting that companies that have more fun have the greatest success. Actively seek out opportunities to have fun. Well-intentioned gag awards and games that are win–win are two ideas some companies use effectively.

The team should also take time to celebrate its success. Again, team members go off-site. The team leader, in the spirit of fun, awards each person a special gag award. A good laugh goes a long way to retaining the positive energy of the experience.

The Least You Need to Know

➤ There are three common problems experienced by a team in the first few meetings.

➤ For most problems, emphasizing the charter and mission is effective.

➤ If a team becomes discouraged, listen closely, recalibrate expectations, and brainstorm for new ideas.

➤ With success comes momentum and higher levels of success.

➤ A successful team enjoys the benefits of the experience well after it is disbanded.

Part 5
The Five-Minute Small Business Manager

The small business poses special challenges for most managers. Managers are usually expected to fulfill more roles and to achieve proportionately more with fewer resources than their counterparts in a large business.

Urgency and the day's goals tend to be very important, especially to generating profitable sales. The focus on the current day often prevents the visioning and planning that can lead to market share leadership and long-term profitability.

In this part, you learn many insights Five-Minute Managers use to manage smaller businesses. The vast majority of the tips are low-cost and powerful. The combination of power and simplicity are hallmarks of the special skills for which Five-Minute Managers are known.

Chapter 17

Rev Up That Sales Engine

In This Chapter

➤ The major myths of selling dispelled

➤ Why gimmicks and aggressiveness are not sales requirements

➤ Adding value to increase sales

➤ Using the Internet to add value to your product or service

The ability to sell its product or service to customers is critical to the success of any company. Although sales is the function that drives virtually every business, it is one of the least understood. The Five-Minute Manager understands the importance of sales and what can be done to optimize its contributions. This chapter also addresses the myths associated with selling.

After dispensing with the myths, the chapter covers one of the most powerful methods of increasing sales—adding value to your product or service. There are several low-cost yet highly effective ways of adding value your customers notice and appreciate.

Sales Myths

Because virtually everyone has had a sales person try to sell them something, most people think they know what sales is about. Unfortunately, this misconception perpetuates several myths about selling.

Myth #1: You Can Be Sold Something You Don't Want

This myth probably has its roots in the experience of purchasing something you later regret buying. Instead of taking responsibility for making the purchase decision, you blame the sales person.

The truth, if you are willing to see it, is that buyers buy and sellers sell. In the moment you buy something, you believe you need or want it. Sometimes the item is something you preplanned to buy, and sometimes your purchase is spontaneous.

In either case, you go through a checklist in your mind before paying for the item. Do you need or want it? This is a tricky question, especially if it is a want instead of a need. Regretting a purchase usually occurs when you confuse a want with a need. Wants vary. One day you want it badly, and the next day you do not want it so much. The regret is generated after you buy the item at the high point of the want cycle, and the next day you are near the low point of the want cycle.

Consider This

In the past, the car dealer held almost all the cards. Buyers knew they could negotiate, but never knew when they had the best possible deal. Today buyers go online and download dealer costs, special dealer incentives, and a compendium of reviews by a wide variety of magazines. Several services have arrangements with dealers to buy a car at a set amount over dealer cost. If you are buying a used car, check the Kelly Blue Book price for your market at www.kbb.com.

Needs, on the other hand, are more stable. The faucet drips today as much or more than it did yesterday. It is likely to drip as much or more tomorrow. You seldom regret buying something you need unless you have misunderstood the need. For example, you think the washer will fit a Delta faucet, but it does not. You remedy any regret by buying the right washer.

Other questions on your pre-buy checklist include "Can I afford it?" and "Do I want or need it right now or can it wait?" Needs and wants are weighed against these questions. You are the only one who knows the answers. No matter what the sales person says, it is ultimately your decision. Sales people are going to make their product look attractive; that is their job. Our job is answering the questions on our checklist; then making a decision.

Myth #2: Success Means Gimmicks

If you look at it from sales people's perspective, they will tell you that they want to make the buying process fun and informative. They know there is sometimes a thin line between entertainment and a gimmick, but sales professionals do not use the latter. Five-Minute Managers insist on presenting the facts in an easy-to-understand and persuasive format. They want to make more than one sale to you.

The most expensive form of selling is television. A 30-second commercial can cost over one million dollars. Even a relatively inexpensive commercial costs at least $200,000. Often a brand wants more than one commercial so that consumers do not tire of seeing one ad. Companies end up producing two or three ads for the brand. As you can see, the commercial production costs are already a large investment.

A company also needs to pay for the 30 seconds to run the ads. Although the cost per 30 seconds of airtime varies dramatically, it can cost over one million dollars for 30 seconds during the Super Bowl. A leading consumer package goods company believes that you cannot have an effective television ad campaign unless you spend a minimum of 20 million dollars.

Speed Bump

You have all had the experience of going to the grocery store when you are hungry. A record number of items not on your original list somehow make it into the shopping cart. The lesson is simple—do not go to buy something when your need is at its highest level. Wait for calm to return. It always does.

Consider This

One test advertising managers use to evaluate advertising is to watch the ad with the sound off. They know that people watching the ad most remember what they see, not what they hear.

After spending all this money, advertisers want you to watch their ad. To do this, they try to entertain you while they are selling to you. Some ads use cute animals; others use stop action photography; whereas still others use a well-known person as their spokesperson. These are not gimmicks. Gimmicks are deceptive, and today's brands know the tremendous risk of deceiving consumers.

As consumers, you know companies attractively present their products to get your attention. They do not spend millions to achieve only one purchase by a consumer. They want repeat purchases because it is the only way they can make back their advertising investment. They know that using gimmicks to trick a buyer effectively limits their opportunity for repeat purchases. A deceived buyer does not often make the same mistake twice.

The Five-Minute Manager knows the difference between a gimmick and an entertaining ad that sells. A gimmick usually has little to do with the actual message. It can be entertaining, but there is little product benefit information. It is used only to get attention. An entertaining ad that sells is all about the product and its benefits.

Myth #3: Gotta Be Aggressive

This myth developed more than 20 years ago; it is based on some hard selling efforts of early advertisers and a few industries that seem to specialize in the hard sell. For instance, the car sales person probably seems to fit best the stereotype of an aggressive sales person. They still exist, but the trend is toward less aggressiveness. Hopefully, they will soon appear on the endangered species list.

Most selling efforts today are not aggressive. Some marketers argue that this is the era of subtlety. How many times have you watched a 30-second commercial and wondered what product or brand was being advertised? Many advertising agencies today believe you need to entertain the consumer, not sell them. Many ads include almost no facts about the product, and there is no request or even suggestion that you buy the product.

You see this approach in sales to the public. Buyers are often more knowledgeable about products than the sales person. This is a big change from even 20 years ago. Two examples illustrate this point.

First, retailers used to be very dependent on suppliers for data on brands and categories. With the advent of the scanner checkout, retailers now have a richness of data that makes them the experts. Suppliers increasingly buy sales data from retailers so that they are at least as knowledgeable as the chain buyer is.

Second, with the growth of the Internet, individual buyers have access to information about products that was not available 20 or even 10 years ago. They can gather information from company Web sites, consumer forums, and rating services. Consumers can check prices at a variety of companies and even participate in an auction for some products.

The era of the aggressive sell is now the era of the informed purchase.

Consider This

When you use a search engine on the Internet, put the phrase you want to search for in quotation marks. For example, a search for "Taurus features" returns only pages using those words in conjunction. If you did not use quotation marks, you would get many more pages returned by the search. These pages would include the words "Taurus" or "features" anywhere in them.

Myth #4: Born, Not Made

A sales person only succeeds because of training, learning, and experience. A sales person is no more born a sales person than a physicist is born a physicist.

Some highly successful sales people are introverted and shy. People with a wide range of IQs succeed in sales. Tall and short people alike succeed in sales.

The sales process as taught by most companies is very logical. They break a sales presentation down into a number of steps. Each step has its key points. There are training programs in many companies that teach the sales process. People learn from studying and doing. It is like any other profession.

The myth that good sales people are born, not made, probably developed from the image of the smooth-talker who people think could sell ice to the Eskimos. If smooth talkers ever did dominate the sales profession, informed talkers who weave a persuasive presentation and meet customer needs have now replaced them.

Myth #5: Forget Ethics

Trust is critical in the sales relationship, maybe more than in most relationships. An untrustworthy sales person does not make a second sale to a customer. Sales people greatly value trust in a relationship.

There certainly are some sales people motivated by greed and the desire to win, people who will act unethically to achieve their objectives. However, this is true in any profession.

Companies are increasingly creating customer teams in which a group of a company's sales professionals work with only one customer or a very small group of customers. The purpose is to build stronger, more informed relationships with customers. The customer's trust in the ethics and the expertise of the supplier is crucial to the success of the relationship. Both suppliers and buyers are increasingly taking a long-term, more intimate approach to their working relationships. The Five-Minute Manager's listening and interpersonal skills serve this effort very well.

Personal Coaching

A good candidate for a sales position in a small business is the most knowledgeable person in the company about your product. You can harness knowledge and belief to basic sales training and have an effective sales professional. It is not surprising that the person who best fits this description in small business is usually the owner.

Add Extra Value for Super Sales

Adding value to your product or service is one of the best ways to rev up your sales. Often you can add value with little or no cost or risk. Added value distinguishes your product or service, especially in a market where many products or services are similar in purpose and cost.

The Five-Minute Manager knows that value drives success. If customers do not see value or see the value of a product decline, they will purchase from another supplier. Value's implications are that direct.

Let New Customers Try Before They Buy

This added value scares many small business owners because of their fear of returns. If they are afraid, then their confidence in their product is low, which may mean there are more fundamental problems. When they have a good product, most businesses experience very low return rates.

Sage Advice

"What we obtain too cheap we esteem too lightly; it is dearness only that gives everything its value."
—Thomas Paine

You offer this added value in a variety of ways. For example, a customer can try a product or service for 30 days and return it if they are not satisfied. Another example might be no charge for the product until the end of the 30 days. When the sale is executed this way, it is like a guarantee.

Many service companies offer a promotional first use of the service at no cost. Companies use the offer to recruit new customers.

Again, small business owners may fear freeloaders, but experience suggests most people taking advantage of the offer are potential customers. Depending on the economics of the company, the break-even point for this type of offer requires converting less than 20 percent of people who try for free into new customers. Some businesses use this as an on-going offer to new customers.

You may need to adjust the offer for some high cost products. Car companies, for example, have occasionally offered free use of a new model over a weekend. They use one car for all the trials.

For years, consumer product companies have invested millions in sending free samples to consumers. If a company has a better product than competitors, it is an excellent method of letting consumers know about the advantages.

The key to using this added-value approach is having a product that consumers want and like. If you have a weak product, this approach is not for you.

Follow Up After the Sale—Are They Happy?

How many times has a company followed up to see how you liked its product? If it happened once, you probably remember it. Follow up after a sale is a powerful way of saying to customers that you care and that you are confident in your product.

This approach is also one of the best methods of collecting valuable information about how consumers like your product. Are they happy they bought it? If they are, share their reasons with potential consumers. If not, you now know where you need to improve your product.

You do not need to follow up with every buyer all the time, unless that is right for your business. Every month you can select 10 percent of your customers to follow up with. The person following up can be the company owner, the sales person (who can ask if the customer knows anyone else who might buy the product), or a research agency, in that order of preference.

Consider This

Large companies not only regularly follow up with their customers; they also invite their customers to call them with any comments or problems. The 1–800 number on the package invites consumers to call. This is a great early warning system to use to spot problems.

Communicate Regularly—Try a Newsletter

Establishing regular communication with customers and potential customers can be a good way of delivering value. What you communicate needs to be truly useful to them.

Car dealers, for example, regularly mail notices of service specials to people who buy a new car from them. Some car sales people also call you after you have owned the car for two or three years to see if you have an interest in a new one.

Personal coaches have effective programs of communicating with customers and potential customers. They use specialized newsletters sent via e-mail. When done well, they present new resources, book reviews, and updates on the coach's areas of special interest. Other personal coaches offer their clients a list of services and products that other clients have found valuable, like a good plumber or electrician

The challenge with adding value this way is to make sure it is something the customer wants or needs. It may be of interest to only some of your customers. For example, heavy users or purchasers of your product are worthy of special focus. Some companies give these customers advance notice of promotions and special promotions for only them.

How Web Sites Deliver Extra Value

The Internet is becoming the newest means for delivering extra value to consumers. Example are the Web sites of Dell Computer and Hewlett Packard.

From Dell's Web site, you customize the computer you want to buy. You can add and subtract features and immediately know the prices. If you are an owner, you can enter your serial number to learn all the capabilities for a system you already own. You can determine if the CPU can be upgraded and how much RAM you can add to your system. You can also have many questions about technical problems answered at this site.

At the Hewlett Packard site, you can learn about all their products, a common feature of many business sites. You can also download the drivers necessary for printers and scanners. This is a great value when your computer crashes, and you need to restore printers and scanners. It is much more convenient than calling and waiting a few days for disks to arrive.

Booksellers, like Amazon.com, deliver great added value from their Web site. You can buy virtually any book in print, and many already out of print. You can search titles, authors, and subjects. You can easily find books similar to ones you like. You can order a book with one click of the mouse. You can have the book sent gift-wrapped with a special message.

Personal Coaching

Select a product you own. Now search the Internet for the product name. Be sure to visit the manufacturer's Web site as part of your search. After thirty minutes of searching, write down the three important things you just learned about the product. You will be surprised.

Yes, you pay for shipping, but you do not pay for gas and wear and tear on your car. You also do not pay sales tax. There is also the convenience of buying whenever you want, even after normal retail hours.

The list of added values you can get from Web sites is a very long one. You can get great prices and often levels of service that are difficult to receive at non-Web sellers. The Five-Minute Manager is a believer in the Web as a means of delivering extra value.

Celebrate Success with Your Customers

Customers love associating with a winner. When you are successful, share the good news with them. When you win an association award as best retailer in your region, for example, share the good news with your customers. You can do this with direct mail or a newspaper ad. Do not just tell people that you won the award; more importantly, tell them why. Maybe it was your superior service or great selection or creative services. Maybe, it was all of these. This is an opportunity for you to tell your customers how you are better then other companies offering the same or similar services.

You see car companies making great use of this approach. If they rank high in J. D. Power surveys, you hear about it. If they are *Family Circle's* "Car of the Year," you hear about it. If an SUV wins "Four Wheeler of the Year," you hear about it.

An anniversary for a business can be a great reason to celebrate and to tell your consumers about your business. It says to consumers that you have been successful for 5, 10, or 25 years. That is quite an accomplishment for most businesses, and it must be because the company offers something valuable to its customers.

Celebrate being awarded a new line of products. The breadth of selection you offer just increased. Having a wide range of product options to choose from is an attractive feature in many businesses. Customers love one-stop shopping.

Ask Your Customers What They Need

Do not guess what your customers need. Ask them what they need from you. Ask them every day. It is that important.

If you do not have any ideas on how to add value to your business, your customers do have ideas. They probably have bought from your direct competitors who do something that you do not. That something keeps them going regularly to your competitor and only occasionally to you.

Customers also have ideas of added value benefits that other types of companies offer. You can ask your customers, "What is the best extra you have had from a retailer of any kind in the last month?" Some will not have an answer, but some will. When you hear about the idea, visit the retailer. Learn all that you can, and think about how it might translate to your business. Think about possibilities. Say to yourself, "If I adopt this idea for my business, what is the best way to do that?" You can transform an idea that does not appear to fit into one that you adopt and use for years.

The Least You Need to Know

➤ Most things you blame on sales people are your responsibility.

➤ The aggressive, unethical image of sales people is rarely well founded today.

➤ Gimmicks may create a first-time sale but not repeat sales, which are the lifeblood of a successful business.

➤ You can add value to a product with low risk and cost. The key is giving people something they value, and it does not always cost money.

➤ Contact customers after the sale to determine how you can improve their experience of the product or service. They appreciate your efforts and you gain a rich source of product improvement ideas.

Chapter 18

Low-Cost, Highly Successful Sales: You Can Have Both!

In This Chapter

➤ Be a super sales person

➤ Sales success is much easier than you imagine

➤ Marketing on a small budget

➤ Personal attention—the '90s power tool of marketing

You look at the super successful sales person and wonder what secrets they possess. The secrets are simple methods that produce spectacular results when you combine them with skill and passion. The good news is that you do not need a personality transplant to be successful. Being you is one of the crucial ingredients to successful sales effort.

When you hear the word "marketing," you often think of something complicated with a large budget. In the 1970s and 1980s when marketing was a blunt instrument, it was difficult for many companies. In the 1990s, rather simple and relatively low-cost marketing methods were found to be the most effective. Part of this is from the proliferation of new, small businesses and some from the discovery that some simple elements are very effective. We can expect to see more of this over the next decade.

Be a Super Successful Sales Person

Everyone, yes everyone, who wants to be one can be a super successful sales person. There are no deep, dark secrets. If anything, you need ask merely, "How would I like someone to sell something to me?" You can also reflect on the best sales person you know and pattern yourself after that person, with a few changes to remain consistent with who you are.

The Five-Minute Manager knows sales skills can be developed. The skills are mostly common sense and can be learned.

Passion for the Product AND People

When you think of the successful sales person, you often think of someone who really believes in the product. That is important, but it is also critical to have a passion for people.

Passion for the product is something that comes with knowledge and experience. Sales people who are passionate about their product invest the effort to become experts. They know how it is made, where it is made, and who makes it. They know the materials, any patents, and special features of the product. They know how you can buy it and ship it. They know its best uses in a wide variety of situations.

Personal Coaching

If you are in sales, subscribe to magazines that focus on your industry. Once a month, search the Internet for newspaper articles and other new references that can help you.

They also use the product and have sought the knowledge of many others who use the product. They have practical knowledge of what to do in different situations. When there is a problem, they know what to do. They have seen situations in which the product does not work well, and they never recommend customers use it in these situations.

As passionate as they are about their product, they are equally passionate about people. They know their product is very good in certain situations, and they want others to experience these benefits. They want to help people. They know when there is a good match between what people need and what their product can do.

What Does the Customer Really Need?

Customer knowledge distinguishes a good sales person from a super sales person. The super sales person uses the same communication skills as the Five-Minute Manager, asking good questions and being an excellent listener.

Many sales people ask questions, however some do not. Those who do not are the "tellers," and they do not last long. Some sales people ask very narrow questions. They want to set up conditions and answers they can manipulate and use in their sales pitches. This approach is more successful than the "teller" approach, but it produces a number of problems and leads to eventual rejection.

The super sales person goes on a fact-finding mission to find out what the potential buyer wants and needs. The person asks questions that might make the product look bad in some cases to find out what has worked and what has not worked in the past.

What is critical is in-depth knowledge. It is OK with this sales person if the answers suggest the product is not the best one to fill the customer's needs.

This in-depth understanding can only be developed by an excellent listener. A good sales person listens to hear the actual words, verbal clues, and tonality by using a variety of listening skills, such as the ones discussed in Chapter 5. Only upon knowing the customer does this sales person consider selling the product.

You can develop this in-depth understanding at any level of sales. In a retail store, just two or three great questions can help you develop this understanding. In a service business, asking questions on all the important considerations and not making any assumptions is critical. Assumptions are a short-hand approach to selling that only alienates customers.

If you want super sales, know your customers.

Speed Bump

Do not try to do consumer research on your own. Consult with a consumer research company on how to best ask questions of consumers. How you ask a question can make a very big difference in the answers you get back. You want your questions to be objective, with no suggestion of what a "good" answer would be.

Speak Their Language

When you know your customers, you can speak their language. Every business has lingo and acronyms that sound like code to the uninitiated. Probably no place has more of this than the federal government, which seems to have an abbreviation for everything.

If your customer uses metric measures, you use metric measures. If your customer talks about different slump grades in their concrete, then you know and talk slump grades.

There are often company-specific terms. As a sales person, if you know them and can use them you have an advantage. For example, if you know a company has a three month ZERO (Zero Errors Requires Observation) program, then you can talk their language to make your product or service more relevant to them and their immediate needs.

Will the Real Buyer Please Stand?

A super sales person knows who the buyer is. This seems obvious, but it is surprising how may times the person making the final decision to buy is unknown.

In a retail example, a sales person spends 20 minutes explaining the benefits of a new appliance to a woman, only to find out that she is only collecting facts that will help her mother to make a decision. Certainly, the daughter will have some influence over the product bought, but she is not the buyer. If the sales person had determined early on that the mother was the buyer, she could have highlighted the benefits of the appliance for an older user and given literature to her to take home.

In non-retail situations, determining whom the real buyer is can be a challenge worthy of Sherlock Holmes. Sometimes the person you think is the buyer only collects information to bring to a buying committee. Buying committees, formal and informal, are one of the conundrums many sales people face. It is difficult to determine if the person you talk to can make recommendations that are approved or if there are other key influences in the group. A negative decision from the committee compounds the challenge because it is often difficult to discover the real reason for the rejection.

Fathoming the workings of a buying committee is one of the biggest challenges a super sales person encounters. A good place to start is learning all you can about the group. Maybe you need to ask who is on the committee and find out if the committee's recommendations need anyone else's approval.

A super sales person expands relationships at a company to include all potential decision-makers. For those who use the committee process to isolate themselves from sales people, the super sales person takes different approaches. If lunch does not work, mailing information with a follow-up call can help. Penetrating the purchase decision process is something the Five-Minute super sales person is skilled at. Those who can do it well experience an exceptional level of success.

Personal Coaching

Outside of business, we are also faced with issues of determining who the decision maker is. When we have a complaint, we can waste a lot of time and energy venting to someone who has to follow procedures. When you have a complaint ask who has the authority to make the decision you seek. Make your case only to this person if it is important to you.

Obstacles Are Your Best Friends

The super sales person adopts the attitude that also enables the Five-Minute Manager to convert goals from masters into servants, viewing every obstacle as an opportunity to learn.

For example, when there is a delay in the buying decision, determine what to do with the extra time. Determine the cause of the delay. Has there been a budget crunch? Maybe a lease makes more sense than an outright purchase if cash flow in the current year is an issue. Has there been a change of objectives? Maybe another model or the same model with different options is a better solution.

Sage Advice

"It still holds true that man is most uniquely human when he turns obstacles into opportunities."
—Eric Hoffer

Sometimes the time delay has little to do with the buying decision. In this case, the Five-Minute Manager can also be a super sales person uses the additional time to build bridges to others in the company. Maybe, talking to the operators of the equipment the company is considering replacing presents new understanding. Though the operators are not directly involved in the buying process, they are the true company experts on what is really needed. If they go to their managers and support your equipment, their input can mean the difference between making and not making the sale.

170

Be You

Being "yourself" is the single most important asset of a super sales person. You are a unique and wonderful person when you live the truth of who you are. Do not try to be someone else. Identify a great sales role model, then emulate that person's skills and approaches in a way that is consistent with who you are.

When you come from the place that you know best, you are your best. When people are in the "flow" or in the "zone," they are who they really are. They are doing what they love in a way that is totally comfortable.

When you come from this place, you are free of fear and anxiety. The absence of fear and anxiety allows you to maximize your potential.

Reflect on when you met someone who was free and happy. That person was not pretentious. The happiness was contagious and you enjoyed that person's company. Communication was smooth and easy.

When you take all the sales skills you learn and adapt them to who you are, you have added a turbo booster to your sales effort. Super sales are just around the corner.

Small Budget Marketing

Smaller companies look at bigger companies and conclude, unfortunately, that it takes millions of dollars to market a product. This discourages some from even trying. Whereas it does take millions to run television advertising nationally, that is not the only form of marketing that works. In fact, there are several more efficient and more effective marketing approaches.

The Five-Minute Manager of a small business is resourceful and imaginative, knowing all the resources to be tapped to have an effective and efficient marketing plan.

Past Customers—"Hello Again!"

One of the richest sources of new business you have is old business. There are two groups of old business. The first group is the customers who now buy from you regularly. The second group includes those customers who used to buy from you but no longer do so.

In a small business, make it your highest priority to obtain information from your customers. The objective is to establish a database. With a database in place, you are ready to mine gold.

In this database you want key information about your customers. The minimum information includes name, mailing and e-mail addresses, and telephone number. If you can collect demographic data, household size and income are important.

With this information you are ready to contact customers. Earlier in this book, you learned the importance of maintaining a dialogue with your current customers.

Consider This

You can buy demographic data that is categorized by zip code. This enables you to pick zip codes in your area and determine which ones best fit your business. For each zip code there is a demographic profile. Select the ones that best fit your needs. With this information you also receive addresses you can use to create a mailing list.

Past customers are a rich opportunity for new business. At one time, they bought from you. Two pieces of news can regain the interest of these people. First, inform them of key changes in your business, such as new products you sell and new services you provide. Second, give them a financial incentive to return to you. For example, design a coupon that represents a significant value. Treat this as an investment in new customers. Recognize that consumers redeem only a small percentage of the coupons you distribute.

With today's software, you can design a mailer, assemble mailing lists, and print out all your materials on a color printer. You save money by e-mailing those people who have an e-mail address.

Mine the gold you have in your database of current and past customers.

Personal Coaching

Visit a printer and examine its sample business cards. Examine the cards you receive from others. Order a catalogue from printers on the Internet. Use all this visual stimulation to create a super hard-working business card for you and your business.

Business Cards and Public Materials—Don't Skimp

The materials that people see the most should put forth your best image. For most people, one of these materials is their business card. For people who have any interest in your business, make your card work hard for you.

There are three elements to consider in creating a great business card. First, it should be simple and small. That does not mean it has to be boring. Consider designing a card that is memorable and has the one graphic or picture that works the hardest for you in your business. You do not want a gimmick. You want an image that delivers your message. For example, if your business name is Pathfinder Coaching, a lighthouse communicates an important, relevant message.

Second, you want color. Use the colors you associate with your business. You want consistency. For instance, Coca-Cola is always red. Color is more expensive, but it works hard for you.

Third, consider adding a picture to your card. It can be a picture of you, your retail store, or a key product. Visuals are very powerful communicators.

You can do all of this design with relatively inexpensive software like Microsoft's Publisher.

Announce Everything

Whenever you have news, announce it. It does not have to be the biggest news in the history of the business to make it worthy of an announcement. It can be anything people recognize as different and better about your business. It can include something as simple as new hours that you are open for business.

Issue a press release for each paper and media outlet near you. Tailor the press release to make it make sense. For example, if one of the first customers for your new product line is in an area or town that has a small paper, include this information for that paper. When targeting new products at certain types of customers, mention them in your release. If the paper publishes it, these companies will appreciate the publicity.

Mail information about your announcement to key potential customers. Use color and graphics in your announcement and develop it using the low-cost software discussed earlier.

Buy newspaper ads. Consider making the ads color, even though it is more expensive. Use color if you have a good graphic or picture that powerfully tells your story. If you do not have either of these, use black and white in most cases. The one exception is when you want to use color in your headline. A good red color in a sea of black and white, for example, will make your ad more noticeable.

Speed Bump

When you run an ad in a newspaper, resist the urge to say everything you know. Carefully choose only the important points. Say them with energy and imagination. Present them in a type style that is bigger than news story print. Make the layout inviting. You do this by making it easy to read.

Seminars and Workshops

Conducting seminars and workshops can be one of the most powerful techniques for building your business. As powerful as they can be, they usually require some testing and experimentation before they work well.

If you have an accounting business, you might say, "What seminar could I put on that would interest people. People think accounting is one of the most boring businesses." You sell yourself short with this kind of thinking.

Target a seminar at small business owners, for example. The seminar title might be "Accounting and the Small Business—10 New Developments to Increase Your Profits." You can charge a low fee for the seminar. In some communities, you can include the course in the community education course curriculum. Often newspapers have a weekly section where they announce these kinds of courses. You can print up flyers and post them at various locations around town, like bookstores and libraries.

Their effectiveness comes from drawing people interested in the topic and who probably do not use the product or service today. In the seminar, you have the opportunity to convince them of your expertise.

Some of the most successful seminars today started very unsuccessfully. Experiment with seminar titles and methods of getting the message out. As you have seen, most of this effort is relatively inexpensive, so errors are not too costly.

Consider This

When you conduct a seminar, use attractive materials. Use color overheads and booklets. Spend time making the information useful and then present it in a high-quality manner. Again, software programs like Microsoft's Publisher and a low-cost color printer are about all you need.

Alliances

Alliances are one of the most cost effective, on-going methods of generating new business. Importantly, they can distinguish you from competitors who do not have them.

What is an alliance? In its simplest form, it is where two or more businesses agree to cooperate in a mutually beneficial manner. For example, a massage therapist and health club can form an alliance. The massage therapist refers customers to the club and the club to the therapist. The therapist might do their work at the club one or two days a week. Now the club offers a service other clubs do not, and the therapist refers people interested in improving their bodies to the club.

The possibilities are almost endless. Almost every product and service interacts with some other product. Thus, by linking them, the customer can achieve greater convenience and value.

To find the alliances that work best for you, think of how people use your product or service. Identify the three other products or services people are likely to use directly or indirectly when they use yours. Now search for companies that offer these and visit them. You want the alliance to be a good fit. The image and functionality need to work together. If they do not, it will not be a match made in heaven and it may not work.

The World Wide Web

The Internet is one of the best venues to use to offer a variety of services and to bring added value to your products. As such, it can play a significant role in your business.

Creating a Web presence does not have to be expensive. You can create the site yourself using powerful Web creation software. Microsoft's FrontPage is a leading product in this industry, but there are several other good options. To speed your learning, buy an instruction book. For instance, Microsoft Press offers a helpful guide to FrontPage that comes with a CD-ROM that animates some of the lessons.

Personal Coaching

Consumer products and fast food companies are forming alliances. For example, in their cinnamon roll product, Burger King aligned with Pillsbury. Because Pillsbury makes a similar product for the home, they brought Burger King instant credibility with their product. In return, Pillsbury received business and advertising.

It costs about $50 a month or less to host your site on a server. You also need to pay for your domain name (less than $100); that is the www.____.com. Do not be surprised if your first few choices are already taken. You can do a minor variation of an existing name. For example, if "www.purity.com" is taken, then "www.purity-az.com" may be available for your business. The final expense you have is regular registration with search engines. This also can cost less than $50 per month. Having a Web site is a great way to utilize a low-cost marketing tool.

The Least You Need to Know

➤ Product and customer knowledge coupled with passion for the product are great ingredients for sales success.

➤ When you know customers' real needs and can speak their language, you are more than half way to making the sale.

➤ Low-cost elements are already available to help you construct an effective marketing plan. Take advantage of these elements and add your imagination.

➤ Invite past customers to a seminar where you announce your latest products and services, along with the new alliances that make buying from you the smart choice.

Chapter 19

Powerful Ideas to Develop Your Business

In This Chapter

➤ How to make personal creativity your strong suit

➤ Tips on how to make an inspiring creative environment—internally and externally

➤ You can have razor-sharp problem solving skills

➤ How to redefine a problem as an opportunity

Personal creativity is one of the most powerful tools anyone in business has. It is also something all are capable of using. Just as every person's natural sales ability must be nurtured to reach its full potential, so natural creativity must be honed.

Creative skills are also excellent problem-solving skills. Energize your problem-solving skills with an attitude that lets you see opportunities, not problems. Problem solving requires some external input, but the quality of your solution is ultimately a product of your own work.

You Are Creative—Discover Just How Creative

Somehow, many people grow up believing that although some people are creative, most of us are not. Because creativity is not taught, they find it difficult to hone their creativity. The limited number of teachers and books on creativity only serve the assumption that people are born creative or not creative.

The Five-Minute Managers, however, are exceptions. They know they are creative and can help others improve their creativity, often dramatically.

See Yourself as Creative

The first step to becoming more creative is to recognize that being born creative or not creative is a myth. Certainly there are different levels of creativity. But just because you are not Monet or Picasso, does not mean that you are not creative.

Everyone is creative. You can see that this is true whenever you come up with a novel idea or solution to a problem. Everyone does it, sometimes several times a day.

Creativity is not found only in writing a book, scoring music, painting, or sculpting. Creativity is developing something unique. It can be a completely new idea or a change to an existing idea. It can be a unique combination of objects or ideas that already exist but are not usually combined as you have combined them. The possibilities are endless.

The crucial starting point is recognizing that you are creative. Do not underestimate your creativity. Instead, celebrate it and recognize you can develop it, just like any other skill. This strong personal belief is a fundamental starting point for all. If you do not recognize your current creativity and ability to make it even stronger, you will not enhance your creative skills.

Start by believing.

Sage Advice

"Whatever creativity is, it is in part a solution to a problem."
—Brian Aldiss (b. 1925), British science fiction writer

Create an Idea-Friendly Environment

To create an idea-friendly environment, make changes to your surroundings. There should sunlight and open windows to let in fresh air but not rain. If these are not readily available in your house or place of work, identify a place nearby where you can connect with nature. Maybe it is a park or a path along a stream.

Bring nature into your place of work. Plants, especially flowering plants, bring a special beauty. Bring in artwork that appeals to you. You are not trying to win art awards here; so make sure it is a painting, picture, and object that uplifts you. Pictures of favorite places and people might make your list. You might call this process "creativity nesting."

When you have this set up, consider bringing music into your space. If playing music on speakers bothers others, then use headphones. The CD drive on most computers plays CD music. On the front of most computer CD players is a plug for headphones. Speaking of computers, you can buy special screen savers that

Sage Advice

"I know no subject more elevating, more amazing, more ready to the poetical enthusiasm, the philosophical reflection, and the moral sentiment than the works of nature. Where can we meet such variety, such beauty, such magnificence?"
—James Thomson (1700–1748), Scottish poet

inspire you. One person bought a Kauai, Hawaii screen saver on their vacation there and relives favorite spots each day.

Finally, add inspiring picture books to your space. Visual elements are one of the most powerful creative stimulants. These are books that calm your energy and bring a smile to your face.

Schedule Regular Brainstorming Time

If you want to get your body into shape, you exercise regularly. If you want to improve your chess skills, you play regularly. The same is true for creativity. If you only try to be creative once or twice a month or every other month, however, your improvement will be slow.

Pick the time of day when you have the most energy. If you are morning person, make it the part of the morning when you are ready to be productive. Pick a subject in which you need more options or you are stuck. Get comfortable. Use a pad of paper, a flip chart, or a tape recorder to record your thoughts. Make recording your ideas easy. You do not want difficulty recording the ideas to stifle their flow.

Invite others to your session. Several brains only aid the process. One rule that everyone needs to strictly adhere to is "No judging allowed." Judging of ideas only inhibits the flow. Have fun being outrageous.

Sage Advice

"True creativity often starts where language ends."
—Arthur Koestler (1905–83), Hungarian-born British novelist,

Bring sure-fire creativity starters to the session. Bring previous ideas and then build on them. Pictures on relevant and not-so-relevant subjects are great idea starters. Invite two people who know nothing about the idea you are working on that day. People with an "uneducated" perspective can be some of the greatest teachers. They see the obvious in some cases and the totally fresh idea in other cases.

Most of all, have fun!

Adapt and Build on Already Good Ideas

Benefit from the good work of other people who have faced similar challenges. For example, if you have a business that got off to a great start but then started to slump, find other businesses that have experienced the same thing. The examples can be in very different types of products, if you cannot find any for your type of business. The potential learnings are often very similar—a competitor is stronger or your service level slips, for example. The responses may be different, but the principles used to guide a response are often similar.

Use a brainstorming session to identify businesses with a similar problem. Then learn all you can about them. Visit the company or talk to owners or managers about the business. What did they do to turn the business around? What were the results? Learn from what did and did not work. When you hear of things that worked, dig in and learn all that you can. Call the company and talk to the most senior managers you can. Search the Internet for magazine and newspaper articles. Collect information from every resource that helps.

Speed Bump

When you build on the ideas of others, be sure to give the originator of the idea credit. With good ideas there is always enough credit for everyone.

When you have the information, conduct a brainstorming session. Adapt approaches that worked for other companies to your situation. Then brainstorm how to make it even better. Maybe you can combine two ideas that worked for other companies and apply them to your situation.

Use the good ideas of other people as building blocks to face your challenges.

Ban Negatives

Earlier in the chapter, you learned the cardinal rule of brainstorming—"No judging allowed."

Nothing stops the flow of creativity quicker than a comment like "You can't do that" or "We tried that before and it didn't work."

Not judging ideas is very tough for some people. For them it is a deeply ingrained habit. If you have these people in a brainstorming session, they may struggle. Raise a red flag every time they begin to criticize. It is so important to avoid judging in a brainstorming session, that if someone cannot control himself, ask that person to leave.

It helps people to understand that ideas in a brainstorming session should not be automatically rejected. Acceptance at this stage encourages the flow of more ideas while judging bogs the process down and discourages new ideas. There is time for judging later in the process.

In the creativity stage, cheering is allowed; jeering is not.

Visual Stimulation and Mixed Brains

This chapter has already touched on the importance of visual stimulation and adding people with fresh perspectives to the creative process.

The addition of visual stimulation should be a part of every creativity session. Go off-site and visit the area of the company where you need new ideas. A conference room is very quiet, but also visually sterile.

If it is a product issue, bring all the competitive products together. Use them as a group. Exchange observations as you examine them. Use the products in the environment in which your consumers use the products. If it is in the kitchen, go to someone's home and use the products there.

Adding people with very different perspectives to the creative process can double and triple the number and quality of ideas you produce. Great people to add to your brainstorming session are real consumers and users of your product or service. Invite them into your group to have fun inventing the future. Now add some people who have never heard of your product or service. When you mix people with diverse backgrounds, you will be amazed at the fun and new thinking you produce.

This is fun; so laugh, smile, and feel good.

Sage Advice

"The Image is more than an idea. It is a vortex or cluster of fused ideas and is endowed with energy."
—Ezra Pound

Curiosity Does Not Kill Humans

Curiosity may kill some cats, but curiosity in humans leads to wonderful discoveries.

Curiosity is an attitude you carry with you all the time. When you see something even slightly perplexing, you ask, "I wonder why that is that way?" You ponder the possibilities. Your mind goes from "I wonder if … " to "Sure, and if … "

Be curious every day. When you read something in the paper and it raises a question in your mind, do not let it stop there. Reflect for a moment. If necessary, look something up in the dictionary or encyclopedia. Follow your curiosity. Have fun wherever it leads you.

When you make curiosity a part of every day, you exercise some of your creative "muscles" every day. There are two crucial steps to nourishing curiosity. First, be on the lookout for questions and opportunities to know more. Second, pursue the questions and find answers, not just one answer.

This approach not only develops personal creativity, it makes your entire life richer. You see new possibilities in everything. Wonderful new paths open to you. You find richness in the previously mundane.

Sage Advice

"I think, at a child's birth, if a mother could ask a fairy godmother to endow it with the most useful gift, that gift would be curiosity."
—Eleanor Roosevelt

Open Door, Open Mind

You have seen it is important not to judge ideas during the creative process. Not judging is a beginning, but it is not a final destination.

Besides not judging, you need to have an open mind. An open mind is a precious gift you give yourself. You allow yourself to see possibilities that have always been there, but that you shut out before.

An important first step is recognizing that new possibilities are not a threat. When you entertain a totally foreign, even repugnant, idea, it does not mean that you believe in it. You can play with the idea, explore it, wonder why it is the way it is, without ever needing to adopt the idea. See the idea in its fullness. Understand all its possibilities; then you can decide if it is right for you.

Shutting your mind precludes many ideas before you know what they really are. Preconceived notions are killers of the creative process.

Sharpen Your Problem-Solving Skills

All businesses, no matter how successful, face problems. There are very good problem solvers in business and some who are not as good. Very good problem solvers have seven characteristics.

Five-Minute Managers have mastered these seven. They use them daily and teach them to others.

The Right Attitude

When you tell someone about a problem, that person may say, "It's not a problem. It's an opportunity."

Sage Advice

"Life has no other discipline to impose, if we would but realize it, than to accept life unquestioningly. Everything we shut our eyes to, everything we run away from, everything we deny, denigrate or despise, serves to defeat us in the end … Every moment is a golden one for him who has the vision to recognize it as such."
—Henry Miller (1891–1980), U.S. author

In that response lies one of the qualities of a good problem solver. When others fear a problem, good problem solvers almost welcome it. They welcome it not just because they enjoy the process of solving the problem; in their experience, solved problems usually make them and the company stronger.

Seeing problems as opportunities requires opening your mind to the possibility that good things instead of bad things are about to happen. It takes a few times walking down this path to develop the confidence needed to fully embrace the approach.

True opportunity thinkers see a chance to learn something new. The prospect excites them. Learning helps them grow as people and as managers. They see the opportunity to succeed where others have failed. The failures of others do not discourage them.

Opportunity thinkers know there is a solution to every problem. In fact, they know there are several solutions to every problem. They do not stop their problem-solving efforts until they discover several potential solutions. They know that the best solution may be a combination of one or more solutions. They know that if they stop after having the first solution they may only perpetuate the problem, not solve it.

Having the right attitude also means knowing there are answers waiting to be discovered. No problem is beyond solving. Certainly, there are tough ones that may take time to resolve. You find answers with an open and creative mind. This deep faith in finding the answer prevents fear and anxiety from overwhelming the situation.

Redefining

The first breakthrough in problem solving often occurs when the problem is redefined. When you see that the problem is not what it first appeared to be, you often take a big step towards solving it. The redefinition can make the problem appear bigger and more serious than the first definition. That is OK. What is important in the early stages of problem solving is having a clear definition of the problem. It is always discouraging to spend hours solving a problem, only to discover it was not the real problem.

Personal Coaching

Maybe the toughest opportunity thinking challenge is between a parent and a teenage son or daughter. Often interpersonal agendas and dynamics can block the free flow of ideas. To reduce these, try writing letters to each other when you have a tough problem that needs some new thinking to solve it.

For example, you receive a report that labels are not properly going onto bottles on the production line. The label machine has been a reoccurring problem for the last several months. You say to yourself, "Not again!" When you visit the site, you see that labels are going on consistently at an angle. As you look closer, you discover that the problem's cause is that bottles are too wet when they arrive at the label machine. Apparently, they are getting too wet in the filling process. When you check further into the production process, you find that a nozzle in the filler is spraying too much liquid onto the bottles. By redefining the problem, you find that you need to call a filler repairperson instead of the label repairperson.

This is an easy example, but the same process works on even tougher problems. The key is to look at a situation and ask, "Is this the problem or symptom?" Even if the immediate answer is not clear, keep in mind the possibility that what appears to be the problem may only be a symptom of another problem. This attitude will unlock the answers to many problems in the early stages of problem solving.

Have a System

Having a system is like a firefighter knowing what to do when called to a fire. Firefighters know exactly what they are going to do before they get to the fire.

As a Five-Minute Manager, when you learn there is a problem, among other responses, you activate your system for solving problems. There are several already developed systems and many books describe them.

One system that many consultants use to solve problems is describe, analyze, conclude, and recommend or solve. It is straightforward and makes sense.

When defining the problem, do not jump to conclusions. As noted in the previous section, the problem may not be what the person reporting the problem thinks it is. You may need to do some redefining. At this stage, several possible problems are defined. Later steps determine which option best defines the situation. Be open to entirely new options emerging as you analyze.

Analysis is a challenge. The toughest challenge for many problem solvers is to remain objective. They need to resist the urge to say quickly, "I have seen this before. I know what the problem is." Seldom are two problems alike. Differences that appear to be minor often end up being critical.

Personal Coaching

Embracing very new and different ideas is a challenge for most people. Take the threat away of something new by playing with it. When you play with a new idea, you can have fun and know that at any time you can put it away. So often you will be surprised how an initial threatening feeling can transform into enthusiasm for a new idea when you take the play and fun approach in the early stages.

Test tentative conclusions before concluding. Which facts and observations support and refute the conclusion? Again, objectivity is critical at this stage. There can be no rush to judgment.

Recommendations often include several options. With each option come tradeoffs. Weigh the costs of each option along with the benefits and risks before selecting one solution.

Systems work when people do their work right. Systems are a process to guide problem solving. They bend and flex to meet changing conditions and to arrive at the right conclusion. All this contributes to the Five-Minute Manager spending less time on problems.

Don't Let Experience Trap You

Experience is a two-edged sword. Experience teaches us valuable lessons that help us make better decisions today. Experience can also help us make poor decisions.

The apparent contradiction quickly becomes clear when you recognize the best use of experience is as a guide to decision making. Experience should not dictate a decision, nor should you ignore the lessons of experience.

Sage Advice

"To most men, experience is like the stern lights of a ship, which illumine only the track it has passed."
—Samuel Taylor Coleridge

Use past experience only as a guide because no two situations are the same. You can use experience to help you resolve the similar elements of the problem and use an open mind to resolve those elements that are different from your experience.

Part of what experience teaches is that there is much more you do not know than you do know. Pride, resulting from thinking you have learned more than you really have from experience, is a major contributor to poor problem solving. On the other hand, humility opens the opportunity to learning new things, which then become a part of your experience.

Value experiences but do not let their value control you.

Tune Into Your Intuition

Intuition defies definition for many people. It has almost as many definitions as there are people trying to define it.

Sages and teachers say that intuition is a function of the higher mind. This book defines intuition as a quiet voice that leads you to win-win solutions. Intuition never suggests actions that hurt others or you. The wonderful power of intuition is that it always leads you to take the right action for the situation.

Many people think they are intuitive, and some truly are. A good way to test your intuition is to try to sense your energy's focal point when you think you have an intuitive insight. Physically, if the focal point of your energy is in your heart, and not your gut, it may be intuition. If the insight is uplifting and has only positive feelings associated with it, it may be intuition. If the suggestion leads to a win-win solution, you are on the right track.

Quieting the inner chatter in your mind so that you can hear the quiet voice of your intuition helps you to develop intuition. Time in nature, contemplating, and meditation develops intuition. Of these, meditation is the fastest and most powerful method.

As you develop your intuition and learn to trust its guidance, you will have a very effective problem-solving tool. If you invest effort in becoming a better problem solver, focusing on a stronger intuition produces the best results.

> ### Sage Advice
>
> "It is our less conscious thoughts and our less conscious actions which mainly mould our lives and the lives of those who spring from us."
> —Samuel Butler (1835–1902), English author

Going Beyond Just a Solution

Great problem solvers do not just solve the problem. They use the lessons and the solution to create more success. This is the leverage that comes from seeing situations as opportunities and not problems.

Often fixing the problem has an immediacy that requires you to focus on defining, analyzing, concluding, and recommending. When there is an agreed-to solution, the next step is implementing it.

When you move to this stage, it is time to start imagining the possibilities the solution presents. To implement a solution, you may need new skills, machines, and suppliers. How can you use them to make the business even stronger? A solution to a problem, no matter how minor, presents new growth opportunities.

One of the most famous problems that resulting in a major improvement in business results happened to Ivory bar soap. Not long after introducing Ivory, workers left the machine that mixes the ingredients on too long. When they shipped the product, they immediately received a flood of consumer compliments. The extended mixing put more air into the product. In an era when most people took baths, this soap floated instead of sinking to the bottom of the tub. Ivory extended the mixing time as a permanent feature. What was initially a mistake and a problem became a trademark benefit.

Agreement

Agreement is often the most overlooked step in the problem solving process. People work so hard and long to find a solution that, when there is even the slightest form of agreement, they believe they have reached the end of the process.

So much hard work is lost when people stop after making only a tentative agreement. Like solutions, agreements need to be tested. An agreement is not when someone says, "Sounds good to me" or "I like it." A solid agreement only comes when the decision-makers thoroughly consider the proposal. They ask penetrating questions that ensure the proposed solution is the right one. They spend time reflecting on the issues before making a decision.

If a decision-maker does not go thorough this process, you risk a change to the "decision" when the implementation is already underway. This often causes a new set of problems.

The agreement part of the process is the most important. It is the culmination of much hard work. Arriving at a solid agreement requires careful consideration.

The Least You Need to Know

➤ Gently mix a positive environment, brainstorming, an open mind, and curiosity to improve your creative skills.

➤ Personal creativity flourishes when you ban judgement and negativity from the creative process.

➤ Combining different perspectives with visual stimulation is the formula for world class creativity.

➤ Be a problem solver with the right attitude, avoiding the experience trap, and using a system that adapts to the situation.

➤ When you have all of the facts and input, turn on your intuition to synthesize and solve your problems.

Chapter 20

The Power of Working Together

In This Chapter

➤ Tips on creating a referral network

➤ A partnership can make 1 + 1 = 3

➤ Tips on surviving a crisis and turning it into more success

➤ How mentors and advisors help in the best and worst of times

---

Networking is one way successful small business owners get their business off the ground and keep it prospering. Through networking, you might meet a partner who compliments your skills and brings your business to a new level. Partnership is a way you can work with others to make your business stronger

Along the way to success, all businesses experience challenges. How you respond to them plays a big role in how successful your business is. The Five-Minute Manager is prepared for those challenges.

Building a Referral Network

Networking is often the foundation of most successful small businesses. The networking can be formal or informal.

A good definition of networking is "the process of gathering, collecting, and distributing information for the mutual benefit of you and the people in your network."

There are two essential elements to this definition. First, there is the collection and distribution of information about who you are and how your business can help others. Second, the network is formed for the mutual benefit of everyone in it. This is critical insight for those who seek only a one-way benefit from networking. The Five-Minute Manager takes into consideration both elements while managing a business.

Consider This

As a small business, budget for networking. It is at least as important as your supplies and other fixed costs. In your budget, include dues and associated costs, such as dinners and travel.

Be Visible

The first rule of networking is that you need to come out of your cave and let people see you. The insight that draws you out of your cave is that you cannot succeed in business by yourself.

For some people, being visible is easy. They enjoy associating with others and would do it all day if they could. These people benefit by learning the skills to make networking a more effective use of their time.

For those who are reluctant to reach out and be visible, the first step can be a challenge. You answer the challenge by seeing the strong benefits of being visible. When the benefits translate into a plan, your confidence builds. As a businessperson, you are accustomed to having a plan and executing it.

Sage Advice

"A right rule for a club would be, Admit no man whose presence excludes any one topic. It requires people who are not surprised and shocked, who do and let do, and let be, who sink trifles, and know solid values, and who take a great deal for granted."
—Ralph Waldo Emerson

Join the Right Groups

After making the decision to become visible, the next decision is where to do so. The tendency is to go where you are already comfortable, although these might not be the places best suited to your purpose. Still, do not rule out these places; instead test them to see if they are the most productive places for you to be.

The important question you need to ask is "Where are my current and potential customers?" Of course, you need to define who your target customer is. Given the benefits you provide consumers, which people are most likely to need and buy your product or service? Take some time to define this; it will make your efforts to find customers more efficient.

Your current and potential customers are probably not all in one place, but you should find be able to find them in a few major groups. One obvious group for many business people is your city's Chamber of Commerce. Find some current members and ask them questions about how active the organization is and what kinds of activities and services it has. Determine if it is a growing vital organization or one that is in decline.

There are many other groups, such as the Lions Club and Rotary Club, in which you can find your customers. Seek out members of these organizations and talk to them. Become an invited guest to learn what kind of organization it is.

There are also networking groups formed for the mutual benefit of their members. Ask about them and seek them out. Remember you are searching for customers.

A secondary networking target is your suppliers. Strengthening relationships with them can provide a competitive edge in some businesses.

Don't Be a Spotlight Hog

Some people jump in with both feet. They want to chair committees and become president of the organization, to be the most visible of the visible.

A certain amount of this effort can be productive. You need to be careful that your involvement does not become all about you. Networking is for the mutual benefit of everyone in the organization. Getting too involved in an organization drains your time and energy, and it takes your focus off your business. You need to find a balance that works for you. Constantly check your balance and personal reserves. When you feel depleted, it is time to pull back.

Personal Coaching

When you are in the spotlight, share it with others. Give credit to others and invite them to participate with you.

Be Prepared

When you enter a group activity, have a plan and stay focused on what you need to do. The following is a list of some elements of an effective networking session:

➤ Have an approximately 25-word introduction that is memorable and quickly communicates how you help people. For example, a personal coach's introduction might go something like this: "I am a personal consultant and life coach. I help people in business and in life get what they want most in life, faster and easier than they can get it by themselves."

➤ When asked, be prepared to give a more in-depth explanation of your expertise and experience.

➤ Always introduce yourself to people, even those you have met before. You do not want people to struggle to identify you.

➤ Have printed materials with you that you can give to people. Your business card is most important, but a brochure is helpful in many situations.

➤ Make notes on the business cards you receive. You do not want to rely on memory.

➤ Be courteous and acknowledge the strengths and accomplishments of others.

➤ Do not be afraid to ask for help. Look for opportunities to help others in the network.

Slow Down, Don't Panic or Rush

Recognize that you do not go to one networking meeting and double your business the next day.

Personal Coaching

When your personal reserves and self-esteem are high, it is easier to be patient. Financial reserves are often critical, so be sure you have live well within your means all the time and make savings your number one "expense." Self-esteem means having a strong personal foundation, something a personal coach can help you with.

Networking is a long-term investment in your business. Trust and knowledge build slowly. It often takes repeated contacts to know people and their businesses. Consistency is often something people look for before they make a decision to do business with someone.

Stay current with prime potential customers in your network by asking questions such as, "What was the best thing that happened in your business this week?" "What is the biggest challenge you face now, and what resources do you need to overcome it?"

Seek out new networking groups. If there is not an association for your type of business, consider forming one of your own. These groups connect you with the broader picture of what is happening. The view from your one business may not be representative of the broader segment. If you are growing at a rate of 10 percent, while others are growing at a 15 to 20 percent rate, it may signal that you need to strengthen some element of your business.

Building a Solid Partnership

A partnership is one of the most effective means of building a business. There are plenty of success models. Procter & Gamble and Hewlett Packard are two great examples.

As good as this approach is, there are also risks. In many businesses, bickering partners hinder growth. The bickering can lead eventually to dissolution of the partnership and maybe the business.

There are steps you can take to minimize the risks and maximize the benefits.

Team Building—Shared Values and Mission

Before deciding to enter a partnership, you have to do your homework. This will be one of the most important decisions you make.

Start by determining where your values are the same and where they are different. Use the values checklist from Chapter 3. You can also retain a personal coach to help guide the process.

Be rigorous in your examination. Where there are apparent similarities, check them out by sharing specific examples. One person's definition of trust, for example, may be very different from the other person's definition. Where there are differences, work to understand how big the differences are. Again, talk about specific situations in which that value is manifested. Only by putting it into context can you understand its full meaning and importance.

Compare your visions for the business. Work independently to create one, using the guidance of Chapter 2 and a personal coach. Carefully compare your visions. How are they the same and how are they different?

Do not rush into a partnership. If you do, you minimize differences and maximize similarities. When you begin the partnership exploration, be willing to accept either a no or a yes.

Personal Coaching

You will see your business partner during more waking hours than you do your spouse or significant other. Before you decide to become a partner, spend time working with him or her on a project. If one is not readily available, consider going camping or hiking, a situation where you need to cooperate to succeed. Think of this as your "business marriage."

Equal, Associate, or Managing

One of the most important decisions partners is how to share power. This can be a tough one for many partners.

Sometimes partners base the power relationship on how much of the company each partner owns. This makes sense in some cases, but it does not in others. Having majority ownership does not necessarily make one person the best leader for the company.

This issue is particularly difficult in companies where an inventor is very technologically savvy but not as skilled as a leader. That person might have a majority ownership, but others would be better at the helm. It takes wisdom on the part of such a majority owner to see the need to have someone else lead the company and to instead focus on developing the company's technological assets.

This issue faces most partnerships, but the solution is simple: the company should be led by the person who has the best skills to perform the leadership function, not who owns the majority of the company.

Sometimes partners try to be co-leaders. This requires a special relationship to be effective. When there are only two votes, it is easy to have ties. Before entering into this arrangement, the partners need a clear conflict resolution plan. They should not rely on their ability to "work it out." Sometimes it will not work out, and they do not want these impasses to cripple the company. The experience of most partnerships is that there needs to be a clear leader of the business, and co-leaderships should be avoided.

Clearly Understand How Money Works

As easily as egos can scuttle a partnership, differences over money can scuttle it even faster. Before entering a partnership, every aspect of the financial relationship needs to be clearly understood.

Consider This

Open Book Management requires companies openly sharing all the important financial data, except for salary information. Among partners, there should always be open books with data updated no less than monthly.

The partners should define the guiding money principles. They need to be clear on the following:

➤ How much equity each partner contributes and how to manage the money. Should it be invested? If so, in what kind of investments will they put their money?

➤ What salaries will each of them earn and how raises are determined. If there are bonuses, what criteria will determine the amount and frequency of the bonus?

➤ How profits will be used. Will they go to pay bonuses, be reinvested in the company, or used to establish reserves?

➤ How they will obtain additional equity, if it is needed.

Whereas a lawyer can assist in formalizing the agreements, the partners need to resolve the substantive issues. An agreement needs to balance being specific without being overly confining. To resolve substantive issues there are numerous books on partnerships, and a carefully chosen consultant can help.

Talk, Don't Assume

Great communication skills make for great partnerships. Partners need to have the attitude of a Five-Minute Manager. They need to preplan what they are going to say and deliver their thoughts in a logical manner that makes it easy for a listener to comprehend. They are also excellent listeners. They enter conversations without expectations and listen actively.

A partner cannot assume that the other partner knows something. A partner cannot rely on someone else communicating important points.

Many successful partners schedule regular update meetings. They can be over breakfast, lunch, or in the office. At these meetings, they discuss current projects on which each is working. they identify the challenges and victories of the previous week. they discuss important objectives for the next week and what resources they need. They especially note times and projects in which both partners need to be involved.

Be sure to schedule as a regular agenda item a discussion of how the partnership is working. Each partner needs to share some point of view. When there are good events, be sure to celebrate them. When things do not go so well, immediately work to resolve them. Often, a trusted personal and business coach can be a part of these regular meetings. A coach can help to make the sharing a constructive process.

Speed Bump

Find the worst thing about your potential partner. However tough it is for you to deal with it today, it will be much tougher when you become partners. Can you handle it?

Role Players

One of the best things people can talk about is their role in an organization.

You read about the great sports teams, such as the Boston Celtic dynasty, where one of the keys to success was each player knowing his role on the team. Everyone sees teams possessed of individuals with great talent that lacked team cohesiveness. One reason they seldom reached the championship level is the players did not have clearly defined roles. If they had them, they did not accept them and internal struggles ensued.

The same is true in a partnership. It helps if the partners bring different skills to the business. For example, one person has strong technological skills, whereas the other person is strong in marketing and general management.

The partners need to agree to their specific areas of responsibility. If there are areas of overlap, even then the partners should identify sub-segments each partner has responsibility for managing.

Even when there is a clear delineation of responsibilities, there are times when responsibilities clash. It is important to have a clear understanding of how joint decision-making works.

Consider This

Partners are going to have differences of opinion and conflicts. Because problems are a certainty, there should be a conflict resolution process that is agreed to before there are conflicts. If not, partners might not be able to agree on a process in the heat of a conflict. Many times, a mutually respected friend, personal coach, or mentor is recruited to assist when there is an impasse. If this is not agreeable, the partners need a plan they agree to when times are calm.

What is challenging in these understandings is making them specific enough to be helpful without making them constraints that hinder doing the right thing. In some ways, this is more of an art than a science. As such, it relies on the strength of the relationship between the partners. The "art" of the relationship is using intuition to guide actions. Ultimately, everything in the partnership relies on this strength.

Survival and Success Tips for All Businesses

When you read the stories of today's most successful businesses, you will find frequently that there was a time in their history when the survival of the company was in question. All companies face these moments. It is how they respond and use their skills and assets that determines their ultimate success. Similarly, there are certain fundamentals that all companies need to consider to succeed.

Technology

Few businesses can ignore technology. The pace of change is so fast in many businesses that failure to be technologically savvy can result in lost business momentum. Even worse, it can result in a healthy business becoming a struggling business in a few months.

Whatever business you are in, plug into multiple resources to stay current with the latest technological developments. For example, if you want to stay current on computer developments, both in hardware and software, consider these resources:

➤ Subscribe to one of the leading magazines, like *PC Magazine*. It is published every two weeks and includes tests of the latest hardware and software. It also includes a recommendation on what is the best according to the tests and reviews very recent introductions.

➤ Subscribe at no cost to ZD Net's daily e-mail letter discussing the latest developments. ZD Net is a resource-rich site of reviews, free utilities, and shareware.

➤ Subscribe to other daily e-mail services that collect and publish technological stories. Infobeat.com has a good daily service.

➤ At the major news Internet sites, like cnn.com and msnbc.com, you can create a customized news site that displays the kind of new stories you are most interested in reading. You can even make these sites your home page so that you start there every day.

Sage Advice

"Men are only as good as their technical development allows them to be."
—George Orwell

For technological information, you can also get regular catalogues from hardware and software mail order companies. Companies like the highly rated PC Connection have extensive catalogues and very easy ordering and shipping procedures. You also can visit local retailers and join the clubs or associations that best meet your needs.

The ability to stay current with virtually any subject is relatively easy with the Internet. As we have seen in earlier chapters, it allows you to conduct very broad and fast searches.

Have Financial Plans and Forecasts

A cash forecast is one of the easiest ones to construct, but one that many businesses fail to use. A cash forecast is a day–by–day estimate of cash inflow and outflow and the impact it has on your daily cash balance. When you have a cash forecast, you have an estimate of how much cash will be in your account every day.

When you construct a cash forecast, you know when the crunch periods occur each month. Payroll time is one for most companies. When you know the crunch periods, you can plan. The following questions will help:

➤ Is there an opportunity to move an important cash receipt up a few days?

➤ Is there a risk that a receipt will be delayed?

➤ Should you use your line of credit, and if you do not have a line of credit, should you get one?

Cash crunches can hurt a company when they are unexpected and there is little time to respond. Fail to meet one payroll and you will make everyone in the company nervous and less productive. That is a big price to pay for something that can be avoided.

Consider This

Because cash flow is king in many companies, there need to be multiple options defined about what to do in a cash crunch. Options include a line of credit, delaying selected payments, speeding up receipts, a second mortgage on homes or businesses, and liquidating selected assets. Although there are many options, there needs to be an agreed-to plan developed while emotions are calm.

There are many other forecasts that can assist a company in effectively managing its finances. In some businesses, a capital forecast is critical. It tells a company when to expect large cash outlays. The capital forecast derives from the capital budget.

The most fundamental financial tool is the annual budget for every area of expense. Build budgets from the bottom up, with some general guidance from senior management. Once the budget is agreed to, publish it and track progress. People need to know they are responsible for the budget through regular reviews and adjustments where necessary.

Mentor and Advisory Board

A great management supplement to a small business is the adoption of a mentor or the establishment of an advisory board.

A mentor works occasionally with the senior manager. A mentor may be a trusted friend who manages another business, an experienced retired manager, or a much younger person who helps senior manager stay current with important trends. A mentor provides a fresh independent perspective, providing expertise and experience that the manager does not have. In some cases, the mentor is a personal coach who has relevant business experience.

Another approach, and these approaches are not mutually exclusive, is an advisory board. The board is made of a mix of experiences and skills. For example, your accountant, lawyer, and personal coach may be on the board. It may include people who fit the mentor profile discussed above.

The board meets about once a month. The senior manager shares current developments and plans. This helps the board have the context necessary to assist the manager. The manager then shares between one and three issues with which help is needed. Leave time for board members to offer their thoughts independent of the manager's topics.

The board's advice is nonbinding, which differs from a board of directors. They provide advice that you may not be able to get from any other source.

Are You Doing What You Love?

If not, find out how you can. When you do what you love, you do your best work. Your best work is what you do better than anyone else. It is how you help people the most.

Pause and ask yourself, "Do I really love what I am doing?" If you hesitate, the answer is at least a qualified "No." If you are not doing what you love, make it your highest priority to discover what that is and do it.

Personal Coaching

Both retired executives and the Small Business Administration are excellent sources for potential mentors and advisory board members. Your Chamber of Commerce can also be a source of ideas.

It may be that with some adjustments, your current job can become the job you love. This is especially true if you once loved what you were doing, but it has become less fun over time. This suggests that the core essence of what you love might be waiting to be rediscovered. Maybe it requires fewer hours so you are not tired most of the time. Determine what it is you loved in the past and assess your options for bringing more of those elements into what you are doing today.

The current job may not be what you can love doing. Use the visioning process outlined in Chapter 2 to discover what you love doing. Again, a personal coach can be a wonderful facilitator and guide in this process. When in the visioning process, remember do not judge if it is possible. Holding the dream and the intent to manifest it are the keys to taking the first steps to what you really love. Lao Tzu is famous for saying "The journey of a thousand miles begins with a single step."

Don't Gloat

Successful managers do not gloat. They do not believe they are any better than they really are. They have a healthy respect for what they do not know. Their humility is their strength.

So many businesses achieve spectacular success, and then let success "go to their heads." They think that once they are on top that they will stay there. They fail to learn the immediate lesson, that they just dethroned a business that probably thought it would remain Number One.

Businesses that do not gloat are committed to learning. They seek out knowledge and share all that they learn. They invest in the key leverage points of their business. They know people are their most important asset and every action is consistent with this principle—not just some of their actions.

The Least You Need to Know

➤ Effective networking results from having a plan and seeing networking as a mutually beneficial process.

➤ Use great care in selecting your partner because it is your "business marriage."

➤ To survive a crisis you need to be current with the latest technology and have financial plans ready to meet any crisis.

➤ Recruit a mentor and advisory board to provide broad-based diverse advice.

Chapter 21

Supercharge Your Business

In This Chapter

➤ How to be seen and heard to help your business

➤ Tuning up your product for super results

➤ How the big picture makes for better results

➤ Super charge your business with a little help from your friends

---

Most businesses wonder about what can take them to the next level of performance and sales. The answer to the question is a combination of little and big things that work together to consistently contribute to growth.

You start by taking care of some basics and then recharging your business. When you discover the hidden leverage in your business, you will take your first big step forward in your first week of trying. The Five-Minute Manager masters the basics and uses the leverage daily to build a vital, opportunity-driven business.

Become More Attractive

Sometimes businesses exist on a sales plateau that provides for their needs. As needs change and opportunities emerge, they discover a need to resume growth. To continue or accelerate growth in a business also requires reviewing some of the basics of the business. The next section addresses some of the basics of making your business more attractive.

Let Your Customers See You

A frequently forgotten basic of business is being seen by your current and potential customers. Conventional wisdom says "Out of sight, out of mind"; it is true.

How well are you seen? Evaluate the location of your business first. Determine if your business is easy to find. Over time, roads and highways might have changed, leaving your business in a seldom-traveled part of town. If this is your situation, consider finding a new location.

As you consider options, think about where your customers are today. If they are mostly near your current location, do not move too far away. Convenience often ranks near the top of the list of reasons people buy or use a service. Also, consider your competition's location. You do not want to move and leave them a business bonanza.

In addition to considering current customers, determine where your major potential customers are located. Sometimes, if you become significantly more convenient than a competitor, that alone is the reason a customer will begin using you. Are there some potential customers who now have to drive some distance to get a product or service that would switch to you if you were close to them?

Consider This

In television advertising, the general rule is that if you want consumers to remember your ad, they need to see your ad a minimum of three times a month. Television is the most powerful advertising medium; other mediums are less intrusive and less memorable, so the frequency needs to be higher. Even award-winning print advertising campaigns can take three or more years to have a measurable effect on the business.

You need to consider all these factors when selecting a new, more visible and convenient location. Take out a map and plot all of the critical information. Locate your and competitors' businesses, as well as some important potential customers. Draw some circles around potential new locations and explore the areas. If necessary, recruit a commercial real estate agent's assistance.

Before you make a decision, talk to your current major customers about a potential move. Determine their concerns and how to address them.

Often a move to a new location is an opportunity to offer more products and services. Combining a more visible location with one that is easier to get to makes it attractive for current customers to stay with you. The one caution is to make sure you understand their views. You may be missing a crucial perspective.

With this basic handled, look for other ways to be visible to your customers. There are some obvious next steps. If you are not in the Yellow Pages, you may need to be there. Keep track of where new customers learned of you. Many businesses find the Yellow Pages are an important source. If you are not a believer in them, consider experimenting for a year with a quality display ad in color. Track the difference in customer inquiries to determine if it is a worthwhile investment.

There are other very simple, low cost ways of getting your company name in front of people. Put your name on coffee mugs and T-shirts and give them to customers as part of a promotion. These are inexpensive enough that they can be gifts. Depending on your target customers, you may want to put your ad in symphony programs or a program for an auto show.

Personal Coaching

Use the same business logo on everything. Invest in creating a quality business logo. A graphic artist can help. Choose your colors carefully. Make sure the colors you select are consistent with the message and image of your business. Finally, remember that as pretty as pastel colors can be, they can also be hard to see.

Speak Out

Speaking out is one of the best ways to increase your business. This improves your credibility while informing people of your company's capabilities.

Consider developing contacts with key people in your local media. Identify the business editor and writers on your newspaper. In addition to the business section, there might be an opportunity to work with the local news reporters. Read the paper and determine who writes articles on local business issues. From your network, determine the best method of developing a relationship with them. Maybe the key people are part of another organization or one of the people in your network can introduce you to them.

When you contact a person in the media, be prepared. Being prepared begins with having printed materials about your business. Identify a reason for publicizing your business. A popular way is to find a link between a broader news story and your business. For example, if you are a supplier to NASA or a subcontractor to a NASA supplier, you may want to suggest a story about your business in conjunction with the next launch. Linking your story to a regional, state, or national story is often a good reason to do a story about a company.

Sage Advice

"All publicity is good, except an obituary notice."
—Brendan Behan (1923–64), Irish playwright

Another hook is being the first to do something. It can be new technology or an innovative technique. Even better is a story about the growing acceptance of your company's invention.

Remember that the newspaper wants to sell, too. Find an angle for your business that will interest their readers.

Speak publicly about your business. Determine its most interesting aspect. What about it would interest and benefit other people? Now, how can you take the information and weave it into a captivating or fun talk? Later, this book addresses how to be a great speaker, but you can learn the basics now.

Who will listen to you? Many clubs are constantly on the lookout for speakers at their regular meetings. Again, use your network to help identify opportunities. Target those groups that are most likely to include your target customers.

Be a Special Volunteer

You join groups to widen your networking circle and out of your desire to serve others. You become a special volunteer when you take volunteering to the next level.

First, determine what organizations connect with your heart. For example, the Red Cross offers excellent opportunities to be an active volunteer.

Many people associate the Red Cross with major disasters and forget that in most counties there is a local chapter of the Red Cross. That chapter is the center for many volunteer activities. You can become a disaster services volunteer. In this role, you may be called upon in the middle of the night to assist a family that has seen their house burn down. They need food and shelter immediately. The local Red Cross provides that help.

Sage Advice

"I will get things done for America ... Faced with apathy, I will take action. Faced with conflict, I will seek common ground ... Faced with adversity, I will persevere. I will carry this commitment with me this year. I am an Americorps volunteer."
—Bill Clinton, swearing in members for his national service program

Disaster Services also serves as the backbone of volunteers who respond to a larger disaster in their area. Although national Red Cross volunteers eventually arrive for a major disaster in your area, the first line of assistance is a group of volunteers associated with a local chapter. With training and service, you can become a part of that effort.

There are additional opportunities at your local chapter. You can volunteer to assist military families, teach Red Cross classes, and lead as a board member. The Red Cross illustrates the richness of volunteer opportunities of which many people are not aware. When you explore other organizations like the Salvation Army or Boy and Girl Scouts, you may be surprised at the diverse number of opportunities to help others.

You can become a special volunteer by sponsoring an activity. For example, many Red Cross chapters conduct an annual CPR Saturday, an opportunity for people to learn CPR. They recruit company sponsors for the event. This is a wonderful opportunity to be a sponsor and have your company's name on all the banners, T-shirts, and printed materials for the event.

The point is to make a heart-felt connection with an organization. Then discover the way you can become a special volunteer. What unique and special contribution can you make? When you make a contribution, you do your best work and make you and your company more attractive to others. Follow your heart and do what is right for those needing help. When you help others, your business might receive some ancillary benefits. For example, you may significantly expand your network with quality contacts.

Product or Service Evaluation

Put your product or service under the microscope. Give it its annual "physical."

Often a business pays only casual attention to the health of its product or service. People are so busy executing that they take their eyes off the ball. It is easy to do. Filling orders, paying people, and solving problems can consume you. These and other on-going issues can take up 100 percent of every waking hour, if you let them do it.

If you want a long-term healthy business, you need to routinely pull back and dedicate quality time to examining the product or service you provide. Start the process by collecting information. You want to know everything about your competitors. Collect product and service descriptions. If practical, purchase their product or use their service. Make sure you have their price lists.

Now collect all the information that you can about the category of product or service you provide. You want to know the latest developments in technology. Also, learn about what the major companies in the category are doing. Use the Internet as an efficient way to search for this information.

When you have this information, begin an evaluation of your product or service. How has it changed? What are your customers saying about your product or service? This is where a formal survey of your customers or your constant interviewing of customers becomes very helpful. Think about your potential customers. If they purchased from you, why did they choose you and not a competitor? If they chose your competitor, why did they do this? These are some of the most important questions you can ask when evaluating your business.

When you have all this information, take a day to evaluate it. You may want to have senior managers and advisory board members join you for the process. Among your senior managers, make sure you have someone from sales who has regular

Sage Advice

"The ultimate umpire of all things in life is Fact."
—Agnes C. Laut (1871–1936), Canadian journalist and author

contact with customers. It is important that you have both expertise and objectivity in this review.

There will always be differences in services and products. You need to understand where you are strong and where you need to improve. Be sure that you note these. This can be difficult. For example, it may be difficult to measure the importance and value of a competitor's more convenient location. It helps if you know how important convenience is for customers. A general rule is that convenience in all its forms is usually much more important to your customers than you think it is.

In your review, pay close attention to the value equation. What are you and your competitors asking customers to pay for what they are receiving? Do your best to lay out a side-by-side comparison of all products and services. Solicit the help of everyone in your group to assemble the best possible approximation.

When you have quality understanding of the status, look for opportunities to improve. There may be helpful suggestions from your review of developments. There may have been some added value ideas discussed earlier that you want to add to your value equation. It is important to remember that customers buy for a variety of reasons. If you are weak in one area, you have the opportunity to gain an advantage in another important area. Before you make the investment, make sure that you know it is important to your customers.

Consider This

A good consultant combines expertise and objectivity. Use your network and industry connections to identify consultants and interview the most highly recommended ones. Consider using a consultant in your annual evaluation every two to three years.

Every time you conduct the review, there will be opportunities to improve your product or service. When you make the improvements, announce them to the world. They will make your company and its products more attractive.

Business Recharge Kit

In the last section, you made a good start to recharging your business. You are now ready to expand your efforts to create excellence in every important area of your business.

The Five-Minute Manager knows this kit is one of the most valuable assets. The Five-Minute Manager wants to take the business to a level of world class excellence. Often they start by examining themselves.

Personal Values Inventory

Now that you have completed an assessment of your product or service, it is time to update your values and those of your business. As noted in Chapter 3, values are dynamic. They can change over time.

For example, as you embark on a spiritual journey, there are major changes to your values. The importance of helping others and building your connection to spirit may move from secondary to primary values over a period of a few years. When this happens, you may keep all of your old values and add the new ones. This can create conflicts and inconsistencies that result in not fully living any of your values. It may be time to demote some values so you can develop the new ones.

Examine the checklist of values from Chapter 3 and update what is really important to you. This process asks you to identify your top five values. When you have identified them, ask yourself the following series of questions:

➤ Are you surprised by any of the values that made your top five? How did the "surprise values" end up on your list?

➤ What values are you living today and how are they different from what is really important to you? Are the differences caused by personal growth or are there other reasons?

➤ How do you start fully living and honoring your top five values? What needs to change? Specifically, on what will you spend more time or less time to honor your values?

Speed Bump

When you inventory your values, be sure to be honest with yourself. Do not include values you only believe you should have. Include only those that actually guide your daily life.

360 Degree Review

In recent years, conducting 360 degree reviews have become an increasingly useful tool. When used in personnel reviews, a 360 degree review collects the thoughts of your boss, subordinates, and lateral, cross-functional contacts. The goal is to gather the thoughts of every key person that you interface with regularly.

Two 360 degree reviews improve the health of you and your business.

First, conduct a review of your business. This review evaluates all people and organizations with which your business interfaces.

Evaluate your suppliers.

➤ Are your suppliers the same ones you have had for years?

➤ Why did you choose your current suppliers?

➤ How strong is your partnership with them? How have they made your business stronger in the last year?

➤ Are there new suppliers? What are the advantages and disadvantages of alternative suppliers?

➤ Finally, conduct one or two interviews with alternative suppliers to see if there are reasons to switch now.

This book has discussed customers already. It is essential that you not assume that because some customers stay with you that your relationship with customers is strong. Of all the assumptions you should avoid, this has to be first on the list.

Speed Bump

People need to know they can share positive and negative feedback in their reviews and not face negative consequences for doing so. Making the feedback anonymous can help if it truly is confidential.

Review the strength of the people in your organization with the following questions:

➤ As your business has grown, have they grown with it?

➤ As your business has changed, are there new skills needed that current employees do not have? Can current employees be trained to develop the needed skills?

➤ If you lost an important person, how would you replace him or her?

➤ Are you investing in training and development programs? Should you increase the training budget and refocus it on new skills?

Second, conduct a 360 degree review of how you are doing. This is a personnel review by all the important people with whom you interact. You want to inventory how strong your relationship is with them. You want to know what is working and what is not working.

You do this by having people in the company and outside the company, such as suppliers, anonymously complete an evaluation. For example, you want to know if your Type A personality has weakened relationships. What should you focus on in the next year to make you a more effective manager?

The Really Big Picture

Sometimes you focus only on your small part in the world, and miss the big picture. Pull back and evaluate the world in levels.

At the first level, evaluate recent developments in your category. For example, if you are in accounting, what are the latest developments in rulings and technology? What trends do you see with the largest firms and how might that influence your work? Tap into associations and Internet research to discover this information.

Consider This

Do not rely on an annual review to update yourself. Subscribe to newsletters and join associations that keep you abreast monthly. Examine both closely before subscribing or joining. It is easy to get too many and be so overwhelmed that you give each only cursory review.

At the next level, pull back and examine what is occurring in your state and region. Examine employment trends, demographics, and the kinds of new businesses that seem to be flourishing. Are there new competitors expanding in the region that may move into your city? Are there parts of the region that are growing faster than others, and is there an opportunity for your business there? What new laws are under consideration by the state legislature? Are regulatory agencies considering any changes you should be aware of now?

At the next level, examine national events that potentially affect your business. What are Congress and regulatory agencies doing that may change the way you do business? What societal trends will influence your results? What can you learn from the major companies in your category?

At the final level, conduct a review of international events that may influence your business. A couple of decades ago, this might have been a frivolous investigation, but not today. Developments in another part of the world can directly influence your business in the next year. Perhaps, there are new services or product improvements in other countries that you can adapt to your business to make it stronger.

Backup Plans—A Through D

For businesses that have almost no backup plans, the thought of having multiple backup plans may appear to be unreasonable. In fact, there is great immediate value to the exercise of developing backup plans.

Sage Advice

"Chief among our gains must be reckoned this possibility of choice, the recognition of many possible ways of life, where other civilizations have recognized only one ... a civilization in which there are many standards offers a possibility of satisfactory adjustment to individuals of many different temperamental types, of diverse gifts and varying interests.
—Margaret Mead

You start by asking what important area of the business may be vulnerable to a serious problem, even a disaster. The answer is likely to be that almost every major area of your business is susceptible.

If you ask, "What would I do if our computers crashed and we could not process customer orders," you will develop some very interesting answers. First, if you cannot process customer orders, you have a serious problem. It is not just a short-term problem, because it invites customers to buy from a competitor and some percentage of those customers will be lost.

Personal Coaching

Your computer only has to crash once for you to become convinced that backing up your personal computer files is critical. A complete crash can wipe out all programs and files. A virus not handled correctly can cause this. If you do not have a high capacity backup drive, such as a Zip drive, then backup all your files on floppies. Do it at least once per month.

Sage Advice

" ... No two people see the external world in exactly the same way. To every separate person a thing is what he thinks it is—in other words, not a thing, but a think."
—Shippey in Penelope Fitzgerald's book *The Gate of Angels*

The backup plans you develop to answer this question will surprise you. For example, you may find a service company that can help you. Working with the telephone company, you can switch your incoming calls to the service company that has your software systems loaded and in reserve. With a couple of hours of lead-time, they call in additional people trained in your system to start taking incoming orders. Or your order takers can go to the service company's office. What may surprise you is that they can handle your order processing at a lower cost and more efficiently. What started as a backup plan might become a better idea for your business.

The advantage of developing backup plans is that doing so forces you to examine alternatives you would not otherwise consider. In almost every case, you will discover a backup idea that you promote to the primary way of performing a function. That makes the process of developing backup ideas a payout proposition.

Objectivity Versus Interpretation

Facts are seldom just facts. People tend to interpret facts so that the interpretation becomes a fact. There is danger in this.

For example, if sales are down 10 percent over the last two months, that is a fact. If your interpretation is that this is just a short-term lull that will pass like the one last year, then this sometimes takes on the status of a fact, even though it is clearly not a fact.

The interpretations we give facts can be our worst enemies. They can obscure the truth and get in the way of taking necessary action now.

Although facts usually need some interpretation in most cases, do not elevate an interpretation to the status of a fact. When you want to interpret facts, it is critical that you not develop just one interpretation. Develop three or more different interpretations. They can differ greatly. Any interpretation is a guess, even if it is a educated guess, about what a fact implies.

In the "sales are down 10 percent over the last two months" example, one interpretation can be that it is a lull. If this is so, the interpretation suggests the necessary actions. Another interpretation is that it could be the beginning of a new trend, and that would require certain other actions. A third interpretation might be that the facts are misleading because in the previous year's two months there was an abnormally high level of sales due to a one-time event. Whatever the interpretation, recognize that is not a perfect analysis of the situation. If it is important, continue to watch for additional facts to indicate which, if any, interpretation is correct.

Personal Coaching

When you interpret a fact, invite others to share their own views. Do not rely on one person's view. After you have collected various views, see if there is a consensus. If there is, be careful to not confuse a consensus interpretation with truth.

The Least You Need to Know

➤ Low cost ways of being can pay big dividends.

➤ Complete a thorough and objective evaluation of your product or service annually; also determine the health of your organization and its ability to grow.

➤ Developing backup plans identifies ideas that can become your preferred method of doing business.

➤ It takes five minutes to violate trust, and it can take years to rebuild.

➤ Do not confuse interpretations with facts, or you may make a major mistake.

Chapter 22

Leap Forward

In This Chapter

➤ The seven sources of hidden leverage in your business

➤ How to dramatically increase your effectiveness in a week

➤ The path to having your best year ever

Every company has hidden leverage it can use to improve its business. Finding and evaluating these strengths is not difficult. When you are ready, you can take a significant leap forward in your business in a week. Now that you have experienced success, are you ready to have your best year ever?

The Five-Minute Manager loves finding hidden leverage because it is already available. The Five-Minute Manager knows how to take that big leap forward and loves setting new records each year.

Discover Your Company's Hidden Leverage

Whereas there is danger in overestimating your company's abilities, there is also danger in not seeing real strengths that can be used to take your business to the next level.

Customers Are Your Best Friends (No Offense, Fido)

It is easy to undervalue customers, and difficult to overvalue them. They are a unique asset. If you followed earlier suggestions, you know who your customers are today. You have vital information about them, and you regularly monitor how well your business meets their needs.

With this information in hand, you have the best asset to increase your sales. Because your customers already know about you and trust you enough to buy from you, they are a prime audience for any new and improved products you decide to sell.

Look at it this way, a new business would love to have your customer base. You already have a positive relationship with customers, and this base is an essential leverage point for selling new products.

Targeting existing customers for additional sales is the number one growth opportunity for most companies. Even when a company has a new major product, existing customers tend to be its earliest adopters. Whereas it might eventually appeal to many new customers, existing customers are the early purchasers who help you spread the word.

Cash Is a Pretty Good Friend, Too

Cash is an asset everyone recognizes. But sometimes people fail to understand what its greatest leverage point is for a business. This can happen when all parts of the business need cash infusions.

Speed Bump

What is cash and how much of it do you have at your disposal? You often need an accountant to help determine the answers to these critical questions. For example, some of your cash on hand is needed for cash flow and to maintain reserves and is not available for investment.

Look around your business and determine which one part of your business you would invest cash in today if you had to make the decision. Carefully examine the range of expected returns from investment opportunities in your business. Then, factor in the range of risk each represents.

With this picture, ask the bold question, "What would happen if I gave the highest return opportunity in the business all the cash it needs?" It is another way of determining what it would look like to really go for your number one growth opportunity, instead of spreading yourself out over a few opportunities.

This can be a provocative question with some unexpectedly positive answers.

Market Share

Market share is often just a number on a report, but it is much more than just a fact. It can be a powerful leverage tool for your business.

When you have the largest market share in a category, it provides a powerful invitation to people or organizations buying from a competitor. If you ask them to consider your company, you receive much more consideration than the fourth or fifth largest company in the category would if they asked the same question. People and companies are curious about why more people decide to buy from the market leader.

Even if you are the number two or three biggest company, you can use your market share position to get new customers to consider buying from you. If you are increasing market share, that can also be an attractive method of interesting new customers.

Consider This

Although you cannot put market share in the bank, it is more important in some ways than sales. Your sales may be growing at 10 percent, but you can be losing market share in a category that is growing at 20 percent. If this trend prevails for a couple of years, you could be on the verge of going out of business, despite the fact that you are growing.

You see companies using their market share in their ads. In automobiles, first Honda, then Taurus, and, most recently, Camry have all called themselves "America's Most Popular Car."

Even if you are not the overall market leader, you may be the market leader of a segment of the category. For example, Dial is the leading antibacterial soap, while Dove is the leading beauty bar. In most cases, if you are number four or five in the overall category you can improve your position to number two or three in an important and recognized segment of the category. You can then leverage this position.

Reputation

Reputation can be difficult to quantify, but when you do measure it, it can become the most important leverage point of your business. Think of the medicines that tout they are the number one hospital or doctor-preferred product. Tylenol, for example, has used this reputation as a cornerstone of its advertising for decades.

What is your business's reputation? You can measure it by having a consumer research organization conduct quantitative research among consumers of products or services like yours. If this research reveals a meaningful win in relation to competitors, consider how you can leverage it to build your business. Imagine what you could do if you had a win for friendliest and most expert service?

If you do not want to pay for quantitative research, ask some of your most well-known customers to give you an endorsement. You have seen businesses

Sage Advice

"Reputation, reputation, reputation! O, I ha' lost my reputation, I ha' lost the immortal part of myself, and what remains is bestial!"
—William Shakespeare, Cassio, in *Othello*

use comments in their ads to convince you to buy their product. Some of the most frequent users of endorsements are movies. You see in print and television ads the superlative comments of critics and even moviegoers caught as they leave a movie.

Knowing what your reputation is and using it to build your business is a smart thing the Five-Minute Manager knows how to do.

Momentum

What is working really well for your business today? How can you make that area of your business grow even faster?

Hal Rosenbluth of Rosenbluth International asked this question shortly after he joined his family's travel agency. As a traditional travel agency, this company was very successful in the Philadelphia market. Hal became involved in some of the agency's early attempts to break into the corporate travel market. At the time, corporate travel was only a small fraction of their overall business.

When he saw the success they had with their first corporate account, DuPont, he focused the company's efforts on developing this segment. Today, this segment represents almost all of their multi-billion dollar business. Hal did this by recognizing the potential in a small but rapidly growing segment. By leveraging its potential, he turned a Philadelphia-focused business into an internationally focused business.

Staff Members with Hidden Skills

You will be pleasantly surprised when you investigate the hidden skills of the people you work with. These people have a richness of experience waiting to be discovered.

The people you work with probably worked at another company before joining yours. Most of the time, you know very little about what they have accomplished in previous jobs. They probably have hidden skills and experiences that can help in your company. They may also have hobbies, areas of interest, and accomplishments outside of work that can help the company.

To discover what hidden talents and experiences exist in your organization, go on a treasure hunt. Meet with each person and reveal your purpose. The questions you are about to ask will seem a little strange to most people if they do not know your motive.

Keep a record of what your learn; then reflect on how you can use these experiences in your business. You will be surprised.

Richard Tuck, president and founder of Lander International, was surprised by what he found. Richard loved the circus, and he discovered a circus that had a great

Personal Coaching

Discover your own personal inventory of talents, accomplishments, and interests. Conduct a life review and write down everything from high school to the present. Your list may surprise you. Record how you feel about each accomplishment today. There may be some interests worth rekindling.

act but was struggling financially. He adopted the circus and began to look for ways to help. As he interviewed the circus performers, he learned that some of them had college degrees from their home countries. One performer had an accounting background, a skill the circus badly needed. With some training from Richard, the circus performer began to assist with the books. Another performer used his non-circus skills to sell an important new account on hosting the circus.

The hidden talents that exist in your organization will pleasantly surprise you. Your biggest challenge is finding ways to use these "extra" talents. It is a nice problem to have.

Unique Systems

Every business takes accepted procedures and systems and customizes them to its needs. The adaptation usually occurs slowly. After some time, the procedures or systems look very different from the original model.

Some of the customized procedures and systems can benefit other areas of a company. Usually, a customized system reflects the ingenuity and creativity of those who developed it. These "new" systems typically perform the designated tasks better than the original model.

In a meeting with other areas of the company, look for an opportunity to share the details of your custom system. It may or may not be of use to those in other areas. In part, your custom system's usefulness depends on how strong the "not invented here" syndrome is at your company. Some companies pride themselves in maintaining an environment conducive to learning, where there is regular sharing among functions and divisions.

You may even consider looking outside the company for opportunities to leverage the custom system. In some instances, it may be worthy of an industry award, which boosts your reputation. There may be a commercial application, as well. For example, you might consult with other companies on how to adapt basic systems to unique situations. This consulting can eventually develop into its own business.

Consider This

Unique and highly valuable systems can be anywhere in the company, though they may be hard to see and appreciate. When you find one, be sure security is established to protect the system. There may be legal protections available, a patent, for example.

Leap Forward in About a Week

Several things you can start doing right now will propel your business forward. If you take these steps, you can look back a week later and see a shift that made a big difference. Many of these are simple actions you probably have not considered until now.

The Five-Minute Manager knows that there is power in what appear to be simple questions, and that the leverage points of business and in life are much simpler than most people think.

Ask for What You Really Need, Not What You Think Is Possible

How many times do you request something you think is reasonable, although it is not as much as you really need? When you do this, you judge asking for what you really need as impossible to achieve. In doing so, you usually preclude any chance of actually getting it. Instead, you set the bar at a lower level, and you ask for what you think is possible. Even that request is many times only partially filled or missed entirely.

Asking for what you think is possible, not what you really need is a losing proposition.

Start asking for what you need right now. In some cases, people with a different perspective see an easy way to achieve what you really need. They may have had a harder time achieving what you thought was possible.

Personal Coaching

Because good, fast communication is crucial to solving problems quickly, make sure you have the systems in place to do that. Can you reach important people all the time? Do they have cell phones and pagers? Is everyone a committed e-mail user? If this is not the case at your company, consider making the small investment necessary to have instantaneous communication with important people.

When you ask for what you really need, you set into motion efforts to achieve it, and not some miniature version of it. You will be surprised that people often love to tackle a challenging goal instead of always doing the routine. They may not be exactly sure how to achieve what you really need, but they are inspired to try. This inspiration can result in achieving something close to what you need. The result will be better than asking for only what you thought possible.

Asking for what you need, not what is possible, is usually a win-win approach. You get exactly what you need and the people responding to the request usually do better work and have more fun doing it.

Get Answers Today, Not Tomorrow

You do not have to be pushy to get answers today instead of tomorrow. When you ask a question, learn what is involved in getting the answer. You will be surprised how often it can take a person only a few minutes to get what you need.

Before asking a question, be prepared. Have the form you need to be completed or the necessary authorization on hand. If the person answering the questions needs materials from you to answer the question, have these available via a fax or e-mail in five minutes or less.

Determine what you can do to help the person preparing the answer. If someone else must be contacted to help with the answer, you call that person. Either alert the person about the need or get the information yourself and pass it on. When you prove your willingness to help in this way, you almost guarantee a quick response.

In addition, share with the person you have asked a question why getting the answer today is important. Importantly, do not make up a story. You are trying to build trust in a relationship. Nothing destroys trust faster than lying or stretching the truth.

If you do not think you need an answer today, challenge that assumption. What would you do with the answer today? There is usually a strong benefit to having a prompt answer. Maintaining a level of urgency creates energy behind a project that produces more inspired solutions and results.

Reduce Appointment Time by 50 Percent

The Five-Minute Manager knows that when someone asks for a 30-minute appointment it can be reduced by at least 50 percent. If you reflect on your appointments, you use at least half of the time discussing unrelated topics and saying what you want to say at least twice, sometimes more.

You will be surprised when you respond to meeting requests by reducing the meeting time by at least 50 percent. You will accomplish all you need to do in that period. People will come to meetings better prepared. They may even send you materials to review in advance.

The Five-Minute Manager uses the techniques discussed in earlier chapters to focus on the issues and resolve them with clear next steps. It takes some training to get to this point, but everyone likes the results.

In most surveys, excessive time spent in meetings is one of the things people most dislike about business. Whereas they dislike it, they do not know how to change it. The Five-Minute Manager does know. Again, this is a win-win solution.

Personal Coaching

You need help to keep appointment times to the minimum. Train administrative help to ask the right questions and to have reviewable materials sent in advance of the meeting.

Over Respond

People usually see being over responsive as a negative. As used here, it is a method of quickly clearing problems so that you can work in a problem-free zone. When you are in this zone, you do your best work.

When a problem arrives on your desk, trigger all problem-solving skills discussed earlier. Add to that the possibility of over-responding. When you over-respond, you launch all available and appropriate resources. You do this because a common characteristic of problems is that they can linger. When they linger, they can disrupt all other activities. This is especially true when there does not appear to be a good solution to a problem.

Eliminate the disruptions that can come from lingering problems. If not, the original problem becomes magnified and affects other projects.

When you over-respond, you signal that you want a quick and immediate resolution. Often it can be as quick as the same day or same hour. When you over-respond, you call the people who have answers or necessary perspective. You go through the problem-solving process with urgency. The urgency propels everyone involved forward towards resolution.

This approach can feel disruptive, but so is a lingering problem. A lingering problem can require solving many times because people forget previous information or agreements. Over-responding can be the most direct route to a solution.

Eliminate Toleration

When you tolerate something, it is like a constant burr in your saddle. You know you do not like it. Whatever the issue, you do not apply the time and energy necessary to resolve it.

The problem with toleration is that it creates constant negative distractions. At a low level in your mind, you grumble and growl whenever you encounter the issue.

Personal Coaching

What are you tolerating at home that you should eliminate? Set boundaries with others so those irritants keep their distance. Work with family members to understand the number one lingering toleration that each of you can eliminate with the help of other family members. Make it a win–win situation.

For example, someone you work with always reacts negatively when you or someone else discusses a specific subject. This person's response is about the same every time, and it triggers negative reactions in others.

You are tempted to deal with those things that you tolerate through compromise. You even make moves to accommodate the irritant. These apparent solutions prove later to not be solutions at all. You continue to be irritated, and when you are irritated, you do not do your best work, nor are you fun to be around.

Resolve to rid yourself of irritants. Treat an issue you tolerate like any other problem that needs a solution. Deal with it honestly and seek a win-win solution. What usually prevents someone from doing this is the idea that a lot of effort and pain will be required to resolve the issue. Again, lessons on problem solving covered in Chapter 19 can help here.

Truth Telling

You often deceive yourself into thinking that accommodation and compromise are the best approaches to situations in which there are apparent differences. If a compromise is not a win-win solution, and it seldom is, it is not the optimal solution. When you do not use the optimal solution to a problem, the problem usually resurfaces later. You end up resolving the problem, sometimes in a different guise, several times.

For example, learn to say no to requests that will burden you unnecessarily. Do not say yes to accommodate. Instead of being brutally honesty, be compassionately honest. Understand the other person's reasons for the request and explain why you cannot do it. Help the other person find another solution to the need that is even better than the original.

Another dimension of telling the truth is doing what you say you are going to do. This not only builds trust, as you learned earlier, it is also the most effective and efficient method of managing. The Five-Minute Manager likes to promise to deliver what another person or organization needs and then over-deliver. Try over-delivering and observe the other person's reaction. When you know the power of over-delivering on your promises, you will want to do it all the time.

Stronger Systems

What can you automate that will save you at least five hours a week? If you ask the question, you will find answers. Act on them when you discover them. The first things you discover are usually routine activities that should have been handled more efficiently a long time ago.

You may have difficulty finding more than one or two things in your life that are better automated or handled by others. If this occurs, it is not because there are not things that qualify for automation. Rather, you are so close to your activities that you cannot see needs and opportunities. Invite someone from your advisory board or your personal coach to assist you with identifying candidates for simplification and automation. Enjoy the process of reinventing and discovering new, more efficient ways of doing routine, time-consuming activities.

Personal Coaching

How can you use a personal computer to create stronger systems at home? Some examples that help people are bill paying, children's homework through CD encyclopedias and the Internet, and online investing.

How to Have Your Best Year Ever

Having your best year ever means having a great year in all areas of your life. Your business, personal, spiritual, and community roles all contribute to your well-being. The following section outlines some important steps a Five-Minute Manager would take right now so the next 12 months are the best ever.

219

Do What You Really, Really Want to Do

Nothing will make this your best year ever more than starting right now to do what you really, really want to do. When you do what you love, you have fun, produce your best results, and it seems effortless.

If you find this hard to believe, reflect back on a time, however brief, when you did what you love doing. Time flew, you smiled, and you probably had more energy when you finished than when you started.

So many of your choices are not something you love doing. You do what you think you have to do or what you should do to please others. These kinds of activities drain your energy, are not fun, and leave you grumpy.

How do you know what you would love doing? In Chapter 2 we outlined the personal visioning process. This is the most powerful process for identifying what you really love to do. This vision involves your whole life and all of your roles.

When you are not doing what you love to do, you try to balance your various roles in life. Some roles are entirely separate from others. Friends from one area of your life do not know friends from other areas. Sometimes, you do not want people at work to know how you are away from work.

Speed Bump

When you discover what you really love to do, do not assume that it is unachievable. Just because it is a big leap from where you are now does not mean that you cannot achieve it. The recipe for achieving it is a combination of clear and consistent intent, action, and a deep faith in its achieveability.

When you do what you really love doing, you do not need to balance the roles. They are no longer separate. Your life becomes seamless and whole. Your various roles blend so much so that it is difficult sometimes to identify them.

When you do what you love, you are more lovable. You are healthier. You help others more than ever before. You use the unique combination of skills and experience only you have to their fullest potential.

Think of someone you know who has this kind of life. If you do not know someone like this, be on the lookout. They are a rare species, but they are there. They are not often the richest people. In fact, they might live very modestly. You usually find them helping others by using their unique skills and experiences. When you meet people who are doing what they love, they make wonderful role models and even mentors.

Personal Power Days

Identify one day each month that is only for you. On this day, you do something special for yourself.

Maybe you have always wanted to fly fish. Take a day off to take lessons. In future months, take advanced lessons; go out to a local stream and fly fish.

You might choose to take time with one of your children. Go to a local amusement park. Play miniature golf, ride the go-carts, and get wet on the bumper boats. Be a kid with your kid. Include all the kids if you want. Watch the joy in their faces and let it be contagious. Do not worry about being an adult.

Schedule your personal power day with the certainty that you schedule your most important business appointment. Once scheduled, do not change it, and tenaciously defend it if you must. Let others know about it, so they know you will not be available for other activities that day.

Look forward to this day. Treat it as a treat. Know what you are going to do or just go with the flow. Do not let it be overwhelmed by the mundane and the routine.

Set a Vacation Record

Building on the personal power day each month, set a personal vacation record in your best year ever. If you have never taken two weeks off at one time, do it this year. If you get antsy after a week; then schedule a second destination for the second week. Do something you have always wanted to do. Have no regrets. If you have wanted to do something for years, there must be a reason. Discover the magic your heart tells you is there.

Vacations do not have to be expensive. Life's most enriching pleasures are often inexpensive. A walk on the beach or along a lakeshore does not cost much. If you are not within an easy drive of a lake or ocean, try camping or going to a cabin in the woods. Mother Nature is one of the most hospitable hosts you can have.

Sage Advice

"Every man who possibly can should force himself to a holiday of a full month in a year, whether he feels like taking it or not."
—William James (1842–1910), U.S. psychologist, philosopher

If you already take the maximum vacation time for your company, you may be able to take additional time off without pay. You will be paying yourself by having time for renewal. You will come away from the experience richer than when you went into it.

Commit to the Dream

There is a project or activity you have always wanted to try, but you have never had the courage or time to pursue it. Go for it now. Use a personal power day or some of your record vacation time to convert the idea from a dream to reality.

Perhaps your dream is to run for local office, mayor or city council. Find out what that takes. When you discover that it is best to have lots of prior experience and money, do not be discouraged. Let Jesse Ventura, the pro wrestler who was elected governor of Minnesota in 1998, be your guide to how to achieve a top office the first time with no prior experience and limited funding. He ran for local office, mayor, before running for governor. Many well-known people today in politics, started as an unknown running for local office. For example, Abraham Lincoln first ran for a regional office and lost.

Maybe you have wanted to learn to ski on water or snow. Find the nearest instructor in the right season and start. That first step can be the toughest, but the next steps are pure fun.

What you want to pursue is that statement you have been making for years, "I have always wanted to …." If you think it will cost too much money, think again. Explore and you will find ways to live your dream for far less than you now believe it costs. Ask people to make their birthday and Christmas gifts to you support your dream.

The important thing is to initiate action. As Nike's ad slogan says, "Just do it."

Expand Your Vision—Buy Four Provocative Books

Open yourself up to entirely new ways of looking at the world. Just because you read a book about something does not mean that you endorse the writer's point of view. Do not view books on new subjects as a threat. Instead, view them as teachers that contribute to making this the best year of your life.

For example, if you are a devout Christian and your spiritual life is important to you, open yourself up to what the great Eastern spiritual teachers have to say. By reading about Buddha or Krishna, you are not forsaking Jesus. You may be surprised how much they all have in common.

If you are interested in personal growth, commit to an exploration of an approach that works for you. Begin your search by spending a couple of hours in a large bookstore. Browse until you find something you feel drawn to reading. If you enter the process with an open heart, you will find authors and books that attract you.

When you find an author that you like, find out where that person is teaching a seminar or speaking. You can write the publisher, who can forward the mail to the author. Make a personal connection with a writer.

Build Your Reserves

When you think of reserves, you probably think of financial ones. Financial reserves are only one of many reserves that contribute to having the best year of your life.

Financial reserves are important. If you have ever lived on the edge financially, you know the pain it can cause. You receive letters and calls asking for overdue payments. Even essential payments, like rent and food, may be a stretch some months. If you find yourself anywhere near this condition, you need quickly to establish reserves so you can devote energy to more than just surviving. There are plenty of books on the subject and financial planners that can help stop the bleeding. Adopt the one that is right for you and act now.

Energy reserves may be more important than financial reserves. You have experienced feeling ragged and depleted of energy. When you feel this way, you cannot do your best work, have fun, or be nice to others. If you have a temper, it is sure to ignite under these conditions.

Examine your life and find the conditions that create a lack of energy reserves. Commit yourself now to not allowing yourself to get into these conditions again. It may require saying "No" to a request or delaying your response until you can accomplish it with greater ease. Build recharging time into your schedule.

Consider This

When energy reserves are low, sometimes expending more energy is the answer. For example, when you have a regular exercise program, it creates more energy, often the kind of energy that helps you do your best work.

The personal power days and record number of vacation days help, but you need a daily process for monitoring and conserving your energy. When your reserves are low, know what you can do right away to recharge yourself. Maybe it means delaying an appointment for which you know you cannot be at your best. Maybe, you take a walk in a park or visit with someone to share a few jokes. You know what you can do to feel refreshed and rejuvenated.

Renew, Rebuild Friends and Family

Where is that best friend from high school? Ever wonder what has happened to him or her? You can find people using a variety of Internet services today. Search for them; it may require help from another person who knows where they are. When you find them, give them a call. Imagine their surprise and have fun with it.

Consider using a personal power day to do something special with a friend you have not seen for a couple of months. Go skiing or choose some other activity you both enjoy. Make sure it is not all activity time. Make sure there is time to talk and reconnect.

Schedule a mystery weekend with your spouse. Let your spouse think you are both going to an event in the city overnight, only to end up on a plane to Vancouver, BC, for a special getaway weekend. It will be a memorable weekend.

Be Kind

Connect with the kindness in your heart. It can be with a smile, a pat on the back, a sympathetic ear, or a good laugh. Think ahead; plan how to be kind to a person you will be with today.

How do you feel when you are kind? Let that good energy recharge you and spread your kindness everywhere. Make it a habit, even when you do not feel particularly upbeat. Just being kind to others can lift you and them.

Plan to be kind to someone each day. It may be with a compliment you would not normally deliver. It can be a spontaneous stop to help someone with a heavy load. Plan your kindness each morning, and then let any spontaneous opportunities be wonderful extras. Random acts of kindness are gifts you give to others. They enrich both of your lives.

When you commit 365 acts of kindness in a year, it will be your best year ever. Enjoy!

The Least You Need to Know

➤ Current customers, cash, and market share can help your business in unexpectedly powerful ways.

➤ The people and systems in your business have strengths you do not see today.

➤ Make urgency work for you, not against you, by getting fast answers and having highly efficient meetings.

➤ When you do what you love to do, it is fun, effortless, and highly productive.

➤ Take a record amount of time off to nourish and recharge your personal batteries.

➤ Building your personal reserves creates a friendlier and more productive life.

Chapter 23

The Effective Home Business

In This Chapter

➤ Working at home requires special skills to succeed

➤ How to make the critical first impression

➤ A polished public speaker knows the steps to success

➤ The telephone is a powerful tool when you know the skills experts use

More people are working out of their homes, either in conjunction with their own businesses or as telecommuters. When a Five-Minute Manager has a home business it poses some unique challenges for them. The person with a home business *is* the business. The impression this person makes on people is the impression the business makes. The person working from home needs to be a good public speaker in both formal speaking situations and informal discussions with customers or potential customers.

Working Effectively at Home

Working at home is different than working in an office. It is difficult for some people to adjust to working at home. The following section shares some tips the Five-Minute Manager uses to be even more effective at home than in the office.

Deadlines as Friends

The first challenge people face when they work at home is the lack of discipline and structure that exist in the office. You can easily address this with what might have seemed an enemy before—the deadline. The deadline is the best friend of many home business managers. It focuses them on needs and provides a precise target time.

Using the deadline as a friend, the Five-Minute Manager at home uses the advantages of being at home to deliver as promised. The lack of distractions allows the Five-Minute Manager full use of all skills and experience.

Of course, there is the same downside to deadlines that existed at the office. You can have too many commitments at once when you promise to deliver a project at a specified time. Commitments require good planning and allocation of resources, but this is the same challenge you face in the office.

You also can set deadlines too aggressively. When you consider what deadline to set, you estimate a range of time when you expect completion of a project. If you constantly set the deadline at the earliest possible completion time to impress the customer, you will disappoint customers more often than you impress them. The Five-Minute Manager remains effective by under-promising and over-delivering.

> ### Sage Advice
>
> "If you want a golden rule that will fit everything, this is it: Have nothing in your houses that you do not know to be useful or believe to be beautiful."
> —William Morris (1834–1896), English artist, writer, printer

Buddy or Coach

Another major adjustment for people moving from an office to a home business is the loss of peers to talk to about life and projects. In an office, you have a network of friends and associates with whom you share ideas and who can help you with your projects.

When you start your home business, the silence can be deafening. In the early stages, people spend hours on the phone trying to replace those lost conversations. Many feel sad because the nature of the relationships changes.

> ### Sage Advice
>
> "Some people go to priests; others to poetry; I to my friends."
> —Virginia Woolf (1882–1941), British novelist

Many home business owners work with a personal coach. A personal coach is a very action-orientated person who helps the home business owner set and then accomplish objectives faster and easier than without a coach. When you work with a personal coach, you usually schedule at least one conversation a week. Often, there are other brief chats and e-mail exchanges. Personal coaches with prior business experience are particularly helpful to the home manager.

Some recruit a buddy to connect regularly with, either in person or over the phone. Often this buddy is someone from your network who is also a home business manager. Buddies can be helpful, but they lack the training of a personal coach. A coach focuses only on you and your needs. A buddy has a significant amount of energy focused on personal issues.

Routine or No Routine

Determining whether you want to have a regular schedule requires knowing yourself and how you do your best work.

Some people like to go with the flow. They have some projects and activities they need to do, and each day they do what needs to be done. If someone calls with a request, that is what they work on at that time. If there are no immediate requests, they determine what they most want to work on that day. They are conscious of deadlines and consistently deliver on their promises. They are careful not to set aggressive deadlines. They know how they do their best work, and they create the routine that enables them to do that.

Others know that they need structure to do their best work. Without structure, they waste a day very quickly. Therefore, they plan their week. Maybe, they use the Stephen Covey system of planning activities for each role they play in life. It is a system that he details in First Things First. The system focuses on a life vision and the part each life role plays in its achievement. Whatever system they use, they usually have a weekly and daily list of things to accomplish. Each day they adjust the plan based on recent developments that require immediate attention. They take great pleasure in crossing items off the list as they accomplish them.

Personal Coaching

A clue as to what works best for you is to look at how you spend your weekends. That is time you are at home. If you work with lists on the weekend, try using lists when you start with your home business. If you are productive on weekends without lists, how can you make this approach work for you in your home business?

Train Your Family

If you work at home, you probably need to train your family. Family members are accustomed to barging in when you are home to discuss any subject on their minds. When you first start in your home business, your increased availability means increased opportunities for family members to share and talk with you.

You need to create boundaries for family members. It may require working with a closed door. If you like an open door, consider posting a sign (a humorous one may help) that alerts family members that you are hard at work right now. Something as simple as a "Do Not Disturb" sign like hotels use can warn people not to interrupt your work.

Besides signs, a conversation that outlines the new situation can help family members. Only telling family members that you are now working at home does not tell them all they need to know to help you. This is a new situation for everyone. With a little coaching, family members can become great allies.

The Perfect Home Office

The home office needs to be equipped like a regular office. The difference is that all the equipment is usually located in a single condensed space. In most cases, you have options on how to meet a functional need. Here is a starter list of considerations for setting up the home office.

➤ A computer—The computer is the backbone of the home office. Unless you are in a business directly related to the Arts, you will want a PC. Even if you are in such a business, a PC may be the best for you. For most business applications, a top end Pentium II or lower end Pentium III are the best values right now. Because business records are valuable, make sure you have a backup system, such as a Zip drive. If you travel, a laptop might be necessary. It allows you to work while traveling and to stay current with your e-mail.

Sage Advice

"Training is everything. The peach was once a bitter almond; cauliflower is nothing but cabbage with a college education."
—Mark Twain, (1835–1910), U.S. author. Excerpted from Pudd'nhead Wilson, "Pudd'nhead Wilson's Calendar" (1894)

➤ Software—Microsoft dominates the suite software, and you risk incompatibility with customers if you use something other than Word or Excel. A current Windows version and the latest browser (Netscape or Explorer) should also be part of your core software capability. Any specialty programs should be compatible with customers. Have an Internet provider. CompuServe is the choice for many businesses because of its rich research capabilities.

➤ Phones—You need a separate line for your home business and perhaps another for your fax and Internet service. A cell phone is also a requirement for most businesses. Evaluate your calling needs closely to determine the type of cell phone billing system you need.

➤ Fax Machine—Most businesses need the ability to send and receive faxes. You have several options. You can have a home fax machine, use an online service like CompuServe to receive your faxes, or have them sent to Kinkos or a similar business.

➤ Printer—A printer is necessary. With current prices, you can afford a color printer for about the same cost as a black and white printer. Ink jet printers are an excellent value, unless you do high volume text printing. If you are going to print text in volume, consider a separate laser printer. The all-in-one option gives you a printer, fax, copier, and scanner all in one piece of equipment. It is much cheaper than buying them separately and it takes up the space of one printer.

➤ Other Stuff—Make sure your desk is comfortable and meets your needs. Explore options before buying. Be sure your chair is comfortable. Use music to enrich your environment.

There are others things you can add to your office that reflect your unique needs as a person and as a business. Make each decision carefully. Do not live with something that only partially meets your needs.

Consider This

Equipment for a home office can be expensive, so be sure to check prices. Mail order is often the least expensive; so be sure to price check sources like PC Connection. With direct sellers of computers, like Dell Computer, you do not pay the middle man or retailer markup. Do not let low price be your only guide. Check the reliability and service record of a potential brand. *PC Magazine* and others regularly report rankings.

Great First Impressions That Turn People "On"

When you are the manager of a home business, you are the business. The personal impression you make is the impression the business makes. Knowing this enables you to use it to your advantage.

Neatness Counts

The first impression that you make is a visual one. People see you before they hear you; so, you want this first impression to count. It should also be consistent with the verbal impression you make.

The precise impression you want to make varies by person and business. In almost all cases, neatness counts. Whether you dress in blue jeans or a blue suit is a decision you need to make to fit your circumstances. In either case, be neat. If you are a man, this means being clean-shaven or having neatly trimmed facial hair. You are clean and sharp. If you are a woman, the makeup must be right for you and the situation. Be conscious of your hairstyle. Your clothes are clean and appropriate for the situation.

Make conscious choices that reflect the impression you want your business to make.

Establish a clothing budget for the kind of clothing that is right for your business. Do not assume that a wardrobe needs to be formal. Casual dressing is widespread in today's business environment. Even when your customers are in suits, you can fit in if your casual dress is appropriate. Do what you want to do and what makes you feel comfortable.

It's in the Eyes

The next aspect of your first impression comes from your eye contact or lack of it.

Eye contact allows you to connect with another person. You want the eye contact to be appropriate to the situation. In most cases, you want smiling, friendly eyes to greet the other person. You do not need to stare directly into their eyes, but do maintain your focus on the area of their face. It communicates to the other person, "I am interested in you and what you have to say." That is a way to begin any conversation.

Sage Advice

"Never try to look into both eyes at the same time. ... Switch your gaze from one eye to the other. That signals warmth and sincerity."
—Dorothy Sarnoff (b. 1917), U.S. publicist

Some people are uncomfortable with eye contact. You can help them with the friendliness of your own eye contact. Make sure there is nothing threatening in your eyes, even if you are uneasy with the conversation. Help them with the friendliness of your words and tone.

When you accomplish this, you are beginning to make the good first impression you want to make.

Shake Like You Mean It

Shaking hands is a Western tradition. It is a greeting that is often overlooked. Some people fail to use it to their advantage.

Shaking hands is a way of connecting with the other person. You do not need to crush the other person's hand to connect, but do make the handshake firm and appropriate for the person you are greeting. A "fish handshake" does not make a good impression with most people. It suggests a lack of interest and involvement. Although the handshake is only a small element of the impression you make, you want each element of your effort to connect with people to represent your best.

When you leave, also shake hands. This is a way of thanking the person and confirming the value of your discussion. Make it appropriate to the situation. Not shaking hands suggests for some people a lack of closure and agreement. This can leave a poor final impression.

SMILE!

When you greet someone, smile. It takes fewer muscles than a frown, and it is fun and easy.

It sets the tone for even a difficult conversation. In a difficult conversation, it communicates positive intent, which can smooth the way for that tough talk.

You have met people who did not smile when you greeted them. Maybe you wondered if they were in a bad mood or they entered the conversation with anger. In either case, a frown triggers negative feelings in the other person, which will not make the conversation easier or more productive.

To appreciate fully the power of the smile and the frown, observe your reactions to this one element with the next five people you meet. Also note the power your smile has to transform and uplift another person's apparent negative feelings.

Listen 75 Percent, Talk 25 Percent

If you want to be a great communicator, listen 75 percent of the time and speak 25 percent of the time. When you listen well, you speak well. Listening allows you to learn about the other person's point of view. Because you already know your preliminary point of view, being an active listener is important to being a great speaker. This was demonstrated earlier in the chapter on listening.

Listening may be especially important to the Five-Minute Manager who works in a home business. Unlike a corporate counterpart who has many people to listen to for new information, the home businessperson has very few people. Because home business Five-Minute Managers are about the only listeners in their business, they need to do it right all of the time. They are listening for a wide range of information. They are interested in competitive developments and customer attitudes. They want to know how people react to their product or service. They want to know what can they do better to present their product or service.

Relax and Live Your Truth

It is very important that you remain yourself. In a home business, you always need to do your best. Doing your best is effortless when you remain yourself.

When you try to act the way you think a sales person acts, you will not make many sales. When you sell from your heart and with compassion, you will make more.

When starting a home business, there can be tension and anxiety. Will you succeed and be able to pay the bills? Being tense and anxious actually works against what you want the most. When you relax and follow what Robert Fritz calls "the path of least resistance," you experience your greatest success. Trust your heart to show you the way to the flow or, as they say in sports, to the zone. That is the path of least resistance.

Speed Bump

Bragging is not only unattractive, it often involves lying. People have a sixth sense for lying, and it can put you out of business faster than any other action.

Bragging and Name-Dropping Not Allowed

Bragging and name-dropping can wipe out all the good impressions you have made so far. Usually, people brag and name-drop because they think it makes them look good. They think because they know certain people this reflects favorably on them.

To understand the impact your bragging and name-dropping have on others, reflect on how you feel when it happens to you. Bragging often suggests that a person cannot be trusted. It usually involves some degree of exaggeration or truth-stretching. You may impress inexperienced people by such actions, but most are not impressed. Bragging and name-dropping are signs of insecurity.

People want to know you, not who you know. Do not work to impress people. Be yourself. Living honestly is the most attractive thing you can do.

The Power of the Compliment

Sincere compliments are powerful. How do you feel when someone gives you a compliment? If it accurately reflects what you have done, it feels good. It also feels good to deliver a sincere compliment. A compliment is a mini-celebration of a good discovery.

Sage Advice

"There is nothing you can say in answer to a compliment. I have been complimented myself a great many times, and they always embarrass me—I always feel that they have not said enough."
—Mark Twain

Looking for the good things people do is fun. Too many people are judgmental, always looking for what they consider to be wrong or bad. The next time you judge, examine the energy behind your comment. It does not feel right. Now, your energy when you look for good deeds or share a compliment. It feels much better.

As demonstrated in Chapters 11 and 12, compliments are a power skill for the Five-Minute Manager. Compliments reflect your knowledgeable interest. They are a gift to another person, often the best possible gift you can give. They help another person appreciate their own qualities.

Become a Confident Public Speaker and Deliver a Great Presentation

The Five-Minute Manager at home needs to be a confident public speaker in both formal and informal situations. In an earlier chapter, this book discussed how public speaking before groups or in a seminar setting is a great marketing tool for your business. Even in informal conversations, the skills that make an excellent public speaker contribute to being a very good one-on-one communicator.

Prepare Early

Begin your preparation early. If you have a month lead time, use it to your advantage. Do not wait until the week or a few days before.

Nothing builds confidence more than being prepared. Confidence is the one ingredient that is essential for a great presentation. You gain confidence by knowing your material. You know your material by having sufficient time to research, assemble, and learn it.

Jot and Jog

Once you agree to speak, be prepared for ideas to pop into your head. As your subconscious and conscious minds reflect on the project, they will supply you with ideas.

Your job is to be ready for them. You do this by expecting the ideas and capturing them as they appear. Keep a notepad and pen or pencil around to write them down as soon as you have them. The ideas might come in the middle of the night; so keep the pad with you at all times. Do not judge the ideas. Just be grateful and accept them as gifts.

The Outline

As ideas come to you, assemble them into an outline. Begin by clearly identifying your purpose. If you leave your audience with just one message, what should it be?

First, align the essential building blocks in logical order. Look at what you have. Is it easy to follow? Is there a better way, a shorter way? Simplicity and clarity are essential to a good presentation. If there are three points you want your audience to take away, phrase them in a concise, memorable way.

Is there a theme that can help deliver the message? Sometimes a sports analogy works. Other times, linking it to the messages of a couple of great writers is better. Mark Twain is a favorite of many people because of his simply stated, yet profound wisdom and humor.

Add a Dose of Humor

You have attended presentations before. The speaker who used appropriate humor to deliver the message is probably one of the speakers you remember most.

There are several sources of humor. Books can help, but one of the best sources is the Internet. There are many humorous sites. The challenge is finding humor that is appropriate to your message. Do not tell a joke only to tell a joke. Be sure to link it to your message.

Provide a dose of humor at critical times. You can get attention and uplift your audience with an

Personal Coaching

Sometimes you are asked to speak with little or no time to prepare a response. A common reaction is fear, but this only shuts down your ability to creatively respond. Let go of fear and become as calm as you can. From a center of calmness trust that the right response will flow through you.

Sage Advice

"The wit makes fun of other persons; the satirist makes fun of the world; the humorist makes fun of himself, but in so doing, he identifies himself with people—that is, people everywhere, not for the purpose of taking them apart, but simply revealing their true nature."
—James Thurber (1894–1961), U.S. humorist, illustrator

opening joke. In the middle, just before you deliver an important point, consider another dose of humor. It wakes your audience up and gets members in a positive frame of mind for your point. Close on a positive note.

Even a very serious message benefits from the right kind of humor. Humor wakes us up and establishes a positive listening environment. A great speaker needs both of these.

Practice; Then Let It Flow

So far, you have prepared early, collected ideas, constructed an outline, and added humor where appropriate. Your presentation is coming together; now is a good time to practice. This requires standing up and giving your presentation.

When you do this, you immediately note some things that felt good on paper but do not work so well in the spoken word. The first several practices are actually opportunities for revision.

When it sounds right, give your talk from beginning to end with no interruptions. You can use a printed script or notes. If using a script, be sure the type is large enough and that it is double-spaced. At this stage, it begins to flow. Eventually, you may want to consider converting your script back into an outline of important points. Then, you can deliver the presentation more as a conversation than a stiff, scripted talk. This is the highest level of effectiveness for many speakers. You need to select the method you are most comfortable with delivering.

Sage Advice

"An audience is never wrong. An individual member of it may be an imbecile, but a thousand imbeciles together in the dark—that is critical genius."
—Billy Wilder (b. 1906), U.S. film director

Your Audience Wants You to Succeed

It may be difficult to believe, but your audience does want you to succeed. When you are in the audience, you want the speaker to do a good job, because it is entertaining and informative. The audience has expectations, and those are for you to succeed.

Knowing this, look at the audience as a group of friends or cheerleaders. They do cheer when you do well. They are pulling for you, not against you. If you stumble, they will feel badly for you. Use their good wishes and positive energy to your advantage. Remove all sense of negativity from your consciousness. Negativity only serves you negatively. It is counter to the positive energy of the audience. When you combine your positive energy with the audience's positive energy, you serve your highest communication purpose—making the sharing of ideas fun and memorable.

Physiology—Breathing and Eye Contact

You have to breathe, so do it right. Before you speak, take several deep breaths. Each time you breathe out, imagine you are exhaling any nervous or negative energy. When you inhale, bring in positive energy and smile. Do this until you feel your energy shift to the positive.

When you begin your presentation, be conscious of breathing slowly and deeply. Shallow, quick breathing means there is more negative energy, fear, and anxiety. Slow down your speaking pace to accommodate a better breathing pattern.

When you speak, make eye contact with your audience. Do not freeze your focus on your script or notes. Remember that you have practiced this many times. You know your material and are very comfortable with it. When you make eye contact, make sure you spread it around. Look left, center, and to the right with equal regularity. Look to the back of the room as well as the front rows. You make contact with your entire audience by doing this, and it improves their comprehension. It does this in part because it wakes them up.

Audience Participation

When your confidence in yourself and your material grows, you are ready to invite the audience's participation. Before you reach this point, the thought of an unscripted portion of the presentation only creates fear about being out of control of the situation.

There are levels of participation. The first level requires asking a question and asking for a show of hands from people who have had an experience or who agree with a point of view.

The next level requires asking your audience to perform some activity. For example, you might ask them to reflect on how what you have just said affects their lives. You may even ask them to take notes.

At the next level, you invite members of the audience to share relevant experiences. When they share, highlight points that connect with your message.

At the most challenging level, ask for questions. This is when you can expect the unexpected to happen. Questions can reflect disagreement with your views and put them to the test. It might be difficult to give a complete reply to a question. You might need more facts, or the question may be so personal that it is inappropriate to discuss at length before the group.

Personal Coaching

Practice your talk with your family as an audience. Allow them to ask questions. It will help you develop a sense of what thoughts your presentation triggers. At the end of the presentation, ask them to ask their toughest questions. Practice listening, pausing to prepare your answer, and responding in a way that does not make the questioner wrong.

Despite these challenges, an adept speaker loves questions. Questions reflect engagement and interest of people in the audience. No question is a threat. They are opportunities for two-way learning and a chance to underscore your most important points. They help you to demonstrate to the audience your expertise and confidence in your message.

Stop on Time

If your audience expects you will finish at a certain time, over-deliver by finishing early. You make a positive impression on those who were not very interested, and you leave those with interest refreshed and uplifted. You may even leave the latter group wanting more, which is usually good. If you have written a book, it may lead to a sale.

At least make sure that you stop on time. Some people have other meetings or rides to catch. Even people who loved your talk will be upset if you exceed this expectation.

Make the Telephone a Powerful Asset

The telephone is a power tool of the Five-Minute Manager at home. As important as a computer is, business is usually conducted face-to-face or over the phone. E-mail does not have the same power, at least not right now. Even when business is done in person, there is usually a phone conversation that precedes it. Having good telephone skills is a great success aid.

Have a Purpose

Before you reach for that phone, stop. Do you have a plan? If the answer is something like, "I want to talk to John about my big project," do not make the call right now.

Personal Coaching

Keep notes to refresh your memory. Record your perception of a person's values and how they make a decision. Be sure to note how they like to make decisions. Do not rely on memory for this critical information. Review it before you call. Several scheduling software programs include a page for these observations.

Define specifically what you want to accomplish by calling John. List one to three objectives for the call. It can be informal, but make it specific and measurable.

Reflect on the objectives. Are the items on the list the most important ones you need to talk about now? Plan to say what you need to say in five minutes or less. Be sure the items are listed in priority order and, if they are interrelated, that this order is logical. Having them listed in priority order is important in case the call is cut short for any reason.

You must have a plan, and not a casual one. Most people are busy and difficult to reach. When you do reach them, you want the call to be highly productive. By doing this, you will make a positive impression on others. They know that you do not waste their time, which makes them more likely to answer your future calls.

If you call with your plan and the person is not there, leave a message. Keep your written plan close to the phone so you can easily access it when they call back.

Know Your Audience

One more thing to do before you call—think about whom you are calling. Do not think only about your needs. Put yourself in the other person's shoes for a few moments.

What pressures do they face? What was on their mind the last time you talked? What is most important to them? What is their role in your project? What can they do and what is beyond their scope of responsibility?

Be sure you refresh your memory fully so that you can use the information to have a productive call.

First Words

You are ready to call. Your first words are the first impression you make on another person during a telephone call. Choose them carefully.

Start by identifying yourself. Make your greeting positive and clear.

Then, determine if now is a good time to talk. You may want to tell them that you need five minutes to discuss your topics. Admit you do not know how much total time is required for discussion. If now is not a good time, agree on a specific time and date when you will resume the conversation.

This step is often critical to the success of the call. Do not assume or hope the person has time to talk. If you just charge ahead and call at a bad time to talk, the other person will feel pressure and resentment for being put into an uncomfortable position. You may say what you have to say, but you will not have a productive call.

Judge Your Tone and Theirs

In telephone conversation, you do not have all the clues available in face-to-face conversation. You do not see facial expressions and body language, for example. These can be clues to how a person is reacting.

Because you cannot use these clues, listen from the beginning to your tone and their tone. If it is neutral or friendly, proceed. If not, pause to determine what is happening to the other person. The person may have said it was OK to talk now, but the tone suggests otherwise. Ask a question such as, "John, are you sure this is a good time? I can call back later today, if that is better."

If there is a tone shift by either party, be alert to its meaning. Is it communicating something different from the words? Work to clarify what is happening. People usually appreciate it when someone is sensitive to what they are feeling.

Consider This

Record your phone calls (where legal) for later review. Small recorders that double as dictation devices easily and inexpensively enable you to record a call. Review how your call went. Did you follow your plan? Were there tonality shifts you missed? How would you change the way you conducted the call? You will learn at least two ways to make the call better the next time.

Assertive, Not Aggressive

Ask for what you need, not what you think they will agree to now. This lesson was covered in Chapter 22.

When you are assertive, you ask for what you need, but you do not try to force agreement. When you use force, you are being aggressive. You are putting your needs ahead of the other person's needs. You are seeking a possible win-lose decision.

When you are assertive, you seek a win-win decision. You are clear about your needs, and you invite other parties to be clear about their needs. You make it clear that you want a win-win solution.

Of Course, Listen

As in any communication process, you need to be a great listener for the process to work well. You use all the listening skills discussed in earlier chapters.

The phone does present one special listening advantage. While you are on the phone, you can take notes. They can be hand-written or typed on the computer. If you use the phone frequently, consider buying a comfortable headset so that your hands are free to take notes. A headset is much more comfortable than a phone cradle, which helps you to wedge the phone between your head and shoulder.

The Least You Need to Know

➤ Assistance from family and a coach, plus a highly functional home office, make the Five-Minute Manager at home a super success.

➤ Remember to be neat, make friendly eye contact, firmly shake hands, and smile from your heart, all make great first impressions.

➤ The successful public speaker recipe: Prepare a month in advance. Add a dose of humor. Understand your audience and have the right attitude about them.

➤ Make the phone a power tool by having a plan, knowing your audience, and being assertive but not aggressive.

Chapter 24

Avoid Potholes and Mistakes

In This Chapter

➤ Preventing business disasters

➤ Your best helpers to avert a disaster

➤ How to spot accounting fraud

➤ Five ways to detect weak thinking in others

➤ Mistakes that can cripple an entrepreneur

Every business faces tough times. It is how well prepared they are and how they react that determines if a tough time will be a minor scratch or a mortal wound.

You need to be ready, vigilant, and alert. You need to be alert for accounting fraud and other disasters, especially in small and medium-size businesses. Fortunately, the warning signs are easy to spot when you are alert.

You Can Prevent Business Disasters

This is the first thing that you need to know: Most disasters are preventable. You will not prevent all of them, but the ones you do prevent can often mean the difference between success and failure. You can anticipate some disasters. For these, you should have plans and systems ready to respond when disaster strikes.

Who Is on Your Disaster Team?

Until now, you may not have associated a disaster team with business. The Red Cross and fire department have them, but not businesses. If this is how you think, you need to update your perceptions.

The Tylenol tampering case alerted many companies to the need to have a disaster plan and team in place and ready. To respond quickly and effectively to disasters, you need to be prepared. If you start preparations after a disaster strikes, you will be late and ineffective.

A disaster team identifies the major types of disasters a company might face. They use their experience and that of other companies to build their list. They make an effort to estimate the probability and impact of each disaster. They then prepare plans and reserves to respond to the most likely and most harmful disasters.

The team consists of important managers from the functions likely to be impacted by a potential disaster. They are experienced and knowledgeable managers who understand the scope of a potential disaster and how their function can best respond. Consultants and business coaches can also be valuable additions to disaster teams. They add objectivity and the experience of how other companies have responded to disasters.

Disaster teams do more than write plans. They recommend the purchase of special equipment and the taking of steps to prepare the necessary backups when disaster strikes.

Sage Advice

"Calamities are of two kinds: misfortune to ourselves, and good fortune to others."
—Ambrose Bierce (1842–1914), U.S. author

Vital Records

You only need to experience a crash on your personal or business computer once to know the value of protecting vital records. If you were not prepared, you know the panic and frustration of not being able to restore important files.

Most vital records today are on computers. Fortunately, you can backup files regularly and at low cost. On non-networked computers, you can simply backup files on floppy disks, but in most cases, you will want a high-capacity backup disk system, such as a Zip drive. There are many good ones, and they are worth every penny that you spend to protect vital records.

Network computers often use tape drives to backup vital records. They also use other high capacity storage disks and sometimes a separate computer system.

How often you backup files depends on how often major files change. Network managers usually backup files daily. On personal computers, the backup can be daily, weekly, or monthly. Many backup systems are automated to backup designated files at specified times. With such help, there is no excuse not to backup your files.

Speed Bump

The systems for backing up vital records are relatively straightforward. It requires personal action and discipline to make sure the systems really are used to backup vital records.

Now that you have your backup files, where do you store them? Right now, you probably store them near your computer. What would happen, however, if there were a fire or major water damage? These are two of the most frequent disasters, yet many people lose both their main and backup files when these disasters strike. The safest action is to store your backups of vital records in a different location.

For noncomputerized records, make sure you have copies of important documents. Again, store them in a different building from the original document.

Assets—More Than Insurance

Assets can take a long time to replace. Even proving that you had a certain asset can be a challenge in certain types of disasters. For example, in a fire you can lose any trace of an asset.

You can protect assets by ensuring that you have a complete record of them. You want to have all the details of the purchase—when, how old, price, condition, and exact manufacturer make and model. It is also helpful to have a video or photographic record of the asset. Be sure to include all assets, not just the visible or expensive ones. This includes the office furniture, water cooler, and accessories.

Protect important electronic equipment with surge protectors. If you live in area where there are thunderstorms, lightening can create a powerful surge that kills all electronic equipment that is plugged in to an ungrounded power source, including computers.

Of course, you need comprehensive insurance. Many insurance companies have asset protection plans and advice that can be very helpful to a small business owner.

If you think that disasters only happen to other people, then you risk disastrous results when one does strike you. There will be at least one; it is impossible to define when and where. Will you be ready?

Sage Advice

"Seeing is believing, and if an American success is to count for anything in the world it must be clothed in the raiment of property. As often as not it isn't the money itself that means anything; it is the use of money as the currency of the soul."
—Lewis H. Lapham (b. 1935), U.S. essayist, editor

Natural and Self-Inflicted Disasters

Disasters come in all shapes and sizes. They can also be self-inflicted. They can include internal fraud as discussed in the next section or an oversight or mistake, such as accidental flooding or misuse of equipment.

People tend to think of disasters in Red Cross terms—hurricanes, tornadoes, and earthquakes. Of course, these should be on your list of things to be prepared for, depending on where you live.

The worst kinds of disasters are those in which people are hurt. You can replace machines and computers. Although you can replace a person who is hurt on the job, you may not be able to help them fully recover from an accident on the job. Everyone in your organization needs to know basic disaster plans. If there is a fire or earthquake, what should people do? There are legal requirements for this in many areas, but you should plan on going beyond the minimum requirements. Determine what is unique about your work environment. Involve everyone to help you design your special plan.

Spotting Accounting Fraud

One of the worst disasters is accounting fraud. One morning you can wake up with no cash in the bank and inaccurate records. Worse yet, your accounts payable and receivable are disorganized or even missing. To make matters worse, you can have legal problems with suppliers and taxing authorities like the IRS and various state groups. This is not a pretty picture, and unfortunately, it is a picture that too many businesses face, especially small and medium-size businesses.

Consider This

Though there are ways to spot possible fraud, a strong set of checks and balances is a great dose of prevention. Consult a trusted CPA; then insist that the systems never be bypassed. Just a few exceptions can turn into an excuse to bypass the systems at will.

The good news is that there is a profile for people who commit accounting fraud. The following section addresses some of the frequent symptoms.

Never Takes a Vacation?

Most tend to view someone who seems extra dedicated to be a very loyal employee. In many cases, this is true, but there are some instances when it masks problems.

Those committing accounting fraud want to be on the job all the time to intercept troublesome phone calls and letters. They do not want someone else snooping around in their records while they are on vacation. The burden of committing fraud is that their personal cash flow is increasing, but they do not have any time to enjoy it.

Certainly, not everyone who foregoes all their vacation time is committing fraud. If you have employees who take little vacation time, you should encourage them to take time off for their own mental and physical health. Not taking vacation is one of several telltale signs of possible accounting fraud. When you see a combination of them, conduct an investigation for your financial and mental health.

A similar symptom is someone who always works late or wants to take work home. Someone committing fraud wants the chance to do their deeds when people are not around. They will do almost anything to reduce the chances of discovery.

Blames Others

Those committing fraud love to blame others for mistakes, setting themselves up as the most trusted and competent. Anything they can do to have management rely on them more serves their fraudulent purposes.

They also tell on others, so that if something goes wrong, the blame falls on those who have made mistakes in the past. This approach tends to make them unpopular, which also serves their purpose of working in isolation as much as possible.

Sage Advice

"Secrecy is the badge of fraud."
—Sir John Chadwick (b. 1941), British judge

Volunteers to Handle Important Details

Employees committing fraud also volunteer to handle as many of the details as possible. Anything that enables them to control completely all of the steps in the accounting process without intervention from others serves their purposes.

They also volunteer to handle tasks that mangers handle. They might say, "You are very busy, why don't you let me handle that for you?" This can sound like a quality of a great employee. In many cases, it is, but not when someone is intent on committing fraud. If they can control their responsibilities and those of their boss somewhat, they widen the scope of possible fraud. The widened scope usually means they have access to more money.

Picks Up the Mail

This may sound like a small thing, but to someone committing fraud it can be critical. By controlling the mail, they control accounts payable and some receivables. They also intercept potentially embarrassing inquiries from suppliers and vendors.

If someone else picks up the mail, they react very defensively. They move to reprimand the person and strongly signal that picking up the mail is their responsibility. They can be tenacious in their defense of this function.

Makes Bookkeeping Complex

Those intent on committing fraud want to make their work appear to be complex to others. By making it complex, they make it necessary for themselves to personally explain any inquiry. They never hand over their records to let others find an answer.

To make it complex, they might quote government regulations by chapter and number. They might point to accounting standards in great detail to impress others with

Personal Coaching

The principles for spotting accounting fraud are good to keep in mind for all your critical dealings. Be involved and be alert. Do not assume that you can perform less than prudent oversight and not be hurt.

their expertise. The more complex they can make their job, the bigger the barriers they create.

Accounting is not complex. It is exquisitely simple in its fundamentals. If you have someone trying to make the job sound complex to keep you from being personally involved, begin your own learning effort. Talk with others in accounting and read some basic books. With a couple of hours of intent effort, you can become conversational in the basics. With additional effort to understand specifics, you can conduct an intelligent inquiry.

Anyone who tries to make it sound too complex for you to personally understand is putting up "Do Not Enter" and "No Trespassing" signs. Tear these down and move in quickly.

Feels They Are Owed Something

So far, you have learned symptoms, not motives. People commit fraud for a variety of reasons.

One of them is a belief that the company owes them money for some reason. The reason does not have to make sense to you, and probably will not when you learn it.

Sage Advice

"The man who is admired for the ingenuity of his larceny is almost always rediscovering some earlier form of fraud. The basic forms are all known, have all been practiced. The manners of capitalism improve. The morals may not."
—John Kenneth Galbraith (b. 1908), U.S. economist

They might have worked for the company for a long time. They feel they have made unnoticed, important, and unrewarded contributions. Therefore, they start rewarding themselves for these contributions with company funds.

The reasons can also relate to personal financial needs. There can be personal bankruptcy, pressure from home to earn more money, or gambling debts. The list of possible reasons is long. In wandering, the Five-Minute Manager gets to know people and their special circumstances. When the Five-Minute Manager notices multiple symptoms and some personal history suggesting motive, it is time to take action. The Five-Minute Manager can consult with an independent auditor to the suspected function. They need to be cautious at this stage, because hasty, ill-conceived actions might trigger a final stage of fraud; the destruction of vital records by a desperate person.

Recognizing Bad Thinking When You Hear It

One of the best ways to prevent disasters is to be alert to the bad thinking that eventually leads to self-inflicted disasters. The Five-Minute Manager heeds the old adage "an ounce of prevention is worth a pound of cure."

Question, Question, Question

Questioning is a skill discussed earlier in Chapter 5 on listening. The Five-Minute Manager does not question to test a person's knowledge. They question to learn substantive information that leads to making the right decisions.

Being a good questioner is an art and very valuable skill. The art involves reading how a person reacts to questions. The Five-Minute Manager wants to maintain an openness that allows the free and candid flow of information. The Five-Minute Manager does not want questions to be threatening. To accomplish this, the Five-Minute Manager closely monitors their tonality and the other person's body language and tonality. When the Five-Minute Manager detects a person feeling uneasy or threatened, they soften the questioning and reaffirm the learning intent. Often there is an ebb and flow to the exchange.

The questions seek the truth as best it can be known. The focus is on having the best information to make the right decision. Often, this can lead along a winding path, with occasional detours and tangents. Knowing the art and skills of asking questions enables the Five-Minute Manager to discover bad thinking in many cases.

Just the Facts and All the Facts

Bad thinking is often disguised as fact. People report something as a fact, which is really their interpretation of some other facts. It may not even be an interpretation, but a guess.

When someone is a good speaker and delivers a strong and convincing presentation, it is tempting to believe everything the person says. The Five-Minute Manager knows that to make the right decision, you need to start with the right facts. Whereas the right facts may not directly lead to the right decision, if you do not have them subsequent steps will be flawed. With the right facts, interpretations, and guesses, if needed, it will be better.

As part of the Five-Minute Manager's questioning process, they carefully identify the difference between facts and personal interpretations. Questions like "How do we know that?" help clarify what the Five-Minute Manager hears. They also signal to the other person the importance of separating facts from interpretations. The Five-Minute Manager highly values interpretations, but only upon knowing the facts used to arrive at the conclusion. Interpreting facts is a valuable skill, requiring the ability to synthesize facts. Because a part of interpretation is adding experience to factual understandings, it is important for the Five-Minute Manager to know the experiences that lead a person to their conclusions. They can then better evaluate the quality of the facts and the experiences supporting the interpretations.

Consider This

Successful managers have mastered the important facts, which are the ones most likely to be indicators of future business result, and they know the strengths and weaknesses of their sources. They know how to ask penetrating questions because they have personal experience with the sources. If you do not have this experience when you became a manager, get the formal or informal training necessary to be an expert.

What's That Source?

Another way the Five-Minute Manager understands facts is by understanding the quality of the facts.

For example, assume a assistant marketing manager reports that 70 percent of consumers prefer an improved product over the current product. At first this sounds impressive. Some managers might be inclined to take action based on this "fact."

The Five-Minute Manager needs to know the source before ascertaining the value of the information. The Five-Minute Manager asks questions about what specific research reports this fact. After learning that it was focus group research in which 7 of 10 people liked the new product, the manager determines that the fact is not worth much. If the source had been a nationally representative panel of about 200 consumers using accepted methodology, then the fact would have been very valuable.

Sometimes, the value of a source is immediately evident, although sometimes it requires further inquiry. The Five-Minute Manager always seeks to understand the methodology used to determine a fact. Good managers remain open to new sources, but need a personal understanding before they can evaluate the strength of the fact.

They may not immediately be able to evaluate the source. It may require further investigation. The Five-Minute Manager knows that even their best sources are not infallible. Knowing this, they try to determine the value of the source.

Seek Other Perspectives

The Five-Minute Manager knows the need for multiple perspectives to make the right decision. The importance of these perspectives increases with the magnitude of the decision and the softness of the facts.

Decisions that can alter the future of the company need careful consideration. Careful consideration usually means consulting trusted advisors inside and, where necessary, outside the company.

An interesting story illustrates the point. A crew was in Africa doing a census of wild animals. Three groups took position on separate hills overlooking a flat area where animals congregated. The group's leader asks each group what kind of animals are in the center of the flat area. One observer group radios in that they are rhinos; another says the same group is hippos; the third group is not sure.

This happens with facts also. When people look at them, what they see varies from their interpretations. When there are significant differences, the Five-Minute Manager knows to take a closer look. Either ask your first respondents to look closer or ask others to examine the same set of facts.

Speed Bump

When you seek the perspectives of others, know their strengths. Some people can be especially helpful in one functional area but be of limited help in others. Interestingly, people who know nothing about your business can have some of the most innovative perspectives.

Verify

Five-Minute Manager verifies what they hear and read. They do not verify because of a lack of trust. Rather the Five-Minute Manager recognizes two important reasons to verify.

First, there is a chance that the facts have changed or are not complete. The Five-Minute Manager wants to ensure they are working with the most up-to-date version and that they have all the relevant facts. Sometimes a person quotes something from a report, but has not closely examined all of the relevant facts in the report. A simple question like "What other conclusions did the research make?" helps the Five-Minute Manager put the conclusions into the appropriate context.

The second reason is that the Five-Minute Manager recognizes the possibility of misunderstanding what someone said. A simple statement like "I understand that the facts are … and concluded with …," confirms or clarifies what the Five-Minute Manager heard. This does not have to be done for everything a person says. Rather, they use this approach for the critical points in a conversation. This helps both the Five-Minute Manager who is listening and the person who is speaking. It helps the latter because they may have been unintentionally ambiguous. This is an opportunity to make an important clarification.

By taking all of these steps, the Five-Minute Manager clears out most of the bad thinking. The more adept the Five-Minute Manager is at the art and skills of discovery, the better their decisions.

The Least You Need to Know

➤ Backup all vital records and keep the backup in a separate location.

➤ A disaster plan and team prevent many disasters and quickly resolve most other disasters.

➤ The person committing accounting fraud wants total control of their job and will do almost anything to keep people from reviewing their work.

➤ Recognizing bad thinking requires asking good questions, focusing on the facts and their sources, and obtaining multiple perspectives on important issues.

➤ When you believe you are thinking the right way, verify that it is right; do not assume it is right.

Chapter 25

Why Be Number Two When You Can Be Number One?

In This Chapter

➤ How to avoid the mistakes which prevent a company from becoming number one

➤ Chaos—a business friend or foe?

➤ Avoiding the glamour of new business opportunities

➤ The mistakes that can cripple an entrepreneur

➤ The benefits of failure and positive thinking

Companies often experience great success for a few years and eventually become number two in their type of product or service. A few more years go by and the company finds itself stuck in the number two spot because of common mistakes that prevent a company from going to the next level.

In a similar way, entrepreneurs struggle and fail. Recognizing and addressing these mistakes helps entrepreneurs to achieve their visions.

Mistakes That Make Companies Number Two When They Can Be Number One

Some very successful companies struggle to grow year by year. After years of effort, they eventually find themselves the second biggest companies in their industries. They set their sights on becoming the largest and continue to expend considerable effort. After years of trying, they are still number two. They may even slip closer to being number three than number one. Often factors associated with early growth are not the same factors a company needs to become number one. If a company does not recognize the need to evolve, it stalls and even slips backwards. This chapter covers some of the common mistakes that companies make as they strive to take the business to the highest levels.

Thinking Chaos Is Creative

Companies who experience early dramatic growth also tend to experience lots of "fire fighting." There is one crisis after another. They tend to thrive on crisis. There is a thrill in successfully resolving the crisis. People pull together to solve the latest problem. This promotes a sense of group cohesiveness. Crisis-solving skills become finely honed. The company takes great pride in these abilities.

Personal Coaching

Although chaos can be ultimately destructive in many situations, a free-flowing, unstructured process can be especially helpful in creative situations. Even here, however, there needs to be a guiding hand that ultimately ensures that it is constructive.

Throughout the period of early growth, managing the chaos of crisis is the primary activity of the company. Crisis and its associated chaos are elevated to the status of a virtue. At this early stage, any suggestion that new systems be established to reduce the chaos is met with disdain. Whereas people complain about the stress and hard work associated with chaos, when pressed they admit to enjoying it. They have become "adrenaline junkies." Turnover increases and people increasingly complain about the stress and anxiety. Management feels people are not as tough as they once were and is not persuaded to change its ways.

When it reaches this stage, a company can be in trouble. It has grown dramatically and the level of chaos had risen proportionately. The founding managers love chaos, but are sobered by the increasing complexity of problems and decreasing rate of effective problem solution.

They reach a crucial juncture. Do they make almost radical changes in their values and how they manage the business or find a way to continue as they have been? This is often a fateful choice. Whatever the choice, the next couple of years will not be easy. If they do not change, they will be managing a large business with small business skills, which ultimately will make them a smaller company.

If they elect to change the way they manage the business, success is not guaranteed. The two major challenges they face are the new management system and new managers. The system may be the easier challenge of the two. There are many books, coaches, and consultants that can help with the selection process. Once a system is chosen, the company will likely find that it lacks the skills necessary to implement the system. Chaos skills are not what most new systems require. The company is faced with re-training and hiring new people. The turmoil during this process can be great. If a company survives the transition, it will be a strong, vibrant enterprise.

Relying on Gut Instincts

In the early stages of growth, the company founder uses limited funds on product development and sales. Prior experience was the primary source of the inspiration that started the business. The founder continues to draw upon this base of experience as the business gets off the ground.

As businesses start to grow, company founders are consumed by the demands. It appears that decisions need to be made fast, so they connect with their gut instincts. Gut instinct is some amorphous collection of prior experiences that you use to guide decision-making. It is amorphous because you cannot always connect an instinct to a specific experience.

Gut instincts can serve you well or poorly. There is no magic correctness with gut instincts like there is with a clear connection to our intuition. Gut instincts typically involve emotions which have great variability. Intuition, on the other hand, is a heartfelt connection to your higher abilities.

A problem develops when the business is success-ful, in part, because of the use of gut instincts. When this happens, the founders give great weight to gut instincts in all the decisions they make. Although gut instincts can be effective early on in a business, they can be a problem when a business is no longer small. If the experiences that form the gut instincts are based on smaller businesses, they may not be as effective with a larger business.

Sage Advice

"What is peculiar in the life of a man consists not in his obedience, but his opposition, to his instincts. In one direction or another he strives to live a supernatural life."

—Henry David Thoreau (1817–1862), U.S. philosopher, author, naturalist

When a company becomes larger, it needs the tools of a larger business to guide its decision-making. For example, formal consumer research is fundamental to most large businesses. It is impossible for gut instincts to consistently replicate the insights gained by consumer research. As a business grows, so does the size and diversity of its customer base. It is the diversity of the customer base that undermines the reliability of the early experience.

As a business grows, however, gut instincts do not cease to play a role in decision-making. Rather, they play a less significant role because additional decision-making tools and guides are developed. This includes the gut instincts of other senior managers. This can be a tough transition for many founders, especially if they let pride get in the way.

Keeping All Eyes on the Competition

Early in a business's life, it learns that it has competition. The learning process can be a painful one for many businesses. For example, the loss of the company's largest customer to a competitor can be very painful when that customer represents more than a quarter of the company's business at the time.

When painful lessons like this are learned and survived, the company focuses increasingly on competitors. You collect data and are sensitive to any changes that the competitors make. When they add a service or value, you make the same or a similar change very quickly. When they hire someone with special talents, you examine your need for those talents and often hire someone with similar skills. You gradually become a mirror image of the other company or companies.

Consider This

Many companies have systems set up to track competition. They have regular collection of price lists, press releases, and institute rewards for reports of new competitive activity. When there is new information, there is a process for reporting it to senior management. The entire organization is alerted to the importance of early notice of competitive actions.

Sensitivity to competition is good to a degree. When it reaches the point that your "innovation" is a reflection of their initiatives, this same sensitivity becomes a serious problem. For customers, there is little difference between two or more companies. Thus, purchase decisions tend to be made on price differences. When a company tries to mirror another company, it runs the great risk of having no real or potential advantages and only being able to distinguish itself with price. This is a long-term recipe for financial disaster.

In an earlier chapter, you learned that a successful strategy has three elements, only one of which involves competitors. A successful business has a healthy competitor perspective. It watches what its competitors do, but does not mimic their every move. Competitors make poor choices and you should not follow them. Competitors make smart moves for their businesses, but these may not be right for our business and its strategy.

The smart business keeps a casual eye on its competitors.

Completing Something Is More Important Than How It Is Done

As a business claws its way up the market share ladder to number two, it often prides itself in its ability to get things done. As issues rise and chaos ensues, the company responds. The fire is put out and the business moves on to the next issue, which is sure to arise.

Managers learn to trust people who can solve problems. The problems and challenges are so frequent that the manager only has time to solve the problem, not monitor the implementation of the solution. As a result, the manager increasingly values those who can execute an agreed-to solution.

People tasked with executing solutions know that they only get criticized when they do not solve the problem. They do not get criticized because of the way they solve the problem. This inevitably leads to problems. As pressures increase, solutions are more likely to be the ones that involve the least effort and are the fastest to implement.

These solutions are not necessarily what is best long term for the company. In fact, the solutions can be off-strategy, which weakens the company's long term viability. Off-strategy solutions take you in a direction that may be interesting, even attractive, but it is not a direction that utilizes your greatest strengths. The solutions can also be at odds with the stated values of the company. Efficient, expeditious, and low profile can quickly lead to a lack of integrity.

When a company values getting things done more than how they are done, it opens itself up to a wide array of problems. This is especially true when a company is young and the culture is still forming. At this stage, there is little to guide the process other than individual decision-making, which may or may not be consistent with the company's values and needs. Legal problems are a frequent manifestation in a company that values results more than process.

When managers of a young, growing company notice that results overwhelm process, they need to inject themselves into the execution of solutions. The Five-Minute Manager does this through goal setting and management by wandering around. In the goal setting stage, agreement on how the goal will be reached is part of the process. Then, managing by wandering around, the Five-Minute Manager observes how well the plan is executed.

A Quick Payoff Is Better Than Making an Investment

In the early stages of a business, when money is tight, the spending of every penny is closely examined. If it is not necessary to make a sale now, the money may not be spent. If a manager cannot see an immediate savings that pays for the investment, it may not be made.

This seems right to many managers in the early stages. Money is precious and is only used to purchase things that bring an immediate return. Unfortunately, money is a limited commodity in most businesses, no matter how large or small. A benefit of looking for immediate payoffs from expenditures is that it focuses the manager's attention on its financial return. The downside is that money is only spent on projects with an immediate return. Other possible good investments are neglected.

Sage Advice

"Sometimes your best investments are the ones you don't make."
—Donald Trump (b. 1946), U.S. businessman

Some of the most valuable expenditures a company makes are on ones that payoff several years later. For example, establishing an ongoing research and development capability requires an up-front investment in a facility and equipment and then an ongoing investment in personnel. The return is usually not immediate and sometimes is difficult to predict. Nonetheless, successful companies are often the ones who make these kinds of investments. How much of an investment is right depends on the nature of the business. In mature businesses, investment in research and development may be a small percentage of sales. In a business like prescription drugs, a large investment in this area is warranted, because the company's future is dependent on a steady stream of new products.

New Business Opportunity Is More Important Than Current Customers

As a company grows, it can become infected with "growthitis." The symptom is an inclination to pursue almost any idea that promises growth. Growth for growth's sake becomes the company's chief goal.

A frequent outgrowth of this disease is the constant pursuit of new business opportunities that are not directly related to the company's core business. The managers see something that appears to be related and pursue it. The pursuit can often consume most of their time and resources. Frequently, the startup of these kinds of projects or businesses requires an extensive learning curve. As a result, it often results in more, not fewer, resources being required.

As a result, managers often find they are no longer paying much attention to their core business. When this happens, the core business often encounters troubles. If the managers do not quickly address them, the core business can quickly begin a decline that is difficult to reverse.

Personal Coaching

A way to avoid becoming too enamored with growth and new customers is to have systems for rewarding old customers. For example, you can provide a one-time discount each year on their anniversary with the company.

There are a couple of important lessons companies need to learn from "growthitis." First, do not become enamored with growth as an end in itself. Growth should be a means to accomplish other objectives.

Second, new business opportunities that directly relate to and strengthen the core business are the best ones to pursue. In most of these cases, the customer base is very similar. Thus, a business can sell more to existing customers instead of needing to find new customers for the business to succeed. In relying on existing customers, you rely on people you know.

Third, when pursuing new business opportunities, make strong provisions to manage and nurture the core business. Do not assume that it can be put on automatic pilot. It is easy to underestimate the amount of effort needed to maintain momentum in the core business. If this step is not taken, a lose-lose situation results—the new business venture fails and the core business falters.

Common Troublesome Qualities of an Entrepreneur

Entrepreneurs are the backbone of the American economy. America has a proud history of innovative and insightful people founding small businesses, some of which grow to become international giants.

As successful as entrepreneurs are in America, there is a very high failure rate among them. Many of the mistakes that lead to failure are avoidable. The following section outlines some of the common mistakes entrepreneurs make that can cripple a great idea.

The Circle Runner

Entrepreneurs pride themselves in having creative ideas. This is a great strength, but sometimes it is carried too far. They generate idea after idea. Each idea is embraced for a moment; then another idea appears. Handled correctly, this can be a great strength.

Handled incorrectly, it quickly wrecks a company. When an entrepreneur generates one idea after another, no one idea is fully developed. Ideas are parked or discarded at the half-baked stage. In the discard pile may be some powerful ideas, but this kind of entrepreneur probably will never know it. Because they do not take the time to develop an idea, they never know its potential. Because they cannot see its potential, they judge the idea insufficient and move on to the next one; then they treat it the same way.

Consider This

One company that was a "circle runner" overcame it by posting a project board in its main office area. It had columns for the various stages: idea, plan, execution, and evaluation. When the idea column became full, people knew it was time to eliminate ideas or plan to implement them. The public display of this information helped the entrepreneurs see how they were accomplishing bringing ideas to life.

This type of entrepreneur is moving in an endless circle. They will have a very difficult time moving forward, because they are frustrated about not having an idea they can get behind. Entrepreneurs typically have lots of confidence and a sense that they are the only ones who truly understand what their business is about. To break the cycle, they usually need someone else to point out what they are doing. This person needs to be strong and respected for an entrepreneur to stop and change.

The first step is difficult. The entrepreneur must reconnect with ideas already developed and discarded, especially if others see strong potential in the idea. It is difficult for an entrepreneur to reconnect with the original inspiration after discarding the idea. If this effort is ultimately not successful, the Five Minute Manager helps the entrepreneur stay connected with a new idea. Use the connection to develop the idea far enough to determine if it warrants further study. The entrepreneur needs to understand that the creative process does not stop with the first blush of inspiration. By staying connected with an idea and playing with it, it can become much greater than it appeared in the beginning.

Details—Not for Me

Details, sometimes too much involvement, and sometimes too little, can kill an entrepreneur's business. This section deals with the common challenge of entrepreneurs who disdain details. They enjoy the big picture issues and think that involving themselves in the details is not worthy of their talents. They may be right, but the details still need to be handled and handled correctly or the business will fail. This can be incomprehensible to entrepreneurs who have convinced themselves that to succeed they just need a big idea and customers will beat a path to their doors.

Sage Advice

"Men who wish to know about the world must learn about it in its particular details."
—Heraclitus (circa 535–475 BC), Greek philosopher

Usually, the best solution for this type of entrepreneur is to find a capable and trusted person to handle the details. The person who handles the details needs to be strong and respected by the entrepreneur or their life will not be fun.

Good Starter, Poor Finisher

Some entrepreneurs love the early stages of idea development. The thrill of a new idea lifts them up and is fun. Taking an idea to the next couple of stages also is fun, because it keeps getting bigger and better.

Part of this entrepreneur's problem is not being able to handle the details that follow. But this case is more severe. The energy and enthusiasm peak in the idea stage. The entrepreneur then moves to execute the idea because it seems the natural next step. This often is the crucial mistake. Maybe what the entrepreneur is really good at and takes joy from is starting companies and then selling them to others. Ideally, the entrepreneur sells them to the operational people who assisted in starting the company.

Many entrepreneurs have difficulty taking this step because of misconceptions about business and themselves. They need help connecting with their true talents and seeing what makes them happy. They need to disconnect from the expectation that they are only successful if they have an idea and fully develop it into a business.

Failure After Failure

When you examine the stories of today's successful entrepreneurs, you often find people who failed several times before they succeeded. Although the previous efforts are seen as failures, they actually were learning steps along the way to success.

For entrepreneurs in the early stages of creating and failing, this is difficult to see. All they can see is failure. They experience the excitement of a big idea and several months later the idea and business are dead.

Two factors separate the ultimately successful entrepreneur from the one who is not successful. First, successful entrepreneurs learn from every step. Failures are only lessons that ultimately help them succeed. Second, they have a deep, abiding faith in self. They know they will ultimately succeed.

Personal Coaching

When entrepreneurs recognize that it often takes a team to get an idea to the finishing line, more ideas get implemented. They can move from the primary mover in the early stage to cheerleader in the later stages.

Super Optimists

Optimism is a two-edged sword for many entrepreneurs. It is very helpful when it reflects their well-founded confidence in their idea. When times are tough, it uplifts others in the business and carries them to the next stage. When optimism is effective, it can carry a business through the bleakest of times.

When it is not well founded, it can tear a new business apart. It is not well founded when the entrepreneur grossly exaggerates expectations. Co-workers can often understand missing an expectation by a small amount, but when the miss is consistently large, it diminishes faith. Again, the entrepreneur is helped in these situations by a good operational manager and coach to help manage personal and business expectations.

Living on the Edge

Entrepreneurs tend to live on the edge in many ways. One way that impacts the business is living on the financial edge. This is especially true when the entrepreneur does handle details well and insists on totally managing the business.

Living on the financial edge can produce jarring surprises. When a payroll is not met or a mortgage payment missed, a small business can be shattered. Missing a payroll can be disastrous because people typically put in more hours than they are paid for and to not be paid is a double loss. Their personal finances often are on the edge, so they do not have reserves to absorb a lost paycheck.

259

Consider This

Some people assume you do not make money in the early stages of a business. This is a dangerous and false assumption. Many companies plan to be very profitable from their first sale. In this way, they do not live on the edge of financial solvency.

Living on the financial edge also undermines the inspiration that created the business. Stress, fear, and anxiety are powerful negative forces. When present, they stifle creativity and productivity when it is most acutely needed.

Many entrepreneurs assume that living on the financial edge is a given when you start a new business. It is not. When well-founded plans are executed with inspiration and skill, a business can flourish from the first day it opens its doors. When the emphasis is on delivering a better product or service than customers can get now, a company starts out in the right direction. When that product or service is also a better value than competitors' products or services, then the company is on solid ground. When these fundamentals are addressed, a business does not have to live on the financial edge, which can cut the vitality out of a company.

Weak Team Members

A challenge for most entrepreneurs is attracting the necessary talent to start a business. The pay is not good; the benefits are sometimes nonexistent; and the future is uncertain.

The solutions are not easy. Sometimes the solution is talented people who help out as their second job before actually joining the new business on a full-time basis. In other cases, the young business contracts with other talented companies to handle some functions, such as billings and payroll.

Entrepreneurs can also be poor people managers who are great with ideas. If this is the case, it can be difficult for the entrepreneur to recognize. Close friends or trusted advisors may be the only people that can help them see their management skills as they are. When they find themselves in this situation, they need to hire a trusted person to manage operations.

The Family Suffers

The family can suffer in any business situation, but it can be acute in an entrepreneurial situation. Entrepreneurs have such strong ownership and identification with the business that the business is like a second family that challenges the number one family position at times.

The hours can be long, very long. A new business can consume almost all the mental and physical energy of entrepreneurs. They justify the costs by saying that the business is for the family's benefit. Sometimes it is. At other times, it is not quite the benefit entrepreneurs think it is. Sometimes, entrepreneurs become unconsciously more concerned with personal image and success.

When entrepreneurs get this wound up in the business, disengaging to any degree can be difficult. Again, it takes a strong, trusted person to partially separate entrepreneurs from their businesses by delegating certain functions to others. This leverage often helps entrepreneurs see that the path they are on may lead to business success and family failure, creating only a hollow victory.

Certainly, not all entrepreneurs take this route. Many go into business so they can better balance their lives. For them, being an entrepreneur means being in control of your life. They are the fortunate ones and can become mentors to others not so fortunate.

The Least You Need to Know

➤ Liking chaos and short-term investment thinking are two major factors that prevent companies from becoming number one in their industries.

➤ Do not make completing a project more important than completing it the right way.

➤ New business opportunities can blind you to current customers whose business pays today's bills.

➤ Common entrepreneurial mistakes include an inability to handle details, the ability to start but not finish ideas, and the habit of constantly running a company on the financial edge.

➤ Learning from failure guides the way to tomorrow's success.

Chapter 26

Profitable Success for the Five-Minute Manager

In This Chapter

➤ Thoughts to consider before writing your business plan

➤ What it takes to be really profitable

➤ How to plan for long term profitability and success

➤ Easy-to-obtain resources that make a big difference

Most definitions of success involve making a profit. Even charities that define themselves as "not for profit" need to have income and expenses balanced. Most of the time, they strive to have small surpluses so they can invest in expanded services and have reserves for replacement of assets and unexpected expenses.

In business, profitability begins with planning for success. Profitability reaches beyond minimal levels through proven techniques that distinguish the Five-Minute Manager's business from all others offering the same or similar services and products. By taking a long-term view of building profitability, a business can remain vital enough to grow to a leadership position in its industry.

A Practical, Powerful Business Plan

Whereas there are success stories of companies whose only planning, they claim, was on the back of a napkin, these are the exception. Most new businesses assemble a version of a business plan. A business plan is a detailed document that lays out all the thinking and planning the owners believe will lead to success.

There are numerous books, consultants, coaches, and Internet sites that provide excellent guidance on how to develop a business plan. The following section provides some guidance on important elements that make the difference between a good and a great business plan.

Dream—Now Make It Bigger

Before setting out to write a business plan, you must consider the dream that inspired you or your group enough to want to take the steps necessary to make the dream a reality. The process of assembling a business plan is an excellent one to address issues and opportunities. It forces you to think through important issues that may not have been obvious in the dream stage. If you need financing from a bank or a venture capital company, a business plan is required.

Before actually writing a business plan, explore ways to make the dream bigger. It may have to remain static while you explore ways to bring it to life. During this time, you can learn more by discussing it with others. The reactions of people you talk to can spark new ideas and concerns.

Use all of this new information to begin the process of making your dream bigger before you prepare your business plan. Assemble a group of trusted advisers and creatively approach opportunities to expand the dream. Consider going to a secluded location, maybe in nature, for a couple of days of focused fun and creatively build on the original idea. During this session, you do not need to make decisions, just develop the dream in detail.

You can take the input and seek additional information and perspectives. It helps you make the decisions about how you can make the dream bigger. Some of the ideas may be second-stage ideas you pursue after you begin working toward the initial dream. When you approach the opportunity to make the dream bigger at this stage, you are virtually assured of developing a stronger idea.

Top 100 Obstacles

As Five-Minute Managers develop a business plan, they start by looking for potential problems. They know that if they anticipate problems they will avoid many and become able to solve the rest more quickly.

They set an objective of identifying 100 potential obstacles. To complete this task, they solicit the help of friends and trusted advisors. Where appropriate, they add other small business owners and a personal coach. They want people who have been through the process of starting a business to assist in this important process.

The list should cover all the functional areas. They might start with the actual product or service, closely examining possible challenges. For example, their product list might include the following obstacles:

➤ Most important ingredient supplier sharply increases prices. Twice in the last three years there have been 50 percent price increases that lasted for two months.

➤ Ingredient shortages develop. A year ago, a minor ingredient supplier had severe shortages for six months. Some analysts predict further shortages over the next 24 months.

➤ Packaging supplier goes out of business. The current first choice is the low bidder, but that company's credit rating is low and there are rumors that it will file for bankruptcy.

➤ Product liability insurance cost estimate dramatically increases. The current estimate is only a rough estimate because a final product prototype is not ready for testing and evaluation. If the final cost is at the high end of the estimate range, it will be 55 percent higher than the current cost assumption.

For each potential obstacle the team identifies, they attach a reason it might occur. Thus, the obstacles are not fanciful but based on real possibilities. The process of identifying obstacles is a very positive experience for Five-Minute Managers. They learn about the risks and begin the process of identifying potential solutions.

Personal Coaching

Obstacles, like problems, can be positive when you learn from them. With a positive attitude, lessons translate into stronger ideas and a stronger company. A positive attitude is critical to the planning process. When you have a good attitude you will be able to find more valid potential obstacles. That is good news.

Top 1,000 Solutions

Five-Minute Managers know for every problem they should think of about 10 possible solutions. Therefore, for their 100 potential problems they develop 1,000 solutions.

The solutions are also based on reality. For example, refer back to the packaging supplier problem.

Ten possible solutions for this problem might be:

➤ The first five solutions are alternative packaging suppliers who are qualified to package the product. Each of these is ranked based on previously provided cost estimates.

➤ Potential solutions 6 through 10 are to revise the packaging specifications and design to become open to another five potential suppliers. These are ranked after they provide preliminary cost estimates. This preliminary data suggests there might be cost and efficiency advantages to redesigning the package. Already, one of the potential solutions leads to consideration of a better idea.

The Five-Minute Manager in this situation calls upon the same people who helped identify the obstacles, plus a few functional experts. The latter provide both ideas and feasibility estimates.

When the Five-Minute Manager completes this process, his confidence is even higher than it was before beginning the process. He understands there can be many problems, but there appear to be more solutions than there are problems. Even if problems not on the original list later occur, he is confident of finding solutions based on this experience. By going through the process, he has also identified some ideas to upgrade his original thinking.

> ### Sage Advice
>
> "The best way out is always through."
> —Robert Frost (1874–1963), U.S. poet

Advice by the Ton—Test Its Quality

In preparing to launch a business, it is helpful to solicit great quantities of advice. Five-Minute Managers who do this recognize that they can accept or reject some or all of it.

There are many sources of advice. One source is books. You can browse a bookstore or search the Internet booksellers. You can go to a library and search a wide range of business books. You can also search for magazine articles on subjects that you are interested in reading about. While you are searching magazines, you may find some that you will want to subscribe to. For example, *Inc. Magazine* runs articles on new and small businesses. You can search back issues of *Inc.* for relevant articles at their Web site, www.inc.com.

Beyond printed advice, you can seek counsel from government agencies. The Small Business Administration is one of the most popular. They have offices in most cities and on the Web at www.sba.gov.

Some chambers of commerce also have groups that assist new businesses. Sometimes, there are groups of retired executives that counsel new businesses. If your local chamber does not have this resource, ask the chamber director to identify some managers in the community who would be helpful with your type of business issues.

For almost every type of business, there is an industry association. These associations are typically great resources for advice and information on the latest trends and issues, especially technological and legislative issues. The library has books listing various associations, and many of them are on the Internet. They often have publications and meetings that can be a source of helpful advice. Identify association members in your area and seek out their advice.

People planning to help you are good sources of advice. For example, your accountant and lawyer can be good direct resources and often can refer you to others who can assist.

The challenge is not in getting advice. The challenge is sorting it out and deciding what to use.

When you collect advice, verify what you think you have learned. You can do this by checking with multiple resources. If the advice is confirmed by several different sources, you can start to rely on it. When there appears to be differences of opinion on important issues, seek the counsel of key sources, ones who have proven to be consistently reliable in the past. Often the differences result from varying interpretations and definitions.

Speed Bump

No matter how much you test the advice you receive, you should never view advice as 100 percent reliable. There is always a margin of error. The best you can do is to minimize error and recognize situations in which the advice might be wrong or inappropriate.

When you seek advice, carefully maintain the confidentiality of crucial elements of your business venture. Indicate an interest in starting a certain type of business, but do not divulge details that are unique to you.

The Path of Least Resistance

When you have an idea, you quickly discover, after you collect all the advice you can find, there are many routes to where you want to go. Which one is best?

For many, the number of routes serves only to confuse. The Five-Minute Manager is encouraged knowing there is more than one way. Advice is encouraging because if you encounter problems you know there are alternatives. While the Five Minute Manager ultimately chooses one direction, from his or her exploration of multiple alternatives he or she has backup plans if they are needed.

There are times when you get advice that suggests you can get to your destination in several ways, but it is more of a hindrance than help. This happens when you try to make the decision using only logic and emotion. Logic is never satisfied. There will always be uncertainty in the facts that will make a logical answer stand on wobbly ground. Emotions are highly variable. What makes sense today will not make sense tomorrow.

The answer lies in your heart, which is not emotional or logical. This provides a feeling about what is the right direction. This feeling is often centered in your heart, which is the seat of your intuition.

Consider This

It is easy to be worn out by the process of starting a new business. Leaders need to monitor their energy and reserve levels. Instead of pushing harder when times are tough, the best decision can be to pull back. You make the best decisions when you are calm and centered. Develop methods to center and calm yourself. Practice these regularly so when you need them you can quickly access your center. Your vision will be broader when you connect with your heart.

For those of us who have difficulty hearing that quiet voice, the intuition provides additional signals. Quiet yourself as you consider multiple options. Calm your emotions and let your logical mind rest. When you are as calm and centered as you can be, consider each option. Understand it. Then observe how your body reacts. If it is dull and heavy, then move on to the next option. When you body reacts with even a glimmer of joy and the faintest of an inner smile, you are getting close. See if you can make the option trigger even more joy. When you have maximized your joy, you know the best option.

You have found the path of least resistance, the path that is best for you and your project right now. A big step in personal growth is learning to trust this decision and follow it wholeheartedly.

Before you reach this point, you rely on your logical mind and emotions to express their perspectives. Most people are familiar with this basis of making decisions. As skilled as you can become with these tools, they have pitfalls that most people are very familiar with. Relying on logic and emotions can cause you to fall back into a state of confusion. As noted earlier, logic is seldom satisfied and emotions are constantly changing. Thus, the decisions you make in this state are riskier.

When you follow the path of least resistance your are connecting with your intuition, which is a higher mind ability that is not subject to the variability of emotions or the never-ending loops that logic can lead to.

Act and Reassess

In the last few pages, you have come a long way. You have collected, assessed, and prepared. Now is the time to act.

You know some important considerations to take before preparing a business plan. You know the path that you want to follow. Now act to make the business plan a reality. Something powerful happens when you act. Momentum is created, enthusiasm is unleashed, and creativity is at its highest.

Work on a section of your business plan and visualize what you are planning. Enjoy developing it. Use words that capture the imagination and excite the reader. Make it something you would want to read.

When you come to logical resting points, pause and reassess. Ask yourself questions. How can I make this stronger? How can this be clearer and more inspiring?

When you ask these questions and listen to your heart, you will get answers that take your ideas to the next level. Sometimes you cannot see the next level until you have actually built the foundation. The same is true for some levels higher than the next. It is important as you write and reassess that you use your powers of visualization. See and feel what it will be like when you create what appears in your business plan. Enjoy yourself and you will create a great business plan.

Personal Coaching

When you prepare a business plan, make the printed report look like an experienced professional developed it. After you have invested considerable time and effort in the substance of the plan, do not skimp on the form it takes. Use quality printers, paper, color where appropriate, and other touches to present your ideas and inspire confidence.

So You Want to Be Profitable?

For many business people, profits are a mystery. They should not be. When you study profitable companies, you find that they are better than other companies at giving their customers what they want. In fact, they go the extra step. They give customers more than expected at a price that is a great consumer value. Almost without exception in free markets, this is the formula for being very profitable.

REAL Customer Benefits

Too often large and small businesses fall in love with product features instead of benefits. They feel good because their product or service has a certain capability. It may even be a capability that competitors do not have. With this, they charge off to get others excited, find financing sources, and launch their business. Only a few days into operating the business, they are amazed and even slightly disillusioned that customers do not beat a path to their door. What went wrong?

It is as simple as this: The company did not offer real benefits to customers. Maybe they have real benefits, but the way they communicate these makes it very difficult for the customers to see these benefits.

One of the most common mistakes is to tell customers about a product or service's features instead of its benefits. A very simple example is when a company focuses on an ingredient and not the benefit of that ingredient. If you only say that a product is sweetened with Nutrasweet, the customer is left to fill in the rest of the details. If instead you say the product has no calories, this is of benefit to those who are concerned with the number of calories. Nutrasweet alone is not a benefit. It is what Nutrasweet does that is a benefit. It sweetens a product without adding calories. Benefit language directly communicates how a product's feature helps the customer. Feature statements are often good explanations or reasons that help the customer know why there is a benefit.

Sometimes providing real benefits is as easy as changing the language used to communicate with customers. In other situations, the problem can be much more serious, if, for instance, there are no real customer benefits.

Sometimes companies add new technology to a product to change the way it performs. For example, an electric toothbrush company decides to add a small computer chip. This chip allows the toothbrush to operate at six different speeds and operates an indicator that tells the number of revolutions per use. The company thinks adding a computer chip, six speeds instead of one speed, and a record of how many times the rotating brush scrubbed the teeth is a great way to distinguish itself from a crowded field of electric toothbrushes. It launches a major advertising campaign lauding it as the toothbrush for the new millennium. Stores are stocked and ready to sell. Unfortunately, two weeks later the new toothbrushes have only collected dust. Although they sell at a attractive introductory price, customers do not want or need the benefits the company has put into its toothbrush for the new millennium.

The lesson? Know what your customers want. It often is as simple as asking them if they want the benefits. Sometimes, just asking is not enough. In this case, you need to run a test market to determine if customers will pay for the benefits and to see if the way you communicate the benefits is persuasive.

Consider This

If you are a small business with a small or nonexistent consumer research budget, go to where customers buy products such as yours. Interview people as they buy a product to learn why they buy a particular brand. Learn how they use it and what is really important to them. Talk to retailers or distributors to learn what they hear from purchasers. When you have this information, recognize that it is helpful but not gospel. Your sample of people is not representative of all your customers.

You must provide real benefits in a way that is easy for customers to understand. This rule is simple but is violated often, to the great regret of many companies.

Companies that do provide real benefits are profitable, often very profitable. Intel and Microsoft provide benefits other companies do not match. The same is true for companies such as Starbucks, Dell Computer, and Wal-Mart. They all give customers more of what they really want than their competitors do. Consequently, they make above average profits year after year.

Value, Value, Value

Great value and profitability are linked. The company that provides the best value is often the market share and profit leader of an industry.

Value can be a challenge to precisely measure and define. It usually is composed of multiple customer benefits, some that may be generic to the type of product and others that are unique to one company.

Toyota is an example of a company with a complex value equation. For the most part, the functionality of its cars is similar to Ford, Chevy, Chrysler, Honda, and Nissan. They are made out of metal, seat four to six passengers, have four tires, and engines with about the same horsepower. The price can vary but there are no major price differences. The main features, such as air conditioning, ABS, and air bags are available in all models.

Despite these similarities, Toyota makes some of the best selling cars. For two years, the Camry has been the best selling car in America. Toyota is also one of the most consistently profitable vehicle companies.

Toyota is an example of a company for which a better reputation makes a big difference in the value equation. Although the raw materials and general functionality are similar, Toyota provides quality that is of great benefit to many customers. Consumers value less frequent breakdowns and the sense of confidence that comes from driving a Toyota.

Speed Bump

Be cautious. Consumer research consistently demonstrates that different groups of consumers buy products for different reasons. What one group values highly is meaningless to another group. Only quality quantitative research can define the types of consumers who buy your product and what they value most.

This is also an example in which it is difficult to measure the value of reputation. In financial terms, how much lower would Ford need to price its Taurus to convert potential Camry purchasers into Taurus purchasers? This is difficult to answer with precision; quality research can only approximate an answer.

The Toyota example is one in which reputation for quality adds value. There are many other ways, including adding improved functionality at little or no increase in price.

When you win the value battle with competitors, you usually win the profitability battle, too.

Service Superstar

The way many companies distinguish themselves to customers and on their bottom line is by becoming service superstars.

So many products today are functionally similar. There is also considerable price parity among these products. To make matters worse, for many products, there is not much hope for a major advancement in functionality. What more can a bar of soap do?

Cars are also an example of mature product challenges. Twenty years ago, only fairly expensive cars had the latest in safety equipment. In this same period, only the most expensive cars, such as Mercedes and BMW, had high quality reputations. Today, new cars at virtually every price level have all the latest safety equipment. Cars of a middle price range, such as Camry, have quality ratings equal to or higher than some of the most expensive cars. There are modest design differences, and the brands still have some image appeal with groups of consumers.

Manufacturers are left with little meaningful differentiation between products. With advances in functionality seeming less likely, some companies have taken a service approach to distinguishing themselves. This approach has been successful for two new car companies. Saturn's cars are good but not functionally exceptional. Their styling is impressive but not extraordinary. Their prices are not a great value compared to their competition.

Saturn was successfully introduced into an industry that has already had many car brands. Their success is built around the proposition that they are a different kind of car company. One of the main differences is in how they price and sell their cars. The sticker price is the selling price, which removes the painful need to negotiate. For many customers, this is a major positive. Saturn has also built a reputation for friendly repairs. These two service elements generate most of their success, which is admirable given they sell parity cars in an already crowded class.

Personal Coaching

One way to become a service superstar is to become faster at a particular function. Twenty-minute oil change companies did not exist 15 years ago in such number. Today, they do the majority of oil changes. The oil change has gone from a half to full day at the new car dealer or mechanic to 20 minutes.

Lexus and Infinity were successfully introduced into a segment that Mercedes and BMW seemed to own. There were several elements associated with their success, and service was only one of them. For example, a new, higher level of quality and very attractive introductory pricing were essential to their early success. Another factor was the level of service they provided in the showroom and in their service operations. In the showroom, their sales people received special training on how to make the purchasing experience a positive one. Surveys rate their sales and service functions among the best. Within a relatively short period, Lexus grabbed the number one luxury car share position and Infinity became a serious contender.

Wal-Mart is an example of a company that dethroned retailers like Sears and K-Mart, using service as an important element of its journey to the top. Its better service comes from little things that do not cost it more. This includes someone greeting you when you come in the store. This is a great help if you do not frequently shop there. There are friendly associates in the departments. They also have great prices and selection; however, Sears and K-Mart were no slouches in these areas.

Superstar service can be as simple as treating people with respect and expressing gratitude for a customer's business. Five-Minute Managers find the best way to develop great service is to be customers of their own businesses. They also become customers of their competitors. They want to know what it feels like to be customers. Not many people in business look at business this way. Five-Minute Managers find it very informative.

They develop compassion for the customer's experience and this spurs their creativity. They develop ways to address buying issues and to make sure the experience is a pleasant one.

Location—Make It Easy

We have already seen the importance of a good location to business success. This section focuses on the role it plays in enhancing profitability.

There are two dimensions to making your business easy to find. The first is how easy it is for customers to find your place of business. Consider the following:

➤ If you have a retail store, visible location, high traffic, and the right kind of traffic are crucial. If you are on a busy street but tucked out of sight, your location is not helping you. If you sell high-priced products in an area with poor demographics, you will struggle.

➤ Invest considerable effort in the store's sign. This starts with the name. If you have a long name, it will be hard to read. Resist the temptation to be clever if it means having a three to five word name. It will seem clever to you, but no one will see it. Learn from names like Wal-Mart, Sears (whose formal name is Sears and Roebuck), Kinko's, and K-Mart. Make the type style bold and easy to read. Fancy type often makes a name hard to read. It needs to be instantly readable. Be sure to have a lighted sign on even during the day, especially cloudy days.

➤ Look for additional sign opportunities. Maybe you can have your name added on the

Speed Bump

You are not the only one who recognizes the importance of location. Consequently, good locations can be costly. Look for hidden visibility potential—erecting a new sign or having an easy-to-remember address, such as 1,200 for the number.

shopping center sign. Where permitted by sign codes, consider special banners announcing sales. Also, consider placing placard signs on street corners. Be creative. Small, highly visible billboards can be helpful. Look around your area and creatively explore every opportunity for helping people find your business easily.

➤ If you run ads in print or television, strongly consider adding a map or some clever reference to your location. It is a waste of money if your ad generates interest in your business only to have the interest vanish because of a perception that you are difficult to find.

➤ If you have an Internet business, consider making your URL your business name. Look at Amazon.com. Their name is their address. If you have a site, regularly register it with search engines. Also explore partnerships with other popular and related sites where you can have your name listed.

Personal Coaching

When your business is small, it can be difficult for customers to find you. When you have a small store or one in a less than ideal location, you need to be creative. Use color to attract people—fire engine red works. Make your windows work creatively for you. Decorate them in highly imaginative ways and change the look every week. Are there opportunities to go further with a sign or floating balloon? Do not let the unusual stop your efforts to be seen.

These ideas are just to make you start thinking. As Five-Minute Managers explore their unique situations, they discover additional possibilities for making their locations well-known and easy to find.

A second dimension of location is making it easy for customers to find what they want once they find you. Clearly marked signs and logical locations help. Consider providing a store map for people, if appropriate.

In a retail store, do not think about how much you can cram into the available space. Rather, think about how you can make products easy to find and examine.

If your business is on a Web site, be sure that people can quickly determine and go to the major sections of the site from the first page. A site map here is very helpful for extensive Web sites. Do what is easiest for customers, not what is easiest for you.

Optimizing these two dimensions of location is a major down payment towards on both immediate and long-term profitability. In businesses where products and prices are at parity, location can be the defining difference.

Innovator

Nothing ensures long term profitability like constant innovation that enhances consumer value and benefits.

Often it is such a struggle to launch and maintain a business that managers forget about investing in innovation. For Five-Minute Managers nothing is more important.

Five-Minute Managers constantly learn from customers and competitors. As they learn, they reflect and turn on their creativity. They love playing with new ideas that will help customers. They are constantly bouncing ideas off customers. They listen well and are excited by co-creating innovative ideas with their customers.

No idea is too small to consider. Think about the following:

➤ The printed instructions on how to use your product may benefit from improvement. Maybe it means replacing words with pictures. Sometimes color or increasing the print size helps. Five-Minute Managers try out the new instructions with new customers.

➤ The packaging for a product is frequently overlooked. Can it be improved to better communicate the benefits of the product? Is it too cluttered? Are there opportunities to replace words with pictures? How can it be made more convenient?

➤ Sometimes increasing the number of product options helps consumers. In other cases, dramatically decreasing options helps consumers who are confused about which is best for them and, therefore do not buy.

➤ One of the biggest and most overlooked innovations is lowering product cost with a less expensive material or method that at the same time improves customer benefits. These win-win ideas are sometimes difficult to find but they are there waiting to be discovered. Five-Minute Managers expect to find one major idea a year.

These are examples of some smaller areas where innovation helps customers. Of course, there are larger areas, such as overall product performance and pricing policies in which innovation can make an immediate difference. Sometimes such innovations occur infrequently, so Five-Minute Managers focus on the smaller areas to maintain a steady stream of improvements. Incrementally, they make a difference. They alter the competitive balance and steadily improve profitability.

Sage Advice

"Most new things are not good, and die an early death; but those which push themselves forward and by slow degrees force themselves on the attention of mankind are the unconscious productions of human wisdom, and must have honest consideration, and must not be made the subject of unreasoning prejudice."
—Thomas Brackett Reed (1839–1902), U.S. Republican politician

Personal Coaching

Experience the benefits of innovation in all parts of your life. For example, explore new ways of choosing a family vacation or organizing family chores. Invite the family to be involved in the innovation process—make it fun.

Reliable

One of the most powerful ways of increasing customer loyalty is by becoming increasingly reliable.

Five-Minute Managers recognize that reliability has several dimensions.

➤ Reliability means having consistent store hours that meet the needs of customers.

➤ Reliability means having the products that customers want when they need them. Out-of-stock situations should be low to nonexistent.

➤ Reliability means quickly fixing or replacing a product when it does not work.

➤ Reliability means telling customers of any important changes before they happen. If you are moving to a new location, your customers can rely on you to tell them and help you find the new location.

➤ Reliability means stable prices. Customers do not like surprises, such as wide fluctuations up or down in prices. If there is a significant increase coming, alert your customers. If a significant decrease is coming, issue credits for customers who bought just before the decrease.

When Five-Minute Managers are viewed as reliable by their customers, loyalty helps insulate the Five-Minute Manager from unexpected competitive moves. This enhances profits.

The Long-Term Success Guide

So often, the focus is on short-term results. For a publicly held company, the focus is usually on quarterly profits. For a small business, it can be on daily receipts. This focus is good, but not when it comes at the expense of the long-term view. The long term is at minimum one year away, but there should also be some thinking about the three to five year horizon.

Sage Advice

"Life is what happens while you are making other plans."
—John Lennon (1940–1980), British rock musician, in the song "Beautiful Boy"

Life Is a Journey

When you start a business, do you expect to be in business for a month or two or a few decades? If the answer is the latter, then act like it. When you are in an already established business the same question is relevant.

Sometimes managers run businesses as if they are running a sprint. In truth, it is more like running a marathon. The training and strategy for running a sprint and a marathon are very different.

By seeing business and life as a journey, you reconnect with the dream that inspires you. When you only focus on the daily or monthly business needs, the mundane consumes you, and you lose sight of the dream.

By seeing life as a journey, you prepare for the long haul. That results in investments in research and development and a commitment to innovation. By truly seeing life as a journey, you greatly increase the likelihood that profits will be steadily maintained and grow over the life of the business.

Learn, Learn, Learn

Besides seeing life as a journey and preparing for that journey, a commitment to learning is the biggest step Five-Minute Managers can take to ensure long-term profitability. Many businesses become complacent or cocky after they achieve success. If you see your competitor do this, it is a sure sign that in the future some of their customers will be your customers—unless you succumb to the same disease.

Other chapters discussed the importance of learning and of staying current with your business. Institutionalize learning in your business. It must not occur vicariously. It needs to be conscious, planned, and honored.

Strong Reserves

Five-Minute Managers know that strong reserves are critical to long-term success. Although there can be brief periods of success when reserves are depleted, routinely low reserves mean that when you need to surge with extra effort there may not be the resources with which to respond.

Maybe the most important reserves are personal reserves. If you are always giving your maximum effort, your body will run down and your mind will not be sharp. You need both to be normally running at about 75 percent. This leaves some reserves for responding to emergencies. More importantly, when a crisis emerges, you can calmly and clearly determine the best response. A tired mind responds, but it is not likely to give the best response.

Other reserves for long-term success are financial. If you have a line of credit, do not use it or use less than half of it. Routinely contribute to reserves for the replacement of important assets. Build retained earnings to provide a cushion for a crisis.

People reserves are also important. If one of your important managers leaves, who will replace that person? Always have backups for key positions. Ideally, it is someone in the company whose

Personal Coaching

You know personal reserves are important, but do others you are close to and depend on know this? They may not. Watch for signs that personal reserves are low—irritability, for example. Help family members see what is tough for them to see— that their reserves are low. Help them immediately re-create their reserves by giving them the rest of the day off, for example.

training enables them to step in if needed. If not, have your eye on someone you would hire if the need arose.

Pick Battles; Don't Burn Bridges

Even Five-Minute Managers find themselves in an occasional serious disagreement. Sometimes a disagreement is the only way to draw out the true differences needing resolution.

Five-Minute Managers are careful not to let a disagreement turn into bridge-burning where a relationship is severely impaired. Burning bridges only creates losers among both parties. This lose-lose method to problem solving can lead to lingering disagreements.

When you have burned bridges during a serious disagreement, it is not unusual for the issues to resurface in a painful way. One party may seek revenge or support from a competitor. When bridges are burned, wounds fester and injuries linger—especially wounded egos.

When Five-Minute Managers are involved in a bridge burning disagreement, they immediately get the repair effort underway. They know the power of forgiveness. They know how to focus objectively on the issues and to find a win-win solution when given a second chance.

Stretch Your Risk Muscles

Risk is an interesting issue all people in business face. How much risk should you take and how do you determine the amount of risk involved in a decision? These are difficult questions, but they can be answered with fair precision with the appropriate resources.

As a business grows, the Five-Minute Manager's knowledge and experience grows with it, which allows for more knowledgeable risk choices.

Consider This

The larger companies manage risk through pre-market simulation models. These models are based on the experience of many previous products. Often if a new idea does not achieve a target score in this test, it is scrapped or revised. Ultimately the simulation is not a replacement for the actual test market, in which the difference is that people need to spend their own money for a product.

Over the long term, their disaster preparation builds Five-Minute Managers' willingness to take risks. They know that if things do not go as expected they have options. They have learned that sometimes the unexpected, even the apparently "bad" unexpected, can lead to better ideas and results. Thus, when they take risks, they think through the downside and prepare for it. Over the long term, they become better at risk management. This reduces actual risk and increases long-term profitability.

How's Your Balance?

Balance in life means that you nurture all your roles. Many people in business find themselves out of balance, primarily because they spend too much time on work.

You need to routinely—once a month, at minimum—check your life balance. If you follow the Stephen Covey time management approach, each week you set goals for each of the roles in your life. Are you achieving the goals you set for all the roles? If not, what can you do right now to get balanced? Often it means you are putting too much energy into one role and need to give greater quality attention to another role.

The benefit of seeing that life has various roles is it allows you to focus on each. Where those roles involve others, like family members, you can involve family members in the objective setting for the week. This team effort helps brings you into balance.

The risks of extended unbalanced periods in your life are great. Divorce, family rupture, dissolved business partnerships, and financial hard times are only some of the more obvious ones. These are well known and predictable if you go through them for extended periods. So, Five-Minute Managers wisely work hard to achieve balance and monitor their effectiveness at achieving it. This is not a hollow goal.

Personal Coaching

Provide services and policies to help associates create balance in their lives. Consider negotiating a group rate with a nearby day care provider. Provide flexible hours whenever possible. Allow associates to purchase more vacation time.

Success Resources You Need But Don't Have Today

You may not have considered some resources. Several inexpensive resources can make a big difference in achieving profitability, often in difficult-to-measure ways.

You can easily access most of these resources. In most cases, they involve taking care of yourself, an area that many business managers neglect.

A Personal Coach

At several times, this book has indicated situations in which a personal and business coach can help. Coaches have multiple qualities. They have quality, relevant life experiences that they have successfully navigated. Their training helps them use those experiences to help others. Maybe more than anything, a coach has an intense desire to help others. Their life experiences, desire to help others, and coaching skills often help people take bigger strides in life.

In business, coaches can help in several ways:

➤ They help with the thinking process on a project. Coaches ask questions and suggest avenues of exploration that managers do not think of themselves. Coaches draw upon their objectivity and business skills to help show the way.

➤ They help with goal setting and achievement. Coaches typically request that a person reach higher than already reaching. Coaches see potential and paths to success that managers alone do not typically see. The result is that most coaching fees are more than paid for by the additional financial gains you achieve.

➤ They help with career management. If managers want to put themselves on the fast track to a promotion or change careers, coaches provide powerful assistance. Their assistance usually involves helping managers discover their own inner wisdom. Coaches seldom tell a person what to do. They make suggestions and ask questions. As managers react to the suggestions and questions, they discover the answers.

➤ They help with life balance issues. Coaches are very familiar with the issues and challenges of achieving balance in life. They usually have a variety of assessment tests that help managers determine where they are today and how they are progressing. Coaches are action-oriented and help managers identify their paths to fuller, more rewarding lives.

➤ They help with the implementation of new concepts and training programs. Introductory meetings launch many ideas with great fanfare. Later, some of these ideas only falter, due to lack of ongoing nurturing and coaching. Personal coaches work with individuals to help them develop the skills and then live them—talk the talk and walk the walk. By focusing coaching on important leaders and getting them to move forward, the momentum necessary successfully to implement a new direction is created.

Speed Bump

When you find a new idea that interests, check it out before you fully embrace it. Often other writers with different perspectives address the same idea. Check out critics of an idea to see if you agree with their thinking. When you have fully researched it, go forth and have fun growing with the new idea.

If you are looking for a personal coach, the Internet is a good resource. Both Coach University (www.coachu.com) and the International Coach Federation (www.coachfederation.org) have coach referral resources at their Web sites.

The Latest and Best Success Books

Many managers develop greater and greater focus on what they are doing. Whereas this feels right, there is the risk of developing too narrow a focus. A coach can broaden your view, but there are also many good books that can help.

Too often, you find reasons not to read. You are too busy, and when you do have time, you are too tired.

Reading the latest and best success books is one of the best investments you can make. It is a form of personal research and development.

Today it is easy to find the latest and best books. If you go to Internet bookstores, you can search by subject, read reviews by other readers, and determine how popular a book is relative to others. There are forums on CompuServe where you can exchange book recommendations. Talk with other readers and check out your local library.

Today there is no excuse. You can always find a good book.

Personal Journal

A personal journal is a hidden power tool of personal growth.

A journal is a place to conduct private explorations that may later have public manifestations. It is where you conduct a personal dialogue. This dialogue is free-flowing and no one can judge it. It is progressive and frequently insightful. A personal journal is often a best friend.

A journal can be a record of events, but its highest purpose is a confidential record of thoughts. These are thoughts that you may not be conscious of until you contemplate and write. By getting in touch with these often subconscious thoughts, you have access to them. When you have access to them, you can change them, if they are not serving your highest good.

If you do not keep a personal journal now, read a book on journaling and talk to someone who has kept a journal for several years. With this input, start doing it your way. Let it evolve to serve your personal growth.

Power Door

Five-Minute Managers use both an open and a closed door as a special tool to help them build their businesses.

Sage Advice

"I am carrying out my plan, so long formulated, of keeping a journal. What I most keenly wish is not to forget that I am writing for myself alone. Thus I shall always tell the truth, I hope, and thus I shall improve myself. These pages will reproach me for my changes of mind."

—Eugéne Delacroix (1798–1863), French artist

They use an open door to invite people to share ideas. Just as they manage by wandering around, they know others reciprocate. They want others to feel free to stop by and share ideas. Five-Minute Managers also tend to work in open environments, such as cubicle office space with no floor-to-ceiling walls. They want the physical openness to invite open relationships.

Five-Minute Managers in non-cubical offices also occasionally close the door. The closed door allows quiet time to focus on an issue. This is especially helpful when they want to let creativity flow. The lack of interruptions allows them to be calm and quiet, two conditions that are conducive to doing their most creative and insightful work.

Many managers do not recognize the power in a door. Five-Minute Managers use their doors as power management tools.

The Least You Need to Know

➤ Determine 100 obstacles you face and, with lots of advice, develop ten solutions for every problem.

➤ Make sure you have real customer benefits that you deliver with great value and service.

➤ A commitment to learning, creating reserves and consistently having a balanced life is crucial to long-term success.

➤ Having a personal coach and reading the best books on success are both great investments in you.

Part 6
The Five-Minute Life

There is much more to life than business. Everyone fulfills many roles in life—parent, friend, and community helper, for example.

In attempting to balance each role, you face many challenges. One challenge is the amount of time you choose to spend on each role. Another is how effectively you use the time you do have.

In this part, you learn how Five-Minute Managers take the powerful, yet simple skills used so well in business and apply them to family, social, and community life. Five-Minute Managers also know many low-cost, simple, and powerful tips on how to "Don't Worry, Be Happy."

Chapter 27

The Five-Minute Parent, Friend, and Helper

> **In This Chapter**
>
> ➤ How the Five-Minute Manager is also a Five-Minute parent
>
> ➤ Praise may be even more effective in families
>
> ➤ Five-Minute principles make social situations pleasant and constructive
>
> ➤ Helping in the community the Five-Minute way

Five-Minute Managers bring the principles that work in business into the rest of their lives. As parents, they understand the benefit of clear communication. Of course, family members love their practice praising them.

In their community roles, Five-Minute Managers find that the principles of Five-Minute Managing are particularly effective. They bring purpose and focus to community events, which make them much more productive for everyone involved. In social situations with friends, the principles enable Five-Minute Managers to take these relationships in new, more joyful directions.

The Five-Minute Parent

Five-Minute Managers love being parents. Other family members eagerly embrace the Five-Minute principles. The boundaries are clear; the feedback is welcomed, and its purpose understood.

When Five-Minute Management principles are first introduced to the family, there is a period of adjustment. Most of the adjustment involves learning the purpose behind actions and how to consistently use the skills.

Goals and Boundaries

In the Five-Minute Family, there is a system of goals and boundaries that enables family members to grow and know what they can and cannot do.

Goal setting is done differently than in a business in that it is less formal, but in most other aspects, it is very similar. The goals are set at a variety of levels.

The process starts with individual goals and builds to family goals. The children's goals are focused on what is most important in their lives during the time period. The period covered by the goals adjusts to meet important events. For example, if a school grading period covers August through November; then all school-related goals are set to coincide with that period.

Academic goals usually focus on achieving a certain grade at the end of a grading period. Goals are based on prior history and importantly include the candid input of the children. Not all goals should automatically become achieving an "A." Recall a very important aspect of goal setting is that the goal be achievable. If a child's grade history in a subject is consistent "C"s, receiving an "A" in the current period may not be achievable, even though it is desirable.

Personal Coaching

With children, there need to be rewards every week. When you review the week's results, celebrate the wins with a pizza party, movie rental, or special event that is meaningful to the children.

Many families establish informal grade goals, but these goals tend to be very general ("You will do better this time."). They might also be at the very high end of what is achievable. When this happens, the child's ownership of the goal is low.

What distinguishes the Five-Minute Family's goal setting is that there is a detailed plan of how the goal will be achieved. If old enough, the child develops this plan. It should include details such as the amount of daily study time, what hours studying should occur, and the kind of help needed. For example, a parent agrees to provide coaching on a specific subject on certain days at certain times. If a tutor is involved, those contributions are detailed.

The plan also includes a tracking system. It can be as simple as a handwritten record in the student's binder, with a copy posted on the refrigerator. For those who enjoy working on the computer, the updates are in an Excel table and color chart that they update and share weekly with their parents.

The goal-setting process begins with the children. They come to a family meeting or private session with parents prepared with their thoughts on goals. When they first begin the goal-setting process, it is a little awkward for some. As they learn the process, they love it when they do it right. Done right, it gives children considerable say on what they are going to do. They set remarkably honest and often challenging goals. They enjoy the process of tracking their progress and seeing the accomplishment of the goal unfold. They often achieve their goals. As a result, confidence builds and children learn that having a plan as a guide is the key to ultimate success.

There need to be goals for children outside of academics. For example, there can be some fun goals. A parent or both parents can agree to a goal to do an activity once a week that is fun for the child and that requires parental support. It could be driving to a local amusement park to play video games, miniature golf, and drive the go carts.

There might be reading goals that are separate from school. A parent agrees to read to a child for a certain period each day. There are bi-weekly library trips and an agreed-to number of pages or books to be read every period. Again, they can use some fun tracking systems.

The parents also set individual goals. For Five-Minute Managers, these might include how they are going to use their special day off each month. Goals can include time for extra self-care—a massage, daily meditation, or daily journal writing.

The goals can also include personal growth subjects. There can be books to read and seminars to attend. A person can use daily affirmations to change bad habits and to adopt new, more joyful ones. As with the children, the goals need to be specific, measurable, achievable, and compatible.

The period for adults' goals is appropriate to their situations. Some can be monthly, whereas others may be weekly or quarterly. They also need to track progress in either a journal or some informal but real tracking system.

Speed Bump

You and your kids both speak English but your versions are probably different. Be sure when you agree on goals and boundaries there is exquisite clarity. A significant difference of understanding over a couple of words can cripple a goal or boundary's effectiveness.

When individual goals are set, consider having a family meeting to set one or two family goals for a period. It can be a fun family vacation—choosing a destination, agreeing on a place to stay, and determining activities. The goals can be about how family members will treat each other. In this case, the specifics and the measures can be tricky. Families should strive to make it specific and measurable. Make sure everyone agrees to and understands the ground rules. To the greatest extent possible, these goals should be set by the group and achievable through group effort, not dictated by one or both parents.

The parents can also set goals. In addition to the types of goals already discussed, they might set saving and spending goals. These are easy to track and can be fun when the goals are achieved.

It is very important to note that the Five-Minute Family's life is driven not entirely by goals. Spontaneity is crucial. Along the path to achieving a goal, the family may learn that the goal needs to be changed or even abandoned.

Strange as it may seem, the purpose of setting goals is not to achieve them. Its purpose is to bring more love and joy into life. It is a means to that, not an end in itself.

Personal Coaching

For parents, financial goals are usually important. Consider having this be a joint project. Read a couple of books, attend seminars, and plan together. When both people develop common understandings, decision-making is easier and more productive.

Look for Opportunities to Praise

When all family members and the family as a whole have goals, there are many opportunities to deliver praise. The tracking systems and weekly reviews present wonderful opportunities for mini-celebrations. Some families designate a certain time on the weekend to review the previous week. It is an opportunity for the whole family to reward and recognize good deeds.

There are also more informal opportunities. A parent, for example, can visit with a child during homework time. Seeing an assignment done well, the parent delivers praise. The praise is specific and notes how the good work is helpful from a broader perspective.

Five-Minute Parents are not locked into recliners with remotes in hand. They prowl looking for opportunities to praise in the same way the Five-Minute Manager wanders around.

The Five-Minute Family knows that praise is not a one-way street. It is not only parents who praise their kids. Children learn the joy of praising. It is a wonderful learning opportunity for kids who often have difficulty praising. Often family meetings are a good place to learn how to do it. Children who praise brothers or sisters and parents learn a skill that serves them well in life.

Negative Feedback Delivered Right

As all families know, there is a time for negative feedback. It is part of the boundary setting process. Children and parents learn what they should not do and where they should not go.

Five-Minute Parents deliver negative feedback using the same guidelines as Five-Minute Managers. They deliver it as soon as the event occurs or when they learn of it. It is clear and to the point. It outlines the impact of the negative act. The negative feedback is objective and not personal. At the end, Five-Minute Parents reaffirm the child's worth and their confidence in using the negative feedback as an occasion to change behavior.

In the Five-Minute Family, negative feedback is not a one way street. Following the same guidelines, children share with their parents those actions that injured or hindered them. Children often find delivering negative feedback to a brother or sister in a family meeting to be especially challenging. Although it is difficult, when the skill is mastered is becomes a valuable life skill.

Consider This

Among children, emotions can be highly charged when negative feedback is involved. Many recommend a very soft, quiet voice when delivering negative feedback. When combined with words that do not put down the other person, the increased effectiveness can be dramatic.

Social Situations—Five Minutes at a Time

For Five-Minute Managers, the same principles seem to be particularly effective in social situations. Social situations have much in common with business situations. Recall the discussion of networking skills, which are called for often in situations that are part social and part business.

Is There a Purpose? Fun Is a Good One!

Do not go into a social situation without thinking about it first. When you do not think ahead, you leave it to your subconscious to make the choices. By default, it makes the choices you have always made. Some of these serve you well, whereas others clearly do not.

Before you even agree to attend a social function, think about what your purpose is and how you will achieve it. Consider the following:

➤ Are there opportunities to further a business project? Are the right people there to discuss this? What is appropriate to discuss and what is not?

➤ What are the personalities in this situation? Do they lift your spirits or do you usually come away grumpy? Are there people there whose interests stimulate and attract you?

➤ Are there any activities planned that are fun? If not, what would be fun to do in this situation?

Personal Coaching

If your social situations are not fun, set the example yourself. Invite people over for fun and games. Consider playing non-competitive games that involve everyone. If there are winners and losers, find a way to make everyone an eventual winner. Laughing is encouraged!

If the situation will not be positive and fun, seriously consider not going. Putting yourself into situations that are not positive only leaves you worse off after going to the event. Life is too short to put yourself into situations you do not enjoy.

If this means that you do not go to many or even most of the social situations that you are invited to, then have the courage to not go. Instead, create your own and invite the kind of people that lift your spirits and with whom you have fun. The difference will astound you.

If you have agreed to attend, reflect on your goals before attending. Let go of any lingering negativity from previous events in the day. Dragging those into a social situation can be recipe for failure. With your goal or goals in mind, reflect on how you will achieve them. What people do you want to connect with and what subjects do you want to discuss?

Speed Bump

When you are in a social situation, be careful about how much business discussion is appropriate. Some people like to get away form business and resent attempts to discuss business away from work. Others do not seem to be able to talk about anything else but work. Gauge what is comfortable to others when setting your goals.

When Five-Minute Managers discuss their subjects, they follow the five-minute rule. They present their views concisely and with purpose. They make it easy for others to comprehend their major points. They do not ramble and talk to hear themselves talk.

When you go in with a plan, you can adjust to the flow of the evening. Be sure to check frequently with your internal dialogue and feelings. If they are not positive, what can you immediately do to change them? Maybe you really did not dispose of feelings related to an earlier negative event. Whatever the cause, it is very difficult to have fun when negative thoughts dominate your internal dialogue.

Positive Power

Being positive is powerful in social situations. When you look for opportunities to praise a person in a conversation, you encourage them to share more with you. Often this increased sharing includes more good news.

In a social situation, Five-Minute Managers follow the spirit of the praise guidelines. Their praise is sincere and purposeful. They make eye contact and their body language is also positive. They praise when they experience the positive event. The praise is specific and the recipient understands its personal importance. It is delivered in five minutes or less.

People love to be around Five-Minute Managers in social situations because of the praise they receive. In social situations, the Five-Minute Manager looks for the positive events in another person's life. These are great opportunities to praise accomplishments.

Five-Minute Managers love social situations because they learn from others and reinforce the kind of positive events that uplift their spirits. As in the workplace, praise is win-win.

Clear, Unmistakable Boundaries

Five-Minute Managers in social situations also make it clear what they do not like. If someone expresses a personal prejudice, Five-Minute Managers do not support it with their presence. They clearly signal that such a discussion is not something in which they want to participate. If the humor is uncomfortable, they also do not support it with feigned laughter.

Five-Minute Managers also set their boundaries very early by what events they agree to attend. If there are some people at the event who create a negative environment, Five-Minute Managers avoid being drawn into situations with them. When appropriate, they provide negative feedback consistent with the negative feedback guidelines previously discussed. They are careful not to make it personal and to provide it privately when appropriate.

Sage Advice

"But the relationship of morality and power is a very subtle one. Because ultimately power without morality is no longer power."
—James Baldwin (1924–87), U.S. author

The Five-Minute Manager Helps the Community

Besides working in business and enjoying home, the Five-Minute Manager helps the community. He or she may serve as volunteers at a hospice or on the board of the local Red Cross chapter.

In their volunteer efforts, Five-Minute Managers use the same skills that make them successful at work and at home. They have clear objectives, enjoy praise, and know how to use negative feedback constructively.

Crystal Clear Objectives

Before Five-Minute Managers volunteer with charity or community organizations, they clearly understand their capabilities and desires. They desire to make a good match between an organization's needs and their possible contributions. A period of contemplation and discussion with a variety of people in the community reveals potential good matches. They then visit the organizations to learn more before making a final decision.

When Five-Minute Managers join an organization, they use their overall objectives to formulate objectives for each time they volunteer. They know the purpose of their time with the organization. Although they have a purpose, it is not unchangeable if they encounter new information. By defining an initial purpose, they make it a goal to be productive and helpful—not just to put in time. They are open to a different purpose if it emerges.

Where Positive Power Really Works

Praise seems to be especially effective when Five-Minute Managers work in the community. People who serve others seem to have a more positive outlook. When Five-Minute Managers initiate praise, it is well received and reciprocated. It even seems contagious.

Speed Bump

For people in business, it can be very difficult to understand fully the mission and activities of a community organization. The values and clients are often very different. To increase your effectiveness, work with an organization for a few days and be prepared to learn a lot.

Praise is greatly appreciated by people needing help. Hospice volunteers find that the dying love to reflect on the good things they achieved in their lives. The Red Cross volunteers who help a family with a burned-down home praise the family for their successful efforts to escape the fire. They keep their comments positive and provide the family with instant shelter and food. When a family has just faced its darkest disaster, positive energy is like a ray of light.

Five-Minute Managers praise other volunteers for their good deeds. Volunteers are special people who love to help others. Often they do not think of themselves. Thus, a Five-Minute Manager's praise is a wonderful personal moment.

How You Can Help

Community organizations often do not have an unlimited depth of available talent; they rely on volunteers to make the difference. For example, it is not unusual for a Red Cross chapter to have a ratio of thirty volunteers for every paid staff member. In addition, the pay in volunteer and charity organizations is lower than for comparable positions in business, often by as much as 25 percent.

Thus, there are wonderful opportunities to help. In an earlier section, the personal introspection process detailed how to find an organization that was a good match between your wants and the organization's needs. When you are in an organization, you will learn more about how you can really help. You will find opportunities to help in areas where you have expertise as well as areas in which you have little technical knowledge. The latter will utilize your general understanding of how to make things happen.

Try staying with an organization for at least five years and discover how your opportunities to help grow. As a skilled volunteer, you can often make a big difference in how much help is delivered to those in need. For Five-Minute Managers, these are some of the most satisfying times.

The Least You Need to Know

➤ The Five-Minute Parent uses goals and boundaries to facilitate growth by their children.

➤ Five-Minute praise principles add new joy to family life.

➤ Delivering family member criticism the Five-Minute way makes it constructive.

➤ Praise in social situations makes them fun and constructive when it is done the Five-Minute way.

Chapter 28

Getting Personal

In This Chapter

➤ Dealing with the challenges of daily life by being centered

➤ A joyful life lived through passion and connection to a higher power

➤ How a personal journal enriches your life

➤ Learn how much you trust yourself

Five-Minute Managers take care of themselves. They know the power of positive energy. As a result, they know what to do to lift their energy.

They know how to become invulnerable to the onslaught of negative energy that occurs at times. If they are stuck, they know how to get unstuck and bring more "delight" into their life. If they have a personal theme song it might be "Don't Worry, Be Happy."

How to Become Invulnerable

Five-Minute Managers know from experience that dealing with people with negative intentions can be unsettling. They have felt their energy shift from positive to negative. They do not like it and, at times, they struggle to return to a positive place. These struggles teach Five-Minute Managers valuable lessons on how to eventually become invulnerable to negative energy.

Be Centered

The number one action Five-Minute Managers take is learning to center themselves on their inner essence. Wherever they are, they connect with their inner wisdom. They want to make conscious choices, not choices out of habit that may not serve their higher good. When they do not make choices consistent with their higher good, they do not make win-win choices.

Personal Coaching

Becoming invulnerable to negative energy and events may sound impossible to some. To recognize that it is achievable, spend time studying and emulate some truly advanced being. For instance, many people emulate the Dalai Lama. His example, and the examples of people like him, is inspiring.

Staying centered all the time is not easy. Five-Minute Managers know two actions that make it easier. First, they create quiet time every day to connect with their inner essence or what some call their inner wisdom. The most effective quiet time activity is meditation. Meditation is a transforming experience. As little as twenty minutes a day, done consistently, will transform your life. The immediate benefit is that it enables you to center on your calm, inner wisdom.

Second, make sure your personal reserves are high. You are off center when you are tired and irritable. When you are calm but energized, you maintain your center even when a storm of negativity rolls into your life.

This is not easy, but focusing on meditation and personal reserves dramatically increases the amount of times your actions come from your deep inner wisdom.

In the Moment

The next steps Five-Minute Managers take are to become invulnerable to negative energy and to be in the moment. Being in the moment means you are totally focused on what is happening to you right now.

You may think that you are aware of what is happening to you most of the time. If you really observe yourself, however, you will find that you are not. Often your inner chatter is still fussing over a previous event. If this event was negative, you bring to the new situation an undercurrent of negativity. You also bring to a new situation your previous experiences with the person or situation. If these were negative, there is another undercurrent of negativity that influences the outcome of the current situation.

These undercurrents prevent you from being in the moment and having pristine awareness. When you are in the moment, you are free of preconceived notions. You are free of the past.

When you are in the moment, you are totally aware of what is occurring and you react with choices driven by your inner wisdom. You no longer react based on habits and preconceived notions. You consciously act with wisdom. Wisdom always leads to win-win results.

Consider This

Give the dishwasher a day off today. After the evening meal, wash the dishes. As you wash, see if you can focus only on the act of washing the dishes. As other thoughts come into your head, release them and bring your focus back to washing the dishes. Do this each time because it will likely happen many times. You have just experienced how difficult it can be to remain in the moment. You have also learned the basic skill of refocusing and letting go of intruding thoughts.

Openness

Openness occurs for Five-Minute Managers when they are free of the internal chatter and are in the moment. They are like blank pieces of paper ready to record all impressions. They hear all that is said and actively work to understand it. They are not in reply mode. They know that they cannot productively reply unless they truly understand.

There are many barriers to openness. Even if you enter a conversation when you are in the moment, you quickly can close yourself off. The easiest trigger is when someone says something that you choose to experience as a threat. It can be as simple as someone saying you did something wrong. You close up and cease to listen carefully. Your heart closes, which means you lose contact with the inner wisdom necessary to discover the win-win solution. If you are aware of the closure when it occurs, you can release the fear and tension and reconnect with your heart to keep it open.

Being in the moment is where you start. You want to stay open to your inner calm and wisdom. You will be amazed when you do this for the first time. You become invulnerable to the attacks if others. You choose peace when they choose anger. You choose the win-win solution, whereas they lose contact with what is right.

Passion

Do not be afraid to be passionate. It is OK to be enthusiastic and to love an idea or your work. If for no other reason, do it for yourself. When you are passionate, you fill yourself with positive energy. By being positive, you connect with more

Sage Advice

"There is only one passion, the passion for happiness."
—Denis Diderot (1713–1784), French philosopher

297

positive energy. When you are passionate, you often do your best work. When you are passionate, you are in the moment and impervious to the negativity of others.

Passion can be a two-edged sword. It helps, but it can hurt. When your passion damages your openness to what is going on around you, compassion and listening reach low levels. Sometimes you want others to share your passion, but they may have their own passions or do not care to share yours. This is OK. Resist the urge to force your passion on others. If it is going to be infectious, it will be. Do not force it.

Personal Coaching

Public opinion surveys and book sales reveal increasing interest in spiritual awakening. If you have wakening interest in the higher power connection that is right for you, start by being more alert to the spirituality around you. When you are in a bookstore, be conscious of what books you are drawn to. If you are reading the paper, check the seminar listing and weekend church section to see what interests you.

Your passionate focus keeps negative energy from penetrating your personal space. Passion does not have to be loud. It can be calm, joyful, and peaceful. Be passionate and let it make you invulnerable.

A Higher Power

Nothing makes you more invulnerable than connecting with a higher power. Meditation and spiritual practice are the best ways of making this connection. Spiritual practice can include church services, personal study, ritual, or nonsectarian practices.

The connection feels very personal and it is. It is also universal. When you connect with a higher power, you recognize the unity of all that is. Ultimately, this sense of unity leads to seeing everyone as your brothers and sisters. When this occurs, your ability to be open with others dramatically increases. Your compassion and wisdom are fully engaged and lead you to win-win solutions all the time.

Let a Personal Journal Help You

A personal journal is like a best friend who is always available and travels with you when you are thousands of miles from home. Everyone knows how helpful a best friend can be.

A personal journal is easy to start and easy to develop into a powerful happiness tool for your life. You will develop your own way of making it work for you.

Speed Bump

Your journal should be private. Alert family members of this and store it in a safe place. You do not want to be less than candid in your journal because you fear someone will read it.

A journal is a place to conduct private explorations that may later have public manifestations. It is where you conduct a personal dialogue. This dialogue is free-flowing and free of the fear of judgement. It is progressive and frequently insightful. A personal journal is often a best friend.

A journal can be a record of events, but its highest purpose is as a confidential record of thoughts. These are thoughts that you may not be conscious of until you contemplate and write. By getting in touch with these often subconscious thoughts, you gain access to them. When you have access to them, you can change those that are not serving your highest good.

Good bookstores carry a wonderful assortment of journals. Pick a style that fits you. Whereas many journals are for written comments, feel free to expand yours. Include friends' letters that you want to save. If you see a picture that attracts you, cut it out and put it in your journal. Take it with you on vacations during which you have the time to be contemplative and introspective.

If you do not keep a personal journal now, read a book on journaling and talk to someone who has kept a journal for several years. Using this input, start doing it your way. Let it evolve to serve your personal growth.

Clearer Goals

Personal explorations in a journal often lead to personal insights. These insights often point to better ways to live your life. It is in this process that the journal becomes a place to set major life objectives. Most people who do not have a personal journal do not have other regular means for exploring and recording major life objectives.

Sage Advice

"Where I would like to discover facts, I find fancy. Where I would like to learn what I did, I learn only what I was thinking. They are loaded with opinion, moral thoughts, quick evaluations, youthful hopes and cares and sorrows. Occasionally, they manage to report something in exquisite honesty and accuracy. That is why I have refrained from burning them."
—E. B. White (1899–1985), U.S. author, editor speaking of his own journals

When you use the journal during times of contemplation and quiet, the insights can sometimes be revelations. Revelations for most people are those moments of profound insight that produce a fundamental shift in their lives. Revelations lead you to more joy and love. They are the best advice of your inner wisdom.

The goals you set in your personal journal are clear and powerful. That is why some people refer to their journal as their personal power tool.

Life Simplification

In the moments you spend with your personal journal, life can become simpler. You see the essential simplicity and beauty of life. You see that what is really important to you is universally important to most people.

These insights lead to greater focus on your inner life and lesser focus on the outer life. The importance of material goods diminishes. You shift from external validation to internal validation. When this shift occurs, you see life can be simpler and happier.

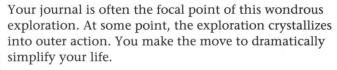

Your journal is often the focal point of this wondrous exploration. At some point, the exploration crystallizes into outer action. You make the move to dramatically simplify your life.

This is currently a national trend and several books and seminars are available on how to simplify life. Most people are amazed at the transformation. They have more reserves, time, and energy. They are happier more often. It may all have started with a few insights recorded in their journal.

A Quieter Life

Life automatically becomes quieter and calmer when you write in your journal. Whatever you did before you spent time with your journal was noisier and more active.

The introspection that occurs when you write in your journal may be new. Before keeping a journal, you may have been very outwardly focused. Beginning a journal may be the first time you look inward.

You enjoy the introspection that occurs while writing in your journal and find yourself being reflective and contemplative even at times you are not writing in your journal. It can be while driving or in a waiting room. Whenever you have idle time, you find yourself turning your focus inward. Many of the thoughts you have during these time eventually end up in your journal. When you embark on keeping a journal, you open yourself to the quiet and wonderful world of contemplation.

Sage Advice

"Simplicity, simplicity, simplicity! I say, let your affairs be as two or three, and not a hundred or a thousand; instead of a million count half a dozen, and keep your accounts on your thumb-nail."
—Henry David Thoreau (1817–1862), U.S. philosopher, author, naturalist

Speed Bump

Create speed bumps in your life that remind you to slow down and enjoy the quiet. Put it in ink on your to-do list. Set an alarm that reminds you that now is the time to be quiet. Signal to family members how important this is to you.

Power

As subtle and cozy as a journal can be, it is also very powerful. It is the only place where you consistently share your inner most thoughts. That sharing often prompts insights, revelations, and actions.

Your journal is the one place you can look back and track steps along your personal evolutionary path. When changes seem to occur at a glacial pace, the perspective of a few years underscores how far you have come. This progress fuels confidence and further commitments to more progress.

The goals set in a journal seem to have special power. The commitments made here are deeply personal. They come from your inner wisdom, so the truth and goodness of the goals resonate strongly. They are in harmony with the person you really are.

Getting Unstuck

Despite their best efforts, Five-Minute Managers sometimes finds themselves stuck in negative energy. It manifests as irritability, anxiety, and even anger. Five-Minute Managers do not like it, but the negative energy seems to hold a special power over these days.

Fortunately, Five-Minute Managers know how to become unstuck. There are simple steps that can help you shift and become liberated.

Sunshine

There is amazing power in sunshine. Some people suffer the blues in winter, when they do not get enough sunshine. Science confirms that sunshine deprivation does cause a chemical imbalance that leaves some people feeling down. Remedy it with sunshine or full spectrum light. Be cautious about spending too much time in the sun. For prolonged periods, use a good sunscreen.

Even if you do not suffer from sunshine deprivation, exposing yourself to the sun for a period each day can do wonders. The next time you feel down, go outside and lay in a comfortable spot in the sun. Spend about 20 minutes. Each minute that you are there, feel and celebrate the rays of the sun. Feel them penetrating deep into your body. They comfort and nourish you. Stay in the moment for the 20 minutes. When you are finished, check your energy level. Most people are uplifted, and some even experience a complete lifting of the negative energy that has plagued them.

Sage Advice

"The Sun, the hearth of affection and life, pours burning love on the delighted earth."
—Arthur Rimbaud (1854–1891), French poet

Call a Friend

Call a friend who always makes you laugh. This person can be someone who is close or someone you have not talked to in a long time. Choose carefully, because you do not want to call someone who will unload negative energy on you. Your purpose is to be uplifted and shift from the negative energy that seems to dominate your consciousness.

When you start the conversation, you may ask, "What good things are going on in your life?" This question gets the conversation going in the direction you need. If you are so inclined, ask, "Have you heard any good jokes lately?" You can ask about good comedy clubs or fun parties a person has been to recently. The whole purpose is to connect you with positive energy.

Consider This

Besides telephone calls, consider a strong e-mail relationship. Some Internet Service Providers and services like AOL and CompuServe alert you when a buddy is online. You can go to a private chat room. As higher speed Internet access expands, you will be able to put a camera on the top of your monitor and have chats with pictures.

Recharge yourself with this kind of conversation, and the person you call is also uplifted. It is a win-win solution.

Rest

When you are in a negative place, it is often because your energy reserves are depleted. When you are tired, you are easily irritated.

The remedy is simple: Get some rest. Take a nap, even if you seldom take one. It can be a delicious experience. After you have recovered from the grog of the nap, you feel fresh. It may take more than a single nap, so plan to sleep in on the weekend and do not schedule any activities. Rest and pick up a book you have wanted to read. If you exercise frequently, it can wear you out, so take a day off and recuperate.

Rest is wonderful elixir that restores the body. You replenish depleted reserves and you feel renewed. Congratulate yourself for the self-care steps you have taken.

Music

You know there have been times when you have listened to music that has completely shifted your mood. You know this, yet you do not use this wonderful experience enough.

Put on some of your favorite music and play it loud. Dance with the music; sing with it. Feel its energy. Play music that reminds you of fun times. Play music that inspires you.

Play music until you notice a smile on your face. Now play it a little longer to let that positive energy become well established. Change gears and play a different kind of music. If you were listening to rock, shift to your favorite country tune. If you do not have a favorite alternative type of music, play a great version of "Amazing Grace." Judy Collins and Cecilia have

Sage Advice

"Music is spiritual. The music business is not."
—Van Morrison (b. 1945), Irish rock musician

great renditions. A song that may surprise you is Dolly Parton's "He's Alive" (referring to Jesus), which she sings as an encore at some of her concerts.

Change the Subject

When you dwell on a subject with negative energy, changing your mood can be as simple as changing the subject to one that is positive.

The tough part of this approach is that the negative energy can feel like it has a tight grip on you. Relax and let go. Visualize breathing out the negative energy as you exhale. On the in breath, replace the negative energy with positive energy.

This loosens the grip but may not entirely remove it. Now think of a fun, positive subject. When you first try, it may be difficult to stay with it. The negative subject wants to dominate. Shift your location. Get up and move about. Now muster your will power and focus on the positive subject. Stay with it. If you are not successful at first, be tenacious. While being tenacious, also be soft and easy. Do not struggle. Let the positive energy flow.

Now that you have the positive subject in your consciousness, act on it. Do something that brings it to life. Maybe it is planning a specific time to do it again. It can be talking with someone about it. Find some action you can take that brings the positive energy even closer to you.

Do a Good Deed

Nothing shifts you from being stuck in a negative place faster than doing a good deed for someone. It can be a very simple act. You can help someone carry a heavy load, open a door, offer a smile, or praise them. It can be complicated act also. You can commit to a walkathon or volunteer at a hospice.

When you see the smile of someone you have helped, notice how your energy shifts. It is as if you have received a shot of positive energy.

Now do another good deed. Good deeds are easy and usually inexpensive. There is no excuse for not doing them. Do not use the excuse that you are stuck in a negative place. It requires a small act of will power to take one step in a positive direction. One step leads to another.

If you are committed to becoming unstuck, these steps will individually and collectively help you shift to a more positive place.

Personal Coaching

Take delight in planning good deeds. Set a day about a week in advance. Then lay out a plan and make sure there is no time pressure involved. Take delight in the planning by visualizing your good deed. It will be a rich and memorable experience for the giver and the recipient.

Add a Strong Dose of "Delight" to Your Life

Five-Minute Managers recognize the power of positive energy. They proactively take steps to nourish constantly the conditions in which positive energy can flourish.

There are specific steps Five-Minute Managers regularly take to stay connected with positive energy. Like the getting unstuck steps, these actions are fun, easy, and cheap. There are no excuses for not taking these daily steps.

Optimism Power

Science demonstrates in several studies that optimists have better lives. Not only are they happier, they are also healthier than pessimists. It seems that positive energy helps your immune system to fight off whatever invades the body.

Consider This

There are many wonderful books on the power of optimism. None may be better that Norman Vincent Peale's *The Power of Positive Thinking*. Reverend Schuller of the Crystal Cathedral also has an extensive series of books on this theme that are easy, inspiring reading.

On a very practical basis, optimism is an undercurrent that keeps Five-Minute Managers connected to positive energy. Five-Minute Managers recognize that they have choices every time they react. They can have a positive reaction all the time if that is their choice.

Positive thinking is not artificial. As you connect with your inner wisdom and recognize the presence of a higher power, you find that all of this points in a very positive direction.

100 Smiles per Day

Smiling, so it has been said, requires fewer muscles and less energy than a frown. If it is easier, why not smile more than you frown. Why frown at all?

Right now, while reading this, pause. Smile. Pay close attention to how you feel. The very act of smiling shifts energy for most people. It can be subtle, but it can also be very noticeable.

The act of smiling brings more delight into your life. Now smile 100 times a day. That is less than 10 times an hour for every hour you are awake.

Smile at strangers, friends, dogs, trees, flowers, cars, and houses. In the next 24 hours, take a smile walk. As you walk, be in the moment, focused only on what you see, hear, smell, touch, and taste. When you experience something that is even slightly positive, smile. Feel the sensation of smiling. It has taken a low-level positive experience and lifted it up to an even more positive one.

You can do this anywhere. If you jog, look at the trees, flowers, and lawns. As you see each of them smile, and say good morning to them. If you are concerned about what others may think, say it only to yourself. Notice how positive it makes you feel. You can get all 100 smiles done on this jog!

Sage Advice

"If you have only one smile in you, give it to the people you love. Don't be surly at home, then go out in the street and start grinning 'Good morning' at total strangers." —Maya Angelou (b. 1928), U.S. author, quoting her mother's advice

A Delightful Group

Find delight in a group of people who lift each other's spirits. Members of a fun group support each other and can laugh together. An especially good sign is when members of the group can laugh at themselves.

If you do not have such a group now, start one. Maybe it is a breakfast or lunch group. The time is less important than who attends. Choose only people who bring positive energy most of the time. You need also to consider how people interact with each other. You can make this complex, but don't. Follow your heart and act. If it is not right the first time, then fix it later.

A Delightful Place

Treat yourself this week by going to the most delightful place you know. This can vary dramatically for each of us. For some it might be near a waterfall in the woods and for others it can be at Nordstrom.

A delightful place is one where smiles automatically appear. It is like nourishment for your soul. You relax and get positive energy from the experience.

If you have only one special place, dedicate your special day for yourself to finding another one or two. Look for places that are close to where you live so that you can connect with them every day or week. Some people establish a sanctuary in their home. It can be where they do their daily meditation and reading. They construct a special place with pictures and music.

Personal Coaching

When you have a special place, consider ways you can make it the most special of places. Some use ritual to make a place special. It can be a place for prayer or meditation. You can keep special treasures and inspiring spiritual items there. Consider using a special prayer or visualization before entering your special place.

Clean Sweep Your Life

A personal coach trained at Coach University has a wonderful program that helps bring more delight into your life. It is a checklist called Clean Sweep that you retake several times to track your progress.

There are a series of questions for the major areas of your life—physical environment, well being, money, and relationships. There are 25 statements for each area and the possible score is 100.

It helps identify areas that, when done right, bring vitality and delight into your life. When you agree with a statement, it means that a small part of your life is in balance and is supporting your efforts to bring even more delight into your life.

Living "Don't Worry, Be Happy"

If Five-Minute Managers have a theme song this may be it. Worrying does not do much good. In fact, most of the time it does no good.

Five-Minute Managers are committed to being happy. You have already figured that out based on all the tips you have already read in this chapter. The commitment is not a forced one. Being happy feels like the right thing to do. It is the path of least resistance. When they are unhappy, life is not easy.

A News Fast

One of the greatest sources of negative energy is the news. The headlines lead with people murdered, kidnapped, raped, or maimed. The other news stories focus on disagreements and lack of progress. It is very difficult to watch the news or read a newspaper and feel like you have connected with positive energy. Most of us are not uplifted by the experience.

Take a news fast. Start by not reading or watching any news—one day a week—no news, sports, or even comics. See how you feel. There may be some withdrawal pains but you will adjust.

Consider This

Consider using the television remote to change stations when bad news comes on. If you can't go "cold turkey" with no news, this interim step can ease the way. A favorite for some is to jump to cartoons where it is usually light hearted and fun. Others jump to sports or the home and garden stations.

After a month of no news one day a week, move to no news for a week. Treat it as if you were on a tropical island with no news sources. That would be nice, and you can enjoy this aspect of the vacation at home.

Now that you have adjusted to a full week, fundamentally alter how and where you receive your news. It is important to stay connected with those parts of your world, including news, that are truly important to your well-being. Good alternative sources are the online news sources, like CNN or MSNBC. There, you can customize a news page to capture only the kind of news stories you are interested in reading.

Random Acts of Kindness

One of the most positive things you can do is to commit random acts of kindness. Random acts of kindness are similar to doing good deeds. The key difference is often the intent to be kind. It is loving and soft. Random acts of kindness can be spontaneous or planned.

When spontaneous, you are alert for opportunities to help another person or to give them a gift of kindness. Acts of kindness can be a simple as a smile, but they are usually more involved. They are helping someone find something they have lost. They are helping someone with whatever kind of struggle they have in the moment.

Sage Advice

"It is futile to judge a kind deed by its motives. Kindness can become its own motive. We are made kind by being kind."
—Eric Hoffer (1902–1983), U.S. philosopher

When you plan random acts of kindness, they are especially fun. There is the fun of planning and anticipation. They can be as simple as delivering a bouquet of flowers and as extensive as constructing something that you know will help another person.

Random acts of kindness come from the heart. It is no surprise then that these acts are win-win acts all the time.

The Least You Need to Know

➤ Become invulnerable to life challenges by being centered, in the moment, and open to life's many possibilities.

➤ Connecting to a higher power can be a personal experience that transforms your life.

➤ A personal journal is cheaper than therapy and a great way to explore your inner thoughts and feelings.

➤ A simpler and quieter life helps you become centered and empowered to address life's challenges.

➤ Simple steps can get you unstuck—a dose of sunshine and fresh air, reconnecting with a friend, or listening to your favorite music.

Finding a Life or Business Coach

Several instances in this book refer to a personal or business coach. Coaching is a relatively new profession that is growing at a very rapid rate.

An analogy that helps people understand the role of a coach is one that relates to sports.

In sports, when you have serious injury, a torn ACL for example, you go to a medical doctor, such as an orthopedic. In life, when you have a serious injury, schizophrenia for example, you go to a psychiatrist.

In sports, when you have minor injury, a pulled muscle for example, you go to a physical therapist. In life, when you have a minor-to-moderate issue, marriage conflicts for example, you go to a therapist.

In sports, when you are healthy and able to do your best, you use an athletic coach to help improve your performance and results. In life, when you are working and living well, you use a personal coach who helps you achieve what you want most in life faster and easier than you can by yourself.

Coaching usually is done over the telephone, so it is not necessary for your coach to live in your area. The beauty of coaching is that you can access the coach that is right for you even if they live three thousand miles away.

If you are interested in learning more about a coach who can help you, you can consult two excellent free referral services. The first of these is the International Coach Federation (www.coachfederation.org). This is the major international organization for coaches. Whereas not all coaches belong to the International Coach Federation, most of the coaching profession's primary leaders do belong.

They have an excellent Web site with a free and powerful referral service. Follow these steps to find a coach that can help you.

1. On the home page choose "Find a Coach!" at the top of the page.
2. On the next page, select "Begin the Search to Find a Coach."
3. If you agree to the statement on the next page click "I agree to the above."
4. Then you are presented with five choices: Corporate Coaching, Small Business Coaching, Personal Coaching, Career Coaching, and Speakers Resource.
5. After you make your choice, you have an extensive list of factors to choose from to find the potentially right coach for you. If you choose "Personal Coaching,"

for example, some of your choices are the areas of life in which you want coaching, the professional experience of your coach, their coaching methods, their country and state, and their fees.

6. You can then review potential coaches. If the fit does not feel right, go back and revise your criteria.

The other Web site is Coach University (www.coachu.com).

Coach University is the largest trainer of new coaches in the world. It trains coaches in North America, Europe, Australia, and Asia. To graduate, coaches complete more than forty courses.

It has an excellent referral site also. To use it, follow these steps:

1. At the Coach University home page, choose "Find a Coach."
2. Do the same on the next page.
3. On the next page, you are given a choice of four different types of coaches: small business, corporate, personal, and creative arts. Choose one.
4. On the next page, a search engine asks you to enter a phrase describing the type of coach you want. There is a list of key words to guide your phrase selection.
5. The search produces a list of coaches ranked by how close they are to the search phrase you entered. There is a brief description of each coach on this page. You access a much more detailed description by choosing one and going to their detail page.

Play with the system and configure your search several ways around different key words and descriptions. Compare the results and look for common coach suggestions. In most cases the initial coach contact is free, so there is no cost or risk in making a getting acquainted contact.

Suggested Reading

This suggested reading list includes mostly books about personal development. As you have learned from this book, when you have great emotional, mental, physical, and spiritual strength you do your best.

> Dr. Alan Loy McGinnis, *Bring Out the Best in People: How to Enjoy Helping Others Excel.* Augsburg Fortress Publications, 1985.

This is a very good book that comes at positive feedback from a different but valuable perspective. Its positive, upbeat message is a breath of fresh air.

> Susan Smith Jones, *Choose to Live Each Day Fully.* Berkeley: Celestial Arts, 1994.

Susan is a gifted teacher and writer whose series of *Choose to ...* books all make great reading. She takes a broad view of life and her insights and suggestions are powerful.

> Neale Donald Walsch, *Conversations With God,* books one–three. Charlottsville, VA: Hampton Roads Publishing Company, 1998.

This best-selling series provides many engaging and provocative insights. You will need to make your own decisions about whether the conversations are really with God, but it is a worthwhile read.

> Drs. Rick Brinkman and Rick Kirschner, *Deal With People You Can't Stand: How to Bring Out The Best in People at Their Worst.* New York: McGraw-Hill, 1994.

Most have encountered people they cannot stand and often they find themselves totally ineffective with these people. This book helps you to deal with difficult people in a way that transforms you and them.

> Stephen R. Covey, A. Roger Merrill, Rebecca R. Merrill, *First Things First.* New York: Simon & Schuster, 1994.

Covey's *The 7 Habits of Highly Effective People* is one of the longest running best-sellers in recent times. This book takes one of the seven habits and turns it into an exceptionally practical and useful life tool.

> Barbara Sher with Barbara Smith, *I Could Do Anything If I Only Knew What it Was: How to Discover What You Really Want and How to Get It.* DTP, 1995.

In several instances, this book suggests that you should try to connect with your dream. Sher and Smith's book provides some additional ideas on how to connect with your dream.

> Wayne W. Dyer, *Manifest Your Destiny: The Nine Spiritual Principles for Getting Everything You Want*. New York: Harper Collins, 1997.

Dr. Wayne Dyer has been a best-selling author for years. This is a wonderful book if you want to connect with the most powerful, proven methods of manifesting your dream.

> Anthony Robbins, *Personal Power!* San Diego: Robbins Research International, 1993.

This is a best-selling tape series. Anthony has a powerful system for changing limiting beliefs—plenty of practical work and strong personal examples. He uses the same techniques to create powerful positive inner states. He uses these techniques to improve relationships, health, personal happiness, and financial results.

> Leo Buscaglia, Ph.D., *Personhood, The Art of Being Fully Human*. Thorofare, NJ: Charles B. Slack, 1978.

Leo was a favorite author and PBS presenter for years before he passed on. This is an excellent book about the stages of life or personhood and the principles that guide life. The section on the key elements of the major religions is one of the best short summaries of this kind. When you read this book, you come away with a good understanding of life's fundamentals.

> Deepak Chopra, *The Seven Spiritual Laws of Success*. San Rafael, CA: Amber-Allen Publishing, 1994.

Deepak is one of the great teachers of this time. For Westerners, this provocative book may be your entry point to an expanded and joyous spiritual path.

> Robert Fritz, *The Path of Least Resistance, Principles for Creating What You Want to Create*. Salem, MA: DMA, 1984.

This is a wonderful book on creativity. Although it is about 15 years old, the message is timeless. It is insightful and practical, a rare combination for a book of this type.

> Sogyal Rinpoche, *The Tibetan Book of Living and Dying*. San Francisco: Harper San Francisco, 1992.

Sogyal has been my personal teacher for years. This book is breathtakingly simple and profound at times and very detailed at other times. If you have started to study Eastern thinking, this book is one of the better ones.

> John Marks Templeton, *Worldwide Laws of Life, 200 Eternal Spiritual Principles*. Philadelphia and London: Templeton Foundation Press, 1997.

312

John founded the immensely successful Templeton mutual funds. He is focused on spirituality, often with its connection to science. This incredibly broad book is a wonderful reminder of the similarities in the teachings of the world's greatest teachers.

Abraham H. Maslow, *Maslow on Management*. New York: John Wiley & Sons, Inc., 1998.

Maslow was one of the great human development thinkers of this time. His thoughts on self-actualization shaped much of the personal growth movement. This book's principles of enlightened management are a must read for any serious student of management.

Index

A

ABC News Web site, 68
accounting fraud, preventing, 244-246
  blaming others, 245
  bookkeeping, 245-246
  mail, 245
  reasons, 246
  vacation, 244-245
  volunteers, 245
action, developing business plans, 268-269
advertising
  product benefits versus product features, 269-270
  television, 200
advice, soliciting for business plans, 266-268
Alta Vista search engine, 69
Amazon.com Web site, 4
appointments, times, 217
assessments, business plans, 268-269
assets, preventing disasters, 243
attitudes
  managerial, 9-10
  negative, management techniques to overcome, 295-298
  positive, techniques for maintaining, 295-298
awareness, focusing on the moment to overcome negativity, 296-297

B

balance, long-term success, 279
BMW, service and profitability, 272

book stores, Amazon.com, 4
books
  advice for business plans, 266
  long-term success, 281
  The Power of Positive Thinking, 304
boundaries
  families, 286-288
  managers, social situations, 291
budgets, marketing, 171-175
  alliances, 174-175
  announcements, 173
  Internet, 175
  materials, 172-173
  past customers, 171-172
  seminars and workshops, 173-174
Business Week Web site, 67
businesses. *See also* companies; organizations
  BMW, service and profitability, 272
  celebrating customers, 256
  community volunteers, 291-292
  creative skills, developing, 177-182
  data summary
    additional input, 83-84
    needs and findings, 82-83
  disasters (preventing), 241-244
    accounting fraud, 244-246
    assets, 243
    bad thinking, 247-249
    teams, 241-242
    vital records, 242-243
  excellence, 204-209
    360 degree review, 205-206

    area and world review, 206-207
    backup plans, 207-208
    objectivity vs. interpretation, 208-209
    personal values review, 205
  goal setting
    action steps toward implementing, 96
    celebrating, 98-99
    compatible goals, 87-88
    learning from implementing goals, 96-97
    measurable specifics, 86
    perseverance, 97-98
    preparation steps toward implementing, 95
    preparing and establishing, 88-90
    reaching goals, 86-87
    reviewing, 93-94
    SMAC, 84-85
  growth, 199-204
    location, 200-201
    networking, 201-202
    product or service evaluations, 203-204
    volunteering, 202-203
  home
    bragging and name-dropping, 231-232
    coach, 226-227
    compliments, 232
    deadlines, 225-226
    eye contact, 230
    families, 227
    listening skills, 231
    neatness, 229
    office, 228-229
    public speaking, 232-236
    relax, 231

routines, 227
shaking hands, 230
smiling, 230-231
telephones, 236-238
success tips, 225-229
improving, 216-219
appointments, 217
getting answers, 216-217
honesty, 219
needs, 216
responses, 217-218
systems, 219
toleration, 218
Ingram Micro
mission statements, 14
vision statement, 14
K-Mart, service and
profitability, 273
leverage, 211-215
cash, 212
customers, 211-212
employees, 214-215
market share, 212-213
momentum, 214
reputation, 213-214
systems, 215
Lexus, service and profitability, 272
logos, 201
managers. *See* managers
marketing
budgets, 171-175
demographic data, 172
mission statements, 4,
12-16, 19-20
The Burlington Northern
and Sante Fe Railway,
15-16
creating, 12-14
Ingram Micro, 14
University of North
Carolina, 14
mistakes, 251-257
chaos, 252
gut instincts, 253
opportunities (new),
256-257
quality of work, 254-255
quick payoffs, 255-256
watching competition,
253-254

plans, 263-269
action, 268-269
advice, 266-268
anticipating problems,
264-265
developing solutions for
problems, 265-266
"dreaming bigger," 264
reassessing, 268-269
networking, 187-190
building, 190
groups, 188-189
involvement, 189
preparations, 189-190
visibility, 188
partnerships, 190-194
communication, 193
money, 192
power positions, 191-192
role players, 193-194
shared values, 191
policy examples
brochures, 160
memos, 8-9
problem solving skills, 194
developing, 182-186
profitability
customer benefits,
269-271
innovation, 274-275
location, 273-274
long-term success,
276-279
reliability, 276
service, 272-273
value, 271
public speaking, 232-236
audience participation,
235-236
audiences, 234
breathing and eye
contact, 235
finishing, 236
humor, 233-234
outlines, 233
practice, 234
prepare, 232
reflect, 233
relationships, long-term
success, 278
review of operations, 61-70
consumer research, 64-66
customer data, 61-62

data analysis, 62-64
internet site research,
67-69
other consumer research,
67
search engine research,
69-70
sales
myths, 157-162
value (product or service),
162-165
Saturn, service and profitability, 272
Sears, service and profitability, 273
social situations
managers, 289-291
strategies
consumer relations, 76-78
determine companies
strengths, 72-73
determine competitors'
strengths, 74-75
implementing gathered
information, 78-79
strengths, evaluating, 72-73
success, sales personnel,
167-171
survival tips, 194-197
financial planning,
195-196
gloating, 197
mentors, 196-197
passion (job), 197
technology, 194-195
team meetings, 147-151
agendas, 143-145
building momentum,
152-153
"I-Don't-Believe-in-This"
response, 150
successful finish, 153
summaries, 145
table shape, 145-146
"What's My Role?" type,
150-151
"Why Me?" response, 149
worker expectations,
151-152
teams
charters, 139-141
mission statements,
141-142

role-players, 142-143
telephone conversations, 236-238
assertive not aggressive, 238
audience, 237
listening skills, 238-239
purpose, 236-237
voice tones, 237-238
words, 237
The Burlington Northern and Sante Fe Railway
mission statements, 15-16
vision statement, 15-16
Toyota, value and profit-ability, 271
University of North Carolina
mission statements, 14
vision statement, 14
values, 21-27
families, 27
identifying, 26-27
Ingram Micro, 27-28
personal, 28-30
vision statements, 4, 11-16, 19-20
The Burlington Northern and Sante Fe Railway, 15-16
creating, 12-14
Ingram Micro, 14
personal, 16-19
University of North Carolina, 14
Wal-Mart, service and profitability, 273
working at home, 229-232

C

cash leverage, 212
CBS News Web site, 69
chambers of commerce, advice for business plans, 266
"Clean Sweep," overcoming negativity, 306
CNNfn Web site, 68
coaches, long-term success, 279-280

commercials, communication in, 6
communication, 5-6
commercials, 6
cooperation
companies, 53-54
developing, 54-55
cooperation vs. competition, 49-50
myths, 50-53
research studies, 50
creative skills, 177-182
brainstorming, 179
curiosity, 181
environment, 178-179
negativity, 180
open minds, 181-182
prior experiences, 179-180
self-affirmation, 178
visual stimuli and adding perspectives, 180-181
e-mail, 302
families, 7
introductory sentences, 7
listening skills
developing, 43-44
first impressions, 231
improving, 42
research studies, 41-42
telephones, 238
learning versus replying, 44-46
negative feedback, 121-124, 133-136
clarity, 122
considerations, 132-133
group dynamics, 125-127
immediacy, 121
lessons learned, 124
patterns, 130-132
performance reviews, 135-136
public or private, 124-125
resolving, 122
understanding the facts, 122
warnings, 133
partnerships, building, 193
personal journals, overcom-ing negativity, 298-301

planning, 6-7
positive feedback, 103-105, 133-136. *See also* praise
benefits, 116
celebrating, 107
group, 109
MBWA (Managing By Wandering Around), 107-108
performance reviews, 135-136
praise, 105-107
where to give, 108-109
who to give to, 116-119
problem solving skills, 182-186
agreements, 186
attitudes, 182-183
defining problems, 183
experiences, 184-185
intuition, 185
solutions, 185-186
systems, 183-184
product benefits versus product features, 269-270
public speaking, 232-236
audience participation, 234-236
breathing and eye contact, 235
finishing, 236
humor, 233-234
outlines, 233
practice, 234
prepare, 232
reflect, 233
sales
personnel, customer knowledge, 168-169
value (product or service), 164
systems, 216
telephone conversations, 236-238, 302
assertive not aggressive, 238
audience, 237
listening skills, 238
purpose, 236-237
voice tones, 237-238
words, 237

trust, 5, 31-32
    building, 34-38
    competency, 33
    integrity, 32-33
    self, 38-39
    values, 21-27
        companies, 26-27
        Ingram Micro, 27-30
        personal, 28-30
    written (memos), 8-9
community volunteers,
    managers, 291-292
    clear objectives, 291
    opportunities, 292
    praise, 292
companies. *See also* businesses;
    organizations
    BMW, service and profit-
        ability, 272
    celebrating customers, 256
    community volunteers,
        291-292
    creative skills, developing,
        177-182
    data summary
        additional input, 83-84
        needs and findings, 82-83
    disasters (preventing),
        241-244
        accounting fraud,
            244-246
        assets, 243
        bad thinking, 247-249
        teams, 241-242
        vital records, 242-243
    excellence, 204-209
        360 degree review,
            205-206
        area and world review,
            206-207
        backup plans, 207-208
        objectivity vs. interpreta-
            tion, 208-209
        personal values review,
            205
    goal setting
        action steps toward
            implementing, 96
        celebrating, 98-99
        compatible goals, 87-88
        learning from imple-
            menting goals, 96-97
        measurable specifics, 86

perseverance, 97-98
preparation steps toward
    implementing, 95
preparing and establish-
    ing, 88-90
reaching goals, 86-87
reviewing, 93-94
SMAC, 84-85
growth, 199-204
    location, 200-201
    networking, 201-202
    product or service
        evaluations, 203-204
    volunteering, 202-203
home success tips, 225-229
improving, 216-219
    appointments, 217
    getting answers, 216-217
    honesty, 219
    needs, 216
    responses, 217-218
    systems, 219
    toleration, 218
Ingram Micro
    mission statements, 14
    vision statement, 14
K-Mart, service and profit-
    ability, 273
leverage, 211-215
    cash, 212
    customers, 211-212
    employees, 214-215
    market share, 212-213
    momentum, 214
    reputation, 213-214
    systems, 215
Lexus, service and profit-
    ability, 272
logos, 201
managers. *See* managers
marketing
    budgets, 171-175
    demographic data, 172
mission statements, 4,
    12-16, 19-20
    The Burlington Northern
        and Sante Fe Railway,
        15-16
    creating, 12-14
    Ingram Micro, 14
    University of North
        Carolina, 14

mistakes, 251-257
    chaos, 252
    gut instincts, 253
    opportunities (new),
        256-257
    quality of work, 254-255
    quick payoffs, 255-256
    watching competition,
        253-254
networking, 187-190
    building, 190
    groups, 188-189
    involvement, 189
    preparations, 189-190
    visibility, 188
partnerships, 190-194
    communication, 193
    money, 192
    power positions, 191-192
    role players, 193-194
    shared values, 191
policy examples
    brochures, 160
    memos, 8-9
problem solving skills, 194
    developing, 182-186
profitability
    customer benefits,
        269-271
    innovation, 274-275
    location, 273-274
    long-term success,
        276-279
    reliability, 276
    service, 272-273
    value, 271
public speaking, 232-236
    audience participation,
        235-236
    audiences, 234
    breathing and eye
        contact, 235
    finishing, 236
    humor, 233-234
    outlines, 233
    practice, 234
    prepare, 232
    reflect, 233
review of operations, 61-70
    consumer research, 64-66
    customer data, 61-62
    data analysis, 62-64
    internet site research,
        67-69

other consumer research, 67
search engine research, 69-70
sales
  myths, 157-162
  value (product or service), 162-165
Saturn, service and profitability, 272
Sears, service and profitability, 273
social situations, 289-291
strategies
  consumer relations, 76-78
  determining company strengths, 72-73
  determining competitors' strengths, 74-75
  implementing gathered information, 78-79
strengths, evaluating, 72-73
success, sales personnel, 167-171
survival tips, 194-197
  financial planning, 195-196
  gloating, 197
  mentors, 196-197
  passion (job), 197
  technology, 194-195
team meetings, 147-151
  agendas, 143-145
  building momentum, 152-153
  "I-Don't-Believe-in-This" response, 150
  successful finish, 153
  summaries, 145
  table shape, 145-146
  "What's My Role?" type, 150-151
  "Why Me?" response, 149
  worker expectations, 151-152
teams
  charters, 139-141
  meetings. *See* companies, team meetings
  mission statements, 141-142

The Burlington Northern and Sante Fe Railway
  mission statements, 15-16
  role-players, 142-143
telephone conversations, 236-238
  assertive not aggressive, 238
  audience, 237
  listening skills, 238-239
  purpose, 236-237
  voice tones, 237-238
  words, 237
Toyota, value and profitability, 271
University of North Carolina
  mission statements, 14
  vision statement, 14
values, 21-27
  families, 27
  identifying, 26-27
  Ingram Micro, 27-28
  personal, 28-30
vision statements, 4, 11-16, 19-20
  The Burlington Northern and Sante Fe Railway, 15-16
  creating, 12-14
  Ingram Micro, 14
  personal, 16-19
  University of North Carolina, 14
Wal-Mart, service and profitability, 273
working at home, 229-232
competency, 33
competition, 49-50
  families, 51-53
  myths, 50-53
  research studies, 50
  system tracking, 254
competitors' strengths, evaluating, 74-75
cooperation, 49-50
  companies, 53-54
  developing, 54-55
  myths about competition, 50-53
  research studies, 50

creative skills
  developing, 177-182
    brainstorming, 179
    curiosity, 181
    environment, 178-179
    negativity, 180
    open minds, 181-182
    prior experiences, 179-180
    self-affirmation, 178
    visual stimuli and adding perspectives, 180-181
criticism, 121-124, 133-136, 206. *See also* negative feedback
  clarity, 122
  considerations for, 132-133
  criticizing the boss, 130-131
  cross-functional criticism, 132
  families, 122, 288-289
  group dynamics, 125-127
    including everyone, 127
  immediacy, 121
  lessons learned, 124
  patterns, 130-132
  performance reviews, 135-136
  privacy, advantages and risks, 125
  public or private, 124-125
  resolving, 122
  small businesses, 124, 130-131
  spouse, 131
  understanding the facts, 122
  warnings, 133
customers
  benefits from products, 269-271
  innovation, 274-275
  leverage, 211-212
  loyalty, 276

D

Data. *See also* key data
  analysis, 62-64
  consumer voices, 67
    focus groups, 67

habits and practices
  research, 67
  listening to, 64-66
  research, 65-66
customer, 61-62
demographic marketing, 172
Internet site research, 67-69
review, 61-70
  consumer research, 64-67
  customer data, 61-62
  data analysis, 62-64
  Internet site research, 67-69
  search engine research, 69-70
  sharing, 62
summary
  additional input, 83-84
  needs and findings, 82-83
decision making, 268
  emotion versus logic, 267-268
disasters (preventing), 241-244
  accounting fraud, 244-246
    blames others, 245
    bookkeeping, 245-246
    mail, 245
    reasons, 246
    vacation, 244-245
    volunteers, 245
  assets, 243
  bad thinking, 247-249
    facts, 247-248
    multiple perspectives, 248-249
    questioning, 247
    source, 248
    verification, 249
  natural and self-inflicted, 243-244
  teams, 241-242
  vital records, 242-243
Discovery Channel Web site, 68
"dreams," developing business plans, 264

E

e-mail, building relationships through, 302
Edgar On-line Web site, 68
Electric Library Web site, 69
emotions versus logic in decision making, 267-268
employees
  leverage, 214-215
  review, 205-206
Entrepreneur Magazine Web site, 68
Entrepreneurs, failures, 257-261
  circle runner, 257-258
  continual, 259
  details, 258
  families, 260-261
  living on the edge, 259-260
  optimism, 259
  start to finish, 258-259
  teams, 260
evaluations
  annual, 204
  product or service, 203-204
Excite search engine, 69

F

failures (entrepreneurs), 257-261
  circle runner, 257-258
  continual, 259
  details, 258
  families, 260-261
  living on the edge, 259-260
  optimism, 259
  start to finish, 258-259
  teams, 260
families
  communication, 7, 38
  entrepreneurs, 260-261
  parents, 285-289
    goals and boundaries, 286-288
    negative feedback, 288-289
    praise, 288

problem solving skills, 183
working at home, success tips, 227
feedback (negative), 121-124, 133-136, 206. *See also* feedback (positive)
  Bill's experience, 122-123
  clarity, 122
  considerations for, 132-133
  criticizing the boss, 130-131
  cross-functional criticism, 132
  families, 122, 288-289
  group dynamics, 125-127
    including everyone, 127
  immediacy, 121
  lessons learned, 124
  patterns, 130-132
  performance reviews, 135-136
  privacy, advantages and risks, 125
  public or private, 124-125
  resolving, 122
  small businesses, 124, 130-131
  spouse, 131
  understanding the facts, 122
  warnings, 133
feedback (positive), 133-136, 206. *See also* feedback (negative)
  benefits of giving, 116
  celebrating, 107
  families, 114
    celebrating, 286
  group, 109
  MBWA (Managing By Wandering Around), 107-108
  performance reviews, 135-136
  praise, 103-107
  small businesses, 106-107, 116-117
  when to give
    customer-service examples, 106
    sales-representative example, 106-107

where to give, 108-109
who to give to, 116-119
    boss, 118
    co-worker to co-worker, 117-118
    everyone, 118-119
finances, family goals, 288
financial planning, companies survival tips, 195-196
first impressions, 229-232
    bragging and name-dropping, 231-232
    compliments, 232
    eye contact, 230
    listening skills, 231
    neatness, 229
    relaxing, 231
    shaking hands, 230
    smiling, 230-231
Five-Minute Managers. *See* managers
Franklin Covey Web site, 19, 68
friendships, overcoming negativity, 301-302, 305

G

goal setting
    action steps toward implementing, 96
    celebrating, 98-99
    companies
        compatible goals, 87-88
        measurable specifics, 86
        preparing and establishing, 88-90
        reaching goals, 86-87
        SMAC, 84-85
    compatible goals, 87-88
    data summary
        additional input, 83-84
        needs and findings, 82-83
    defining to overcome negativity, 299
    families, 286-288
    formalizing agreements, 94
    implementing goals, 96-97
    measurable specifics, 86
    perseverance, 97-98
    personal, 84-86

preparing and establishing, 88-90, 95
    goals as masters, 88-89
    goals as servants, 89-90
    reaching goals, 86-87
    reviewing, 93-94
    SMAC, 84-85
        achieving goals, 85
        compatible goals, 85
        measurable goals, 85
        specific goals, 84
    small businesses, 82
goal statements, written, 94
growth, company, 199-204
    location, 200-201
    networking, 201-202
    product or service evaluations, 203-204
    volunteering, 202-203

H

HotBot search engine, 70
home businesses
    first impressions, 229-232
        bragging and name-dropping, 231-232
        compliments, 232
        eye contact, 230
        listening skills, 231
        neatness, 229
        relax, 231
        shaking hands, 230
        smiling, 230-231
    success tips, 225-229
        coach, 226-227
        deadlines, 225-226
        families, 227
        office, 228-229
        public speaking, 232-236
        routines, 227
    telephones, 236-238

I

Inc. Magazine, 266
    Web site, 69
industry associations, advice for business plans, 266

Information Please Web site, 68
Infoseek search engine, 70
Ingram Micro
    mission statements, 14
    values, 27-28
    vision statements, 14
innovation, profitability, 274-275
integrity
    personal growth, 33
    trust, 32-33
Internet
    creating personal vision statements, 19
    search engines, 69-70
    service providers
        AOL, 69
        CompuServe, 69
    Web sites. *See* Web sites
introductory sentences (communication), 7
introspection, overcoming negativity, 300
intuition, decision making when developing business plans, 267-268
Iquest Web site, 69

J-K

journals, overcoming negativity, 281, 298-301
K-Mart, service and profitability, 273
Kelly Blue Book Web site, 158
key data, 59-61. *See also* data analysis, 62-64
    consumer voices, 67
        focus groups, 67
        habits and practices research, 67
        listening to, 64-66
        research, 65-66
    customer, 61-62
    demographic marketing, 172
    Internet site research, 67-69
    review, 61-70
        consumer research, 64-67
        customer data, 61-62

data analysis, 62-64
Internet site research, 67-69
search engine research, 69-70
sharing, 62
summary, additional input, 83-84
needs and findings, 82-83
kind acts, overcoming negativity, 303, 307

L

Leader to Leader Web site, 68
learning, long-term success, 277
leverage, 211-215
cash, 212
customers, 211-212
employees, 214-215
market share, 212-213
momentum, 214
reputation, 213-214
systems, 215
Lexus, service and profitability, 272
Library of Congress Web site, 68
listening skills
developing, 43-44
expectations, 43-44
clearing your mind, 43
first impressions, 231
improving, 42
research studies, 41-42
learning versus replying, 44-46
location, profitability, 273-274
logic versus emotion in decision making, 267-268
logos, companies, 201
long-term success
See also profitability; success
books, 281
managers, 219-224
dreams, 221-222
expand visions, 222
friends and family, 223
kindness, 224
passion (job), 220

power days, 220-221
reserves, 222-223
vacation, 221
profitability, 276-279
balance, 279
books, 281
business relationships, 278
coaches, 279-280
learning, 277
open door policy, 281-282
personal reserves, 277-278
risks, 278-279
sales personnel, 167-171
be yourself, 171
buyers, 169-170
customer knowledge, 168-169
language, 169
obstacles, 170
passion, 168
working at home, 225-229
coach, 226-227
deadlines, 225-226
families, 227
first impressions, 229-232
office, 228-229
public speaking, 232-236
routines, 227
telephones, 236-238

M

magazines
Inc. Magazine, 266
USA Today, 68
Working Mother, 68
managers, 4-5
analysis of key data, 59-61
as facilitators/coaches, 9-10
communication, 5-6
cooperation, 49-55
e-mail, 302
introductory sentences, 7
listening skills, 41-46
MBWA (Managing By Wandering Around), 107-108
negative feedback, 121-127, 130-136

personal journals, 298-301
planning, 6-7
positive feedback, 103-109, 133-136
product benefits versus product features, 269-270
telephone calls, 302
trust, 5, 31-39
values, 25-30
written, 8-9
companies
excellence, 204-209
growth, 199-204
creative skills, developing, 177-182
data summary
additional input, 83-84
needs and findings, 82-83
decision making, emotion versus logic, 267-268
developing business plans. *See* business plans
disasters (preventing), 241-244
accounting fraud, 244-246
assets, 243
bad thinking, 247-249
natural and self-inflicted, 243-244
teams, 241-242
vital records, 242-243
goal setting
celebrating, 98-99
compatible goals, 87-88
implementing, 95-96
learning from implementing goals, 96-97
measurable specifics, 86
perseverance, 97-98
preparing and establishing, 88-90
reaching goals, 86-87
reviewing, 93-94
SMAC, 84-85
improving, 216-219
appointments, 217
getting answers, 216-217
honesty, 219
needs, 216

responses, 217-218
systems, 219
toleration, 218
leverage, 211-215
cash, 212
customers, 211-212
employees, 214-215
market share, 212-213
momentum, 214
reputation, 213-214
systems, 215
marketing budgets, 171-175
mistakes, 251-257
chaos, 252
gut instincts, 253
opportunities (new),
256-257
quality of work, 254-255
quick payoffs, 255-256
watching competition,
253-254
networking, 187-190
building, 190
groups, 188-189
involvement, 189
preparations, 189-190
visibility, 188
parents, 285-289
goals and boundaries,
286-288
negative feedback,
288-289
praise, 288
partnerships, 190-194
communication, 193
money, 192
power positions, 191-192
role players, 193-194
shared values, 191
personal best, 219-224
dreams, 221-222
expand visions, 222
friends and family, 223
kindness, 224
passion (job), 220
power days, 220-221
reserves, 222-223
vacation, 221
positive feedback
benefits of giving, 116
who to give to, 116-119
one-dimensional,
111-115

problem-solving skills,
developing, 182-186
public speaking, 232-236
audience participation,
234-236
breathing and eye
contact, 235
finishing, 236
humor, 233-234
outlines, 233
practicing, 234
preparing, 232
reflecting, 233
review of operations
consumer research, 64-67
data analysis, 62-64
internet site research,
67-69
search engine research,
69-70
sales
myths, 157-162
value (product or service),
162-165
social situations, 289-291
boundaries, 291
fun, 289-290
positive attitude, 290-291
success, sales personnel,
167-171
survival tips, 194-197
financial planning,
195-196
gloating, 197
mentors, 196-197
passion (job), 197
technology, 194-195
team meetings, 147-151
agendas, 143-145
building momentum,
152-153
"I-Don't-Believe-in-This"
response, 150
successful finish, 153
summaries, 145
table shape, 145-146
"What's My Role?" type,
150-151
"Why Me?" response, 149
worker expectations,
151-152

teams
charters, 139-141
mission statements,
141-142
role players, 142-143
telephone conversations,
236-238
assertive not aggressive,
238
audience, 237
listening skills, 238-239
purpose, 236-237
voice tones, 237-238
words, 237
volunteering (community),
291-292
clear objectives, 291
opportunities, 292
praise, 292
working at home, 225-229
coach, 226-227
deadlines, 225-226
families, 227
first impressions, 229-232
office, 228-229
routines, 227
Managing By Wandering
Around (MBWA), 107-108
market share leverage, 212-213
marketing
budgets, 171-175
alliances, 174-175
announcements, 173
Internet, 175
materials, 172-173
past customers, 171-172
seminars and workshops,
173-174
materials, business cards,
172
product benefits versus
product features, 269-270
MBWA (Managing By Wan-
dering Around), 107-108
Medical Journals Web site, 69
meditation, overcoming
negativity, 298-299
meetings
agendas, 143-145
preparations, 144
presentations, 144-145
summaries, 145

323

teams, 147-151
   building momentum,
      152-153
   "I-Don't-Believe-in-This"
      response, 150
   successful finish, 153
   "What's My Role?" type,
      150-151
   "Why Me?" response, 149
   worker expectations,
      151-152
memos, company policy
   example, 8-9
mentors, 196-197
mission statements, 4, 12,
   19-20
   The Burlington Northern
      and Sante Fe Railway,
      15-16
   creating, 12-14
   Ingram Micro, 14
   teams, 141-142
   University of North
      Carolina, 14
   values, 25-27
      identifying, 26-27
      Ingram Micro, 27-28
      personal, 28-30
mistakes, company, 251-257
   chaos, 252
   gut instincts, 253
   opportunities (new),
      256-257
   quality of work, 254-255
   quick payoffs, 255-256
   watching competition,
      253-254
momentum, leverage, 214
Money, 60
MSNBC Web site, 68
music, overcoming negativity,
   302-303
myths
   competition, 50-53
   sales, 157-162
      aggressiveness, 160-161
      ethics, 161-162
      gimmicks, 159-160
      purchase decisions, 158
      training, 161

N

natural disasters, preventing,
   243-244
negative attitudes, management techniques to
   overcome, 295-298
   bad news, 306-307
   centering oneself, 296
   "Clean Sweep," 306
   defining goals, 299
   focusing on the moment,
      296-297
   friendships, 301-302, 305
   introspection, 300
   kind acts, 303, 307
   meditation, 298-299
   music, 302-303
   openness, 297
   optimism, 304
   passion, 297-298
   personal journals, 298-301
   personal places, 305
   positive thinking, 303-304
   rest, 302
   simplification, 299-300
   smiling, 304-305
   sunshine, 301
negative feedback, 121-124,
   133-136, 206
   clarity, 122
   considerations for, 132-133
   criticizing the boss, 130-131
   cross-functional criticism,
      132
   families, 122, 288-289
   group dynamics, 125-127
      including everyone, 127
   immediacy, 121
   lessons learned, 124
   patterns, 130-132
   performance reviews,
      135-136
   privacy, advantages and
      risks, 125
   public or private, 124-125
   resolving, 122
   small businesses, 124,
      130-131
   spouse, 131

   understanding the facts, 122
   warnings, 133
networking, 187-190
   companies, 201-202
   rules
      building, 190
      groups, 188-189
      involvement, 189
      preparations, 189-190
      visibility, 188
   small businesses, 188
   social situations, 289-291
The New York Times Web site,
   69
news, overcoming negativity,
   306-307
Northern Light search engine,
   69

O

office, home, 228-229
open door policy, 281-282
openness, overcoming
   negativity, 297
optimism, overcoming
   negativity, 304
organizations. *See also*
   companies; businesses
   BMW, service and profit-
      ability, 272
   celebrating customers, 256
   community volunteers,
      291-292
   creative skills, developing,
      177-182
   data summary
      additional input, 83-84
      needs and findings, 82-83
   disasters (preventing),
      241-244
      accounting fraud,
         244-246
      assets, 243
      bad thinking, 247-249
      teams, 241-242
      vital records, 242-243
   excellence, 204-209
      360 degree review,
         205-206

area and world review, 206-207
backup plans, 207-208
objectivity vs. interpretation, 208-209
personal values review, 205
goal setting
action steps toward implementing, 96
celebrating, 98-99
compatible goals, 87-88
learning from implementing goals, 96-97
measurable specifics, 86
perseverance, 97-98
preparation steps toward implementing, 95
preparing and establishing, 88-90
reaching goals, 86-87
reviewing, 93-94
SMAC, 84-85
growth, 199-204
location, 200-201
networking, 201-202
product or service evaluations, 203-204
volunteering, 202-203
home success tips, 225-229
improving, 216-219
appointments, 217
getting answers, 216-217
honesty, 219
needs, 216
responses, 217-218
systems, 219
toleration, 218
Ingram Micro
mission statements, 14
vision statement, 14
K-Mart, service and profitability, 273
leverage, 211-215
cash, 212
customers, 211-212
employees, 214-215
market share, 212-213
momentum, 214
reputation, 213-214
systems, 215

Lexus, service and profitability, 272
logos, 201
managers. *See* managers
marketing
budgets, 171-175
demographic data, 172
mission statements, 4, 12-16, 19-20
The Burlington Northern and Sante Fe Railway, 15-16
creating, 12-14
Ingram Micro, 14
University of North Carolina, 14
mistakes, 251-257
chaos, 252
gut instincts, 253
opportunities (new), 256-257
quality of work, 254-255
quick payoffs, 255-256
watching competition, 253-254
networking, 187-190
building, 190
groups, 188-189
involvement, 189
preparations, 189-190
visibility, 188
partnerships, 190-194
communication, 193
money, 192
power positions, 191-192
role players, 193-194
shared values, 191
policy examples
brochures, 160
memos, 8-9
problem solving skills, 194
developing, 182-186
profitability
customer benefits, 269-271
innovation, 274-275
location, 273-274
long-term success, 276-279
reliability, 276
service, 272-273
value, 271

public speaking, 232-236
audience participation, 235-236
audiences, 234
breathing and eye contact, 235
finishing, 236
humor, 233-234
outlines, 233
practice, 234
prepare, 232
reflect, 233
review of operations, 61-70
consumer research, 64-66
customer data, 61-62
data analysis, 62-64
internet site research, 67-69
other consumer research, 67
search engine research, 69-70
sales
myths, 157-162
value (product or service), 162-165
Saturn, service and profitability, 272
Sears, service and profitability, 273
social situations, 289-291
strategies
consumer relations, 76-78
determine companies strengths, 72-73
determine competitors' strengths, 74-75
implementing gathered information, 78-79
strengths, evaluating, 72-73
success, 167-171
survival tips, 194-197
financial planning, 195-196
gloating, 197
mentors, 196-197
passion (job), 197
technology, 194-195
team meetings, 147-151
agendas, 143-145
building momentum, 152-153

"I-Don't-Believe-in-This"
   response, 150
successful finish, 153
summaries, 145
table shape, 145-146
"What's My Role?" type,
   150-151
"Why Me?" response, 149
worker expectations,
   151-152
teams
   charters, 139-141
   mission statements,
      141-142
   role-players, 142-143
telephone conversations,
   236-238
   assertive not aggressive,
      238
   audience, 237
   listening skills, 238-239
   purpose, 236-237
   voice tones, 237-238
   words, 237
The Burlington Northern
   and Sante Fe Railway
   mission statements,
      15-16
Toyota, value and profit-
   ability, 271
University of North Carolina
   mission statements, 14
   vision statement, 14
values, 21-27
   families, 27
   identifying, 26-27
   Ingram Micro, 27-28
   personal, 28-30
vision statements, 4, 11-12,
   14-16, 19-20
   The Burlington Northern
      and Sante Fe Railway,
      15-16
   creating, 12-14
   Ingram Micro, 14
   personal, 16-19
   University of North
      Carolina, 14
Wal-Mart, service and
   profitability, 273
working at home, 229-232

P

parents (families), 285-289
   goals and boundaries,
      286-288
   negative feedback, 288-289
   praise, 288
partnerships, building, 190-194
   communication, 193
   money, 192
   power positions, 191-192
   role players, 193-194
   shared values, 191
passion, overcoming nega-
   tivity, 297-298
performance reviews, 135-136
personal journals, 281
   overcoming negativity,
      298-301
personal places, overcoming
   negativity, 305
personal vision statements,
   16-19
   creating, 16-19
   creating online, 19
planning communication, 6-7
policy examples (memos), 8-9
positive attitudes, techniques
   for maintaining, 295-298
   bad news, 306-307
   centering oneself, 296
   "Clean Sweep," 306
   defining goals, 299
   focusing on the moment,
      296-297
   friendships, 301-302, 305
   introspection, 300
   kind acts, 303, 307
   managers, 290-291
   meditation, 298-299
   music, 302-303
   openness, 297
   optimism, 304
   passion, 297-298
   personal journals, 298-301
   personal places, 305
   positive thinking, 303-304
   rest, 302
   simplification, 299-300
   smiling, 304-305
   social situations, 290-291
   sunshine, 301

positive feedback, 133-136,
   206. *See also* praise
   benefits of giving, 116
   celebrating, 107
   families, 114
      celebrating, 286
   group, 109
   MBWA (Managing By
      Wandering Around),
      107-108
   performance reviews,
      135-136
   praise, 103-107
   small businesses, 106-107,
      116-117
   when to give
      customer-service
         examples, 106
      sales-representative
         example, 106-107
   where to give, 108-109
   who to give to, 116-119
      boss, 118
      co-worker to co-worker,
         117-118
      everyone, 118-119
positive thinking, overcoming
   negativity, 303-304
The Power of Positive Thinking,
   304
praise, 103-107. *See also*
   positive feedback
   benefits of giving, 116
   celebrating, 107
   community volunteers, 292
   customer-service examples,
      106
   families, 114-115, 288
   group, 109
   MBWA (Managing By
      Wandering Around),
      107-108
   one-dimensional, 111-115
      ideal style, 114-115
      The Body, 114
      The Exclaimer, 113
      The Politician, 112
      The Rare Find, 113
      The Whisperer, 112
      The Writer, 113-114
   sales-representative
      example, 106-107

small businesses, 117
spouse, 118
where to give, 108-109
who to give to, 116-119
    boss, 118
    co-worker to co-worker,
        117-118
    everyone, 118-119
problem-solving skills
    companies, 194
    developing, 182-186
        agreements, 186
        attitudes, 182-183
        defining problems, 183
        experiences, 184-185
        intuition, 185
        solutions, 185-186
        systems, 183-184
    families, 183
problems. *See also* problem-
    solving skills
    anticipating , 264-265
    solutions, 265-266
products
    evaluation, 203-204
    profitability
        customer benefits,
            269-271
        reliability, 276
        service, 272-273
        value, 271
    sales myths, 157-162
    value, 162-165
        celebrating success, 165
        communication, 164
        customer inquiries, 165
        following up, 163
        trying before buying,
            162-163
        Web sites, 164-165
Profitability. *See also* long-term
    success; success
    books, 281
    managers, 219-224
        dreams, 221-222
        expand visions, 222
        friends and family, 223
        kindness, 224
        passion (job), 220
        power days, 220-221
        reserves, 222-223
        vacation, 221

sales personnel, 167-171
    be yourself, 171
    buyers, 169-170
    customer knowledge,
        168-169
    language, 169
    obstacles, 170
    passion, 168
working at home, 225-229
    coach, 226-227
    deadlines, 225-226
    families, 227
    first impressions, 229-232
    office, 228-229
    public speaking, 232-236
    routines, 227
    telephones, 236-238
profits
    customer benefits, 269-271
    innovation, 274-275
    location, 273-274
    long-term success, 276-279
        balance, 279
        books, 281
        business relationships,
            278
        coaches, 279-280
        learning, 277
        open door policy,
            281-282
        personal reserves,
            277-278
        risks, 278-279
    reliability, 276
    service, 272-273
    value, 271
public speaking, 232-236
    audience participation,
        234-236
    breathing and eye contact,
        235
    finishing, 236
    humor, 233-234
    outlines, 233
    practicing, 234, 235
    preparing, 232
    reflecting, 233
publications. *See* books;
    magazines

Q-R

Quicken, 60
reassessing business plans,
    268-269
record disasters (preventing),
    242-243
reliability, 276
reputation, leverage, 213-214
research
    companies, 153
    consumer, 65-66
    focus groups, 67
    habits and practices, 67
    Internet sites, 67-69
    marketing, 169
    search engine sites, 69-70
    studies
        competition, 50
        listening skills, 41-42
resources, review of, 93-94
rest, overcoming negativity,
    302
reviews (companies), 204-209
    360 degree review, 205-206
    area and world review,
        206-207
    backup plans, 207-208
    values (personal), 205
risks, long-term success,
    278-279
role playing
    building partnerships,
        193-194
    teams, 142-143

S

sales
    myths, 157-162
        aggressiveness, 160-161
        ethics, 161-162
        gimmicks, 159-160
        purchase decisions, 158
        training, 161
    personnel
        resources, 168
        success, 167-171
    positions in small busi-
        nesses, 162

Sample Business Plans Web
site, 68
Saturn, service and profitability, 272
search engines, 161
Alta Vista, 69
Excite, 69
HotBot, 70
Infoseek, 70
Northern Light, 69
Sears, service and profitability, 273
self-inflicted disasters, preventing, 243-244
seminars, marketing budgets, 173-174
service
evaluation, 203-204
profitability, 272-273
sales, 162-165
value, 162-165
celebrating success, 165
communication, 164
customer inquiries, 165
following up, 163
trying before buying, 162-163
Web sites, 164-165
simplicity, overcoming negativity, 299-300
sites, Web sites
ABC News, 68
advice for business plans, 266
Amazon.com, 4
Business Week, 67
CBS News, 69
CNNfn, 68
Discovery Channel, 68
Edgar On-line, 68
Electric Library, 69
Entrepreneur Magazine, 68
Franklin Covey, 19, 68
Inc. Magazine, 69
Information Please, 68
Iquest, 69
Kelly Blue Book, 158
Leader to Leader, 68
Library of Congress, 68
marketing budgets, 175
Medical Journals, 69
MSNBC, 68

The New York Times, 69
sales value (product or service), 164-165
Sample Business Plans, 68
Time-Life Publications, 67
USA Today, 68
Virtual Reference Desk, 68
Working Mother Magazine, 68
skills. *See* creative skills; problem solving skills
sleep, overcoming negativity, 302
SMAC (Specific, Measurable, Achievable, Compatible), 84-85
achievable goals, 85
compatible goals, 85
measurable goals, 85
specific goals, 84
smiling, overcoming negativity, 304-305
social situations and managers, 289-291
boundaries, 291
fun, 289-290
positive attitude, 290-291
software
Money, 60
Quicken, 60
Specific, Measurable, Achievable, Compatible (SMAC), 84-85
achievable goals, 85
compatible goals, 85
measurable goals, 85
specific goals, 84
spiritual practices, overcoming negativity, 298-299
statements
business plans. *See* business plans
mission statements. *See* mission statements
vision statements. *See* vision statements
strategies
consumer relations, 76-78
determining companies strengths, 72-73
evaluating competitors' strengths, 74-75
implementing gathered information, 78-79

strengths
companies
consumer relations, 76-78
evaluation, 72-73
implementing gathered information, 78-79
competitors' evaluation, 74-75
success. *See also* long-term success; profitability
books, 281
managers, 219-224
dreams, 221-222
expand visions, 222
friends and family, 223
kindness, 224
passion (job), 220
power days, 220-221
reserves, 222-223
vacation, 221
profitability, 276-279
balance, 279
books, 281
business relationships, 278
coaches, 279-280
learning, 277
open door policy, 281-282
personal reserves, 277-278
risks, 278-279
sales personnel, 167-171
be yourself, 171
buyers, 169-170
customer knowledge, 168-169
language, 169
obstacles, 170
passion, 168
working at home, 225-229
coach, 226-227
deadlines, 225-226
families, 227
first impressions, 229-232
office, 228-229
public speaking, 232-236
routines, 227
telephones, 236-238
sunshine, overcoming negativity, 301

survival tips, companies,
194-197
    financial planning, 195-196
    gloating, 197
    mentors, 196-197
    passion (job), 197
    technology, 194-195
systems
    communication, 216
    competition tracking, 254
    leverage, 215

T

teams
The Burlington Northern and
    charters, 139-141
    disaster (preventing), 241-
        242
    entrepreneurs, failures, 260
    families, 149
    meetings, 147-151
        agendas, 143-145
        building momentum,
            152-153
        "I-Don't-Believe-in-This"
            response, 150
        successful finish, 153
        summaries, 145
        table, 145-146
        "What's My Role?" type,
            150-151
        "Why Me?" response, 149
        worker expectations,
            151-152
    mission statements, 141-142
    role players, 142-143
    small businesses, 140-142,
        148
technology, company survival
    tips, 194-195
telephone conversations,
236-238
    assertive not aggressive, 238
    audience, 237
    building relationships
        through, 302
    listening skills, 238
    purpose, 236-237
    voice tones, 237-238
    words, 237

television advertising, 6, 200
Time-Life Publications Web
    site, 67
Toyota, value and profitability,
    271
trust
    building, 34-38
        multidirectional, 36-38
        sharing ideas, 35-36
        unexpected results, 34-35
    communication, 5
    companies, 31-32
    competency, 33
    integrity, 32-33
    self, 38-39

U

University of North Carolina
    mission statements, 14
    vision statements, 14
USA Today Web site, 68

V

value
    products or service, 162-165
        celebrating success, 165
        communication, 164
        customer inquiries, 165
        following up, 163
        trying before buying,
            162-163
        Web sites, 164-165
    profitability, 271
values, 205
    company, 21-27
        identifying, 26-27
        Ingram Micro, 27-28
        personal, 28-30
    families, 27
    personal, 21-25, 28-30, 205
        company, 205
        small businesses, 23
Virtual Reference Desk Web
    site, 68
vision statements, 4, 11-12,
    19-20

The Burlington Northern
    and Sante Fe Railway,
    15-16
creating, 12-14
families, 16
Ingram Micro, 14
personal, 16-19
    creating, 16-19
    creating online, 19
small businesses, 13, 19
University of North
    Carolina, 14
values, 21-27
    identifying, 26-27
    Ingram Micro, 27-28
    personal, 28-30
volunteering, 202-203
    community (managers),
        291-292

W

Wal-Mart, service and profit-
    ability, 273
Web sites
    ABC News, 68
    advice for business plans,
        266
    Amazon.com, 4
    Business Week, 67
    CBS News, 69
    CNNfn, 68
    Discovery Channel, 68
    Edgar On-line, 68
    Electric Library, 69
    Entrepreneur Magazine, 68
    Franklin Covey, 19, 68
    Inc. Magazine, 69
    Information Please, 68
    Iquest, 69
    Kelly Blue Book, 158
    Leader to Leader, 68
    Library of Congress, 68
    marketing budgets, 175
    Medical Journals, 69
    MSNBC, 68
    The New York Times, 69
    sales value (product or
        service), 164-165
    Sample Business Plans, 68
    Time-Life Publications, 67

USA Today, 68
Virtual Reference Desk, 68
Working Mother Magazine, 68
working at home
  first impressions, 229-232
    bragging and name-
      dropping, 231-232
    compliments, 232
    eye contact, 230
    listening skills, 231
    neatness, 229
    relax, 231
    shaking hands, 230
    smiling, 230-231
  success tips, 225-229
    coach, 226-227
    deadlines, 225-226
    families, 227
    office, 228-229
    public speaking, 232-236
    routines, 227
    telephones, 236-238
Working Mother Magazine
  Web site, 68
workshops, marketing budgets,
  173-174
written communication, 8-9